Truth-Seeking in an Age of (Mis)Information Overload

SUNY series, Humanities to the Rescue

David R. Castillo, editor

Truth-Seeking in an Age of (Mis)Information Overload

Edited by

David R. Castillo, Siwei Lyu, Christina Milletti, and Cynthia Stewart

Cover design by Julian Montague.

Published by State University of New York Press, Albany

© 2024 State University of New York

All rights reserved

Printed in the United States of America

No part of this book may be used or reproduced in any manner without written permission. No part of this book may be stored in a retrieval system or transmitted in any form or by any means including electronic, electrostatic, magnetic tape, mechanical, photocopying, recording, or otherwise without the prior permission in writing of the publisher.

Links to third-party websites are provided as a convenience and for informational purposes only. They do not constitute an endorsement or an approval of any of the products, services, or opinions of the organization, companies, or individuals. SUNY Press bears no responsibility for the accuracy, legality, or content of a URL, the external website, or for that of subsequent websites.

For information, contact State University of New York Press, Albany, NY www.sunypress.edu

Library of Congress Cataloging-in-Publication Data

Names: Castillo, David, editor. | Lyu, Siwei, editor. | Milletti, Christina, editor. | Stewart, Cynthia, editor.
Title: Truth-seeking in an age of (mis)information overload / edited by David Castillo, Siwei Lyu, Christina Milletti, and Cynthia Stewart.
Description: Albany : State University of New York Press, [2024] | Series: SUNY series, Humanities to the Rescue | Includes bibliographical references and index.
Identifiers: ISBN 9781438499246 (hardcover : alk. paper) | ISBN 9781438499253 (ebook) | ISBN 9781438499239 (pbk. : alk. paper)
Further information is available at the Library of Congress.

Contents

Acknowledgments   vii

Introduction
A Convergence Approach to the Mis/Disinformation Problem   1
   David Castillo and Siwei Lyu

Part I
Misinformation and Artificial Intelligence

Chapter 1
It Is Artificial, But Is It Intelligent?   17
   E. Bruce Pitman

Chapter 2
Disinformation, Power, and the Automation of Judgments:
Notes on Algorithmic Harms to Democracy   29
   Ewa Plonowska Ziarek

Part II
Science Communication, Cultivating Awareness

Chapter 3
Communicating Science in an Increasingly Politicized Environment   53
   Yotam Ophir, Raphaela M. Velho, and Lilian Tzivian

Chapter 4
Generative Media and Our Collective Response to the
Ecological Crisis   75
    John Fiege

Chapter 5
SWAMP (Studies of Work Atmospheres and Mass Production)   95
    Matt Kenyon

Part III
Building Trust

Chapter 6
Trust and Confidence in Medicine Among Americans   115
    Jessie Poon and Laurene Tumiel Berhalter

Chapter 7
Practicing Responsible Science through Community Engagement   133
    Jennifer Anne Surtees

Afterword
Trusting Fiction's Truth   157
    Christina Milletti

List of Contributors   169

Index   175

Acknowledgments

We are thankful to Chitra Rajan, Associate Vice President for Research Advancement, whose vision, leadership, and hard work resulted in the founding of the UB Center for Information Integrity in October 2021, with the support of Venu Govindaraju, UB Vice President of Research and Economic Development, Kemper Lewis, Dean of the UB School of Engineering and Applied Sciences, and Robin Schulze, Dean of the UB College of Arts and Sciences. Thanks also to our colleagues in the Center for Information Integrity and the Humanities Institute, especially to our brilliant contributors who represent an astonishing breath of academic departments and fields of inquiry. Finally, our collective thanks to the Office of the Vice President for Research for its generous subvention of this collaborative volume and to SUNY Press for its commitment to research innovation across the disciplines.

Introduction

A Convergence Approach to the Mis/Disinformation Problem

DAVID CASTILLO AND SIWEI LYU

The unprecedented spread of false, fake, and misleading information in our media ecosystem is the flip side of the internet's promise of universal access and information democratization. As an unwanted consequence of the neck-breaking advances of digital technology and artificial intelligence, and the emergence of influential social media platforms, we are experiencing online mis/disinformation with escalating speed, volume, and level of sophistication. The omnipresence of misinformation in our environment is eroding our trust in legitimate sources of information and posing significant threats to consumers/users everywhere in the world. To fully understand the challenges facing our communities and to explore effective strategies for individual and collective action, we need the long view and broad perspective that only collaborative and multidisciplinary approaches (including the full range of scientific, technical, and humanistic fields) can bring.

For context, it is important to keep in mind that mis/disinformation has accompanied the rise of new media throughout history as an unfortunate byproduct of the modern world. The spread of printed materials in the 1500s provided the expanding reading public access to a vast repository of information, but it also made way for opportunists, propagandists, and demagogues, who would quickly learn to exploit the vulnerabilities of the expanding print market to their advantage. Early Modern Europe was flooded with sensationalist and scandalous tales of supernatural occurrences, phony or fake news stories, and baseless conspiracy theories. The "yellow journalism" of the late 1800s, and the arrival of radio and audiovisual media in the first half of the twentieth century are also notable examples of the correlation between the expansion of mass media and the spread of mis/disinformation, including the kind of orchestrated propaganda we associate with the Info Ops of the brutal totalitarian regimes of the 1900s. Yet, the speed of transmission and the volume of mis/disinformation we see in the twenty-first century are without parallel in human history. The exponential increase of corrupt, misleading, manipulative, and exploitative information that's flooding our media-saturated world is causing significant harm to individuals and communities, eroding our trust in democratic institutions, and weakening our ability to respond to emerging crises, such as the recent pandemic or the looming threats of climate change.

The current emergency is at least in part a consequence of the ruthless efficiency of the powerful algorithms that media giants use to optimize user engagement and maximize profits. The data-gathering artificial intelligence (AI) tools employed by Facebook, Twitter (now X), TikTok, and other social media companies work behind the scenes to amplify and personalize sensationalist and polarizing content that attracts more views. Whatever gets a response spreads, and bad actors exploit this vulnerability. It is important to understand that the digital media landscape today is far different from that of the late 1990s, when internet users accessed content through search engines such as Lycos and web directories such as Yahoo. Those early internet services had no embedded mechanism to promote content. Consuming content required users to intentionally search for a keyword or browse to a particular website or forum. That era is basically gone. Instead, today's social media feeds serve up fringe and polarizing content, which users may not be intentionally searching for, thanks to the tech industry's embrace of two key technological developments: personalization, spurred by mass collection of user data through web cookies and big data systems, and algorithmic amplification, the use of powerful AI instruments to select the content that will be shared with individual users based on their interests and search history.

What this means in practical terms is that we can effectively live inside our own media silos, a reality of our choosing that's confirmed on an hourly basis by our AI-curated feeds. In the most extreme cases, these alternative realities can become rabbit holes populated by self-sustaining illusions. One particularly troubling type of audiovisual illusion capable of spreading mis/disinformation and locking us inside AI-generated versions of the world is the DeepFake, featured with increased frequency in recent news and social media posts. The fabrication and/or manipulation of digital media is not a new phenomenon. The synthesizing of realistic audio, images, and videos using algorithms has been an essential task in such fields as signal processing, computer graphics, and computer vision for some time. Yet, with pre-AI tools the creation process was lengthy, costly, and technically demanding for ordinary users. In recent years, however, the developments of AI technologies have significantly lowered the requirements on resources, time, and technical expertise for the creation of convincing fakes. The unprecedented computing power and the powerful AI technology available today, deep neural networks (DNNs) in particular, have made it easier, cheaper, and much less time consuming to generate sophisticated and compelling fakes.

DeepFakes first caught the public's attention in late 2017 when a Reddit account called DeepFake, a portmanteau of deep learning and fake media, started to spread pornographic videos with transplanted celebrity faces created using a DNN-based algorithm. Since then, more sophisticated algorithms to synthesize realistic audio, images, and videos have emerged, along with many open-source software tools and commercial services. In essence, DeepFakes are the tip of the iceberg of the troubling trend of increasingly realistic online mis/disinformation. By creating false records of the words and actions of individuals, DeepFakes can cause significant harm when weaponized. For instance, a fake video showing a politician engaged in inappropriate activity could be enough to sway an election if released at the right time. A falsified audio recording of a high-level executive commenting on her company's financial situation could send the stock market awry. Using a synthesized realistic human face as the profile photo for a fake social platform account can significantly increase the effectiveness of deception schemes. An online predator can masquerade as a family member or friend in a video chat to lure unsuspecting victims.

Left unchecked, DeepFakes can escalate the threat of online disinformation and fundamentally erode our trust in digital as well as traditional media, including reputable news sources and legitimate educational materials. In addition, DeepFakes pose a considerable threat to our cognitive security and could be used in combination with other cyberattacks to breach cyber systems. Working as a form of manipulative disinformation, DeepFakes can "hack" our perceptual system and decision-making process and endanger our personal data. Impersonating someone has become much easier with audiovisual synthesis. We have already seen a few cases of DeepFakes with devastating real-world consequences. GAN-generated face images have been used as profile photos for fake accounts on social platforms such as Twitter, Facebook, Instagram, and LinkedIn. In 2020 alone, 4,000 fake accounts were found on these social media platforms. Using such realistic face images as profile photos significantly increases the deceptiveness of those fake accounts. Another incident involved a scammer who successfully used a synthesized voice to impersonate the CEO of a UK company and mislead an employee to wire transfer a substantial amount of money to the scammer's bank account. Reports show that hackers have used DeepFakes to falsify biometric data to gain access to essential information systems. A particularly insidious case was a DeepFake video of the Ukrainian President directing the Ukrainian troops to surrender to the Russians. The video circulated on social media and Ukrainian news websites before being debunked and removed.

The security threats posed by the availability of increasingly effective DeepFake technologies have received broad attention from lawmakers and government officials worldwide. In the United States, Congress has passed several bills to regulate the use of DeepFakes, including the Malicious Deep Fake Prohibition Act of 2019, the DEEP FAKES Accountability Act, the Deepfake Report Act, and the IOGAN Act, 2019. The European Union and China have engaged in similar legislative efforts. Major social media platforms (e.g., Twitter and TikTok) have followed suit to generate policies aimed at controlling the production and spread of DeepFakes.

As serious as the danger of manipulative DeepFakes truly is, this is by no means the only threat posed by the groundbreaking advances we are witnessing in the field of artificial intelligence. The debates surrounding the recent release of ChatGPT seem to suggest a worsening of the problem in the short term due to the potential of AI technologies to generate convincing illusions that could lock unsuspecting users into alternative versions of reality. As Stuart A. Thompson, Tiffany Hsu, and Steven Lee Myers wrote in a *New York Times* article published on March 22, 2023, "Even as tech giants scramble to join the commercial boom prompted by the release of ChatGPT, they face an alarmed debate over the use—and potential abuse—of artificial intelligence. The technology's ability to create content that hews to predetermined ideological points of view, or presses disinformation, highlights a danger that some tech executives have begun to acknowledge: that an informational cacophony could emerge from competing chatbots with different versions of reality, undermining the viability of artificial intelligence as a tool in everyday life and further eroding trust in society" (Thompson, Hsu, and Myers 2023).

This is where the example of Miguel de Cervantes's most famous character comes in handy for us as a sort of literary analogue and critical caricature. Don Quixote is of course known for living inside a self-sustaining fantasy world (his own chosen reality informed by chivalric illusions) inside of which ordinary windmills can become evil giants. His fictional exploits are the inspiration behind the expression "tilting at windmills," meaning "attacking imaginary enemies or evils." If we can make the leap from the pages of Cervantes's famous novel (and the circumstances of the cultural crisis that inspired it) back to our troubled present, we can say that our media environment is breeding an alarming number of Quixote-style vigilantes (let's call them Q-Knights) intent on charging at all manner of things based on the self-sustaining illusions of conspiracy theories they read about in their media feeds. Like Don Quixote himself, the Q-Knights of our time can live inside a self-sustaining illusion in which the proliferation of mattress stores in close proximity to each other is clear evidence of a money-laundering operation or other nefarious activity possibly linked to a government agency (Hanbury 2018) and the basement of a popular pizza restaurant in Washington, DC, is the headquarters of a child-trafficking ring (BBC Trending 2016). They know what's really cooking "down there," even if there's no "down there" there, because they've read about it online. The fact that the restaurant in question has no basement is only proof of the vast powers of the ring leaders and their accomplices, who managed to cover their tracks so effectively. The resilience of these conspiratorial illusions even when challenged by seemingly incontrovertible evidence is indeed reminiscent of Don Quixote's trademark response to the crashing reality of windmills in the famous scene of the 1605 volume:

> "God save me!" said Sancho. "Didn't I tell your grace to watch what you were doing, that these were nothing but windmills, and only somebody whose head was full of them would think otherwise?"
>
> "Be quiet, Sancho . . . replied Don Quixote. "Matters of war, more than any others, are subject to continual change; moreover, *I think, and therefore it is true*, that the evil enchanter Frestón . . . has turned these giants into windmills in order to deprive me of the glory of their defeat: such is the enmity he feels against me; but in the end, his evil arts will not prevail against the power of my virtuous sword." (146, our translation, our emphasis)

An undeterred Don Quixote would go on to wage war against all manner of evil powers, which he "recognizes" in things that look like wineskins, watermills, and even livestock. In chapter 21 of the novel, Don Quixote and Sancho come across a human figure who is wearing something shiny on his head. The narrator identifies the man as a barber on a mule wearing a barber's basin as a makeshift hat to protect himself from the pouring rain, but Don Quixote begs to differ. The approaching horseman cannot be but a rival knight who is obviously in possession of Mambrino's magical helmet, which Don Quixote is destined to win in battle. When the unsuspecting barber sees Don Quixote charging at him full tilt, he dismounts in a hurry and runs for his life, leaving behind his ride and his headpiece. This is what happens next:

> When Sancho heard the barber's basin being called a helmet, he could not contain his laughter . . .
> "What are you laughing about, Sancho?" said Don Quixote.
> "I'm laughing," responded Sancho, "thinking about the big head belonging to the pagan owner of this helmet, which looks perfectly like a barber's basin."
> "Do you know what I think, Sancho? I think this famous fragment of this enchanted helmet, by some strange accident must have come into the hands of someone who could not recognize or appreciate its value, and without realizing what he was doing, seeing that it was cast from the purest gold, must have melted the other half for its worth, and from this half he made what looks like a barber's basin, just as you say. *But no matter, since I know what it is, its transformation makes no difference.*" (260, our translation, our emphasis)

It bears repeating, for one who "knows" what things really are regardless of their appearance, no amount of fact-checking or "debunking" by the Sanchos of the world will mean a thing. As for the familiar Q-knights of our own day who may consider attacking pizza parlors and mattress stores, they likewise know "the truth" of what is really going on, and no amount of evidence to the contrary will dissuade them otherwise. This is why efforts to combat mis/disinformation and conspiracy theories today and to mitigate their devastating impact in our communities cannot rely on fact-checking and debunking approaches alone. In essence, it is very hard to debunk or fact-check someone out of a conspiratorial rabbit hole, which is why the better approach might be to prevent people, including ourselves, our family members, our virtual communities from falling into those rabbit holes in the first place. But how?

One thing we have learned in the last few years is that there's no technical magic bullet capable of solving the problem of online deception and manipulation on its own. Domain experts in media technologies are the first to admit that even the most effective technical fixes will be at best partial and temporary since they would not be able to get to the root of the mis/disinformation problem. The available research on DeepFake-driven disinformation is a case in point. The mounting concerns over the nefarious use of DeepFakes have spawned increasing interest in counter technologies, with substantial support from government and private companies. Notable examples include the DARPA MediFor and SemaFor programs, the NIST 2018, 2020, and 2021 Synthetic Data Detection Challenge, and the DeepFake Detection Challenge (Meta AI 2020), sponsored by Facebook, Microsoft, Amazon, and Partnership in AI. DeepFake forensics has become an active research area in the past few years in response to the growing concerns. Indeed, it is fair to say that the current efforts in DeepFake forensics heavily tilt toward detection, often looking at the problem in terms of a simple binary classification: real or fake. Thus, we have more than 300 publications focused on this type of classification relying on more than fifty methods with code and datasets. Yet some studies (including Shane et al. 2021) show that the straightforward approach of labeling DeepFakes as part of debunking operations can actually undermine mitigation efforts by not taking sociopsychological considerations into account—users are drawn by curiosity to watch DeepFakes, which increases attention and promotes the spread of the labeled fake content. This is consistent with psychological research data that describes the vulnerabilities and failures of users when facing disinformation while leaving little space for potential solutions (Khodabakhsh et al. 2018; Lago et al. 2021). Taken together, these studies show that we need to think about best practices in intervention procedures, even after a DeepFake is exposed.

Given the complex nature of the challenge and the limited reach of purely technical fixes, we argue that there is a compelling need to refocus our approach, bringing together experts from computer science and engineering with researchers in social and behavioral sciences and the arts and humanities, along with representatives of the user communities. Convergence research, which is inherently multidisciplinary, problem-focused, and solutions-based, offers an ideal framework for the development of a more coherent and comprehensive approach to help guide what we study, whom we study, how we conduct our research, and who needs to be involved in the research process itself. These notions inspired the recent creation of the UB Center for Information Integrity. Our more than forty faculty members recognize that tackling what is clearly a defining challenge of our time requires multidisciplinary teams working together to supplement existing red-flagging and debunking practices with innovative preventative or "pre-bunking" approaches with the goal of raising awareness and increasing resilience. As consumers and users of complex digital products that compete for our attention, we must be able to identify dubious and malicious sources of information and to develop strategies to expose false claims and narratives and build trust in our communities to make effective interventions.

The present collection of essays is an attempt to model a convergence approach involving the Center for Information Integrity and the Humanities Institute at the University at Buffalo. We view this scholarly collaboration as a first step in our efforts to increase awareness and build resilience against the omnipresent threat of mis/disinformation in our media environment. We have structured this volume into three parts dealing with complementary and interrelated issues. Part I, "Misinformation and Artificial Intelligence," deals most directly with the threat of mis/disinformation in the context of what Shoshana Zuboff has called "surveillance capitalism." The essays included in this section reflect on the danger of outsourcing judgment and decision making to AI instruments in key areas of public life, from the processing of loan applications to school funding, policing, and sentencing. Part II, "Science Communication, Cultivating Awareness," is focused on the need to rethink how scientific findings are communicated to the public. We suggest that scientists need to cooperate with colleagues in other disciplines and community representatives to help minimize the negative effects of mis/disinformation in such vital areas as climate change science and public health. The consensus is that no amount of science-explaining on its own will likely work in the absence of a concerted effort to listen to and incorporate community questions, concerns, needs, and aspirations. Finally, part III, "Building Trust," expands on the issues of the previous sections to advocate for and explore instances of trust-building initiatives as a necessary precondition of community-oriented scholarly activity and effective intervention strategies in high-impact areas such as public health. The volume closes with an Afterword by Christina Milletti, executive director of the UB Humanities Institute, in which she foregrounds the power of fiction to hone critical-thinking skills and build awareness and resilience to misinformation.

In the first essay of the collection, E. Bruce Pitman, an expert in mathematical modeling, explains how our trust in AI systems to make critical decisions can lead to fundamentally erroneous, unjust, and potentially catastrophic outcomes for individuals and communities. As he writes, "AI systems are built by humans, are terribly fallible, and do not 'learn,' no matter how generously one defines 'learn,' from their experiences . . . AI systems can provide insight that can be valuable to human decision-makers. But we should not have unwavering confidence in AI systems, on their own, to behave predictably and interpretably." Pitman provides examples of critical areas in which decision making should never be left to unchecked or unsupervised AIs. These areas include the criminal justice system, the financial system, the medical system, and the social services system. He argues that "interpretability of the models used to assist in these critical sectors should be a bare-minimum requirement."

Comparative literature professor Ewa Ziarek takes the baton in chapter 2 with a broad-ranging discussion of disinformation, power, and the automation of judgments with a focus on "harms to democracy." Her starting point is that the current disinformation emergency cannot be understood in isolation. Instead, our disinformation problem must be examined in the larger context of ongoing threats to democracy posed by the rise of new technologies of power emerging from the conjunction of big data, digital capitalism, and the outsourcing of political judgments to algorithmic procedures. In this sense, the current mis/disinformation emergency is but a symptom of the momentous computational transformation of our societies in which algorithms play increasingly critical roles in virtually all areas of human activity, from communications and entertainment to information gathering and ranking, to hiring, banking, health care, and dating.

Ziarek coincides with Pitman in foregrounding the lack of transparency and interpretability of algorithmic decision making, a consequence of which is the erosion of democratic processes inside increasingly opaque societies: "Because algorithmically driven global practices of data collection, user profiling, surveillance, and predictive analytics operated by the digital technology giants—Amazon, Google, Facebook, Microsoft, Apple—are not open to public scrutiny, they constitute 'black box societies' (Pasquale 2015), in which disinformation, distrust, and conspiracies spread 'like a virus.' This global hegemony of private digital technology corporations not only raises questions of data privacy and increased surveillance, but also risks transforming politics and demands for justice into what other scholars and philosophers have called 'algorithmic governmentality' (Stiegler 2019; Rouvroy and Barnes, 2013), in which political and juridical decisions are increasingly replaced by automated algorithms." The risks here are numerous, not the least of which is the replacement of deliberative processes by opaque practices of digital profiling and decision making. The virtual impenetrability of algorithmic modeling makes it harder to question assumptions, challenge potential biases, and impugn faulty processes and unjust outcomes. We would argue that this is indeed the larger context within which the "integrity" of information, its communicability and applicability, should be pondered as we travel deeper into an AI-assisted future.

In chapter 3, Yotam Ophir, Raphaela Velho, and Lilian Tzivian reflect on the politicization of science and lack of compliance with science-consistent recommendations in such critical areas as public health, with the recent pandemic as a glaring illustration. They discuss and ultimately reject the Deficit Model, which explains inadequate compliance with science as the result of a lack of understanding. Instead, they rely on available data from several countries and regions of the world to demonstrate that it wasn't ignorance but politically motivated distrust that most "hampered the global effort to slow down the COVID-19 epidemic." This is why, they argue, scientists must work to (re)build trust, not just by improving their communication strategies and being more transparent about the nature of scientific research but, most importantly, by paying attention to the needs and motivations of their audiences. This requires a better understanding of motivated reasoning and a more inclusive view of potential communication partners: "Importantly, understanding the role played by motivated reasoning in the rejection of science in the face of scientific facts can open doors to more effective science communication (Bisgaard 2019). Groups such as the Evangelical Climate Initiative (Nagle 2008), whose messages explain how protecting the Earth and fighting climate change could be understood through Christian values and perspective, provide an example for effective science communication targeting value-motivated groups and individuals."

In chapter 4, filmmaker and podcaster John Fiege advocates for "alternative" approaches to science communication in the face of resistance to climate action by politicians, business owners, media personalities, and the public at large. His own approach, which he effectively rehearses in his podcast and films, may be best described as deeply personal, inclusive, and conversational: "This essay is about what I have learned in my search for an alternative way to communicate and make media about the ecological crisis—one that brings people together and engages our best thinking, rather than pushing us apart. I am a filmmaker focused on confronting environmental problems through the stories of communities on the front lines of environmental calamity. Feeling the urgency to increase the number of stories I can address, the speed of production, and the frequency of my engagement with audiences, I recently launched a podcast, called Chrysalis, as a way to confront our ecological predicament through conversations with a broad diversity of environmental thinkers. As the title intimates, Chrysalis is a podcast about transformation—the transformation of the podcast guests, the audience, our collective relationship to the rest of nature, and me personally as I engage deeply in conversation."

In chapter 5, art professor and new media artist Matt Kenyon describes his decades-long pursuit to "make visible" the invisible hand of destructive market forces and exploitative power dynamics, which have been normalized by disinformation-filled narratives of progress. Kenyon builds on the sci-fi trope of the classic horror film *The Invisible Man* (1933), which he offers as an analogue for his own public art program: "Through my artwork, I aim to make the unseen visible, much like the way the fresh snow in *The Invisible Man* reveals the hidden protagonist. I strive to highlight the often unseen influence of power and wealth, bringing these forces into focus by making work that might catch the footprints they leave in the snow."

In chapter 6, geographer Jessie Poon and epidemiologist Laurene Tumiel Berhalter team up to examine the influence of socioeconomic, demographic, and institutional factors on trust (or lack thereof) in medicine based on data from the General Social Survey (GSS) and specialized literature on the subject. While a survey of twenty-eight countries conducted by the market research company Ipsos (2021) found the medical profession to be "most trustworthy," the public trust in medical scientists in the United States lags way behind, as only 29 percent of Americans report they have high confidence that members of the medical scientific community will act in the public's interest (Kennedy, Tyson, and Funk 2022). While vaccine misinformation has no doubt exacerbated the problem in recent years, the historical arch provided by Poon and Tumiel Berhalter suggests that there are deeper long-range issues at play that must be understood. As they write, "The American Association of Medical College's Center for Health Justice recognizes the importance of trust in the delivery of quality health care for all and the reduction of health inequity by establishing Principles of Trustworthiness as a guide for health care and public health. Trust has been identified in a burgeoning literature as an important mechanism for combating vaccine hesitancy and misinformation (Franic, 2022). Understanding the influences that explain trust and leveraging existing resources can help inform public policy regarding how trust may be improved to mitigate against misinformation at a time of public health crisis."

This is precisely the starting point of the final chapter of the collection authored by biochemist Jennifer Anne Surtees. In her essay, Surtees makes the point that public engagement is vital to promote mutual understanding between the medical professionals and the communities they serve: "As researchers at a public university, we have a responsibility to engage with our community . . . provide our citizenry with the tools and knowledge to understand, regulate, ensure ethical and equitable use of, and derive maximum benefit from the astonishing advances in these biomedical sciences." Surtees herself has focused her own professional activity on hands on, inquiry-based community engagement practices involving K–16 students and adult populations on issues ranging from genome and microbiome literacy to vaccine education. Her stated goal provides a fitting conclusion to the volume: "to nurture robust community partnerships to better understand the unique crosscutting needs of diverse communities and to develop an infrastructure of trust through which to communicate scientific advances, from genomic medicine to pandemic risk."

As we bring this introduction to a close, Yuval Harari, the historian who authored *Sapiens: A Brief History of Humankind* (2018), Tristan Harris, computer scientist and co-founder of the Center for Humane Technology, and his co-founding partner, mathematician and physicist Aza Raskin, published an opinion piece in the *New York Times*, which includes dire warnings about democracy unless we learn to live with (and protect ourselves from) AI-spread and AI-generated illusions and update our nineteenth-century institutions to cope with twenty-first-century realities:

> The specter of being trapped in a world of illusions has haunted humankind much longer than the specter of AI. Soon we will finally come face to face with Descartes's demon, with Plato's cave, with the Buddhist Maya. A curtain of illusions could descend over the whole of humanity, and we might never again be able to tear that curtain away—or even realize it is there . . . In social media, primitive AI was used not to create content, but to curate user-generated content. The AI behind our news feeds is still choosing which words, sounds and images reach our retinas and eardrums, based on selecting those that will get the most virality, the most reaction, and the most engagement . . . Democracy is a

conversation, conversation relies on language, and when language itself is hacked the conversation breaks down and democracy becomes untenable. If we wait for the chaos to ensue, it will be too late to remedy it . . . The first step is to buy time to upgrade our 19th-century institutions for a post-A.I. world, and to learn to master A.I. before it masters us. (Harari, Harris, and Raskin, 2023)

We would further argue that the first step in protecting human societies against the curtain of AI-spread and AI-generated illusions must include an educational line of defense so that we can be better prepared for not just what's to come but what is already here. Thus, the urgent upgrade of "our 19th-century institutions" that Harari, Harris, and Raskin call for would need to include a revamping of our educational practices beyond the nineteenth-century version of disciplinary silos. We can no longer afford to be segmented into nearly hermetic fields if we are serious about figuring out how to navigate the AI-assisted present-future. It bears repeating that the urgent challenges outlined in this volume are not mere technical problems that can be effectively solved inside technical fields alone. When and where the vital matter of language and communication is involved, the humanities and arts must be key players, along with their partners in the social sciences, as we try to (re)train ourselves in the "art of reading reality" (Castillo and Egginton 2016, 2021). As our contributing colleagues remind us in their own scholarly practices, the kind of collective (re)training we are advocating here requires a degree of disciplinary self-examination and, most importantly, a willingness to engage with colleagues working in other fields and members of the larger community, outside our own academic circles. After all, communication is a two-way street predicated on trust.

References

BBC Trending. 2016. "The Saga of 'Pizzagate': The Fake Story That Shows How Conspiracy Theories spread." BBC (Dec 2). www.bbc.com/news/blogs-trending-38156985

Bisgaard, Martin. 2019. "How Getting the Facts Right Can Fuel Partisan-Motivated Reasoning." *American Journal of Political Science* 63, no. 4: 824–839.

Castillo, David, and William Egginton. 2016. *Medialogies: Reading Reality in the Age of Inflationary Media.* New York: Bloomsbury Press.

———. 2021. *What Would Cervantes Do? Navigating Post-Truth with Spanish Baroque Literature*. Kingston, ON: McGill-Queen's University Press.

Cervantes, Miguel de. 2010. *Don Quixote de la Mancha*, 2 vols. Ed. John Jay Allen. Madrid: Cátedra.

Franic, J. 2022. "What Lies behind Substantial Differences in COVID-19 Vaccination Rates between EU Member States?" *Frontiers in Public Health* 10: 1–15.

Hanbury, Mary. 2018. "Mattress Firm Responds to the Wild Conspiracy Theory about Its Business That People Are Going Crazy Over." *Business Insider* (Jan 24). www.businessinsider.com/mattress-firm-responds-to-conspiracy-theory-about-its-business-2018-1

Harari, Yuval. 2018. *Sapiens: A Brief History of Humankind*. New York: Harper.

Harari, Yuval, et al. 2023. "You Can Have the Blue Pill or the Red Pill, and We're Out of Blue Pills." *New York Times* (March 24). www.nytimes.com/2023/03/24/opinion/yuval-harari-ai-chatgpt.html

Kennedy, Brian, Alec Tyson, and Cary Funk. 2022. "Americans' Trust in Scientists, Other Groups Declines." Pew Research Center.

Khodabakhsh, Ali, Raghavendra Ramachandra, Kiran B. Raja, Pankaj Wasnik, and Christopher Bush. 2018. "Fake Face Detention Methods: Can They Be Generalized?" (Conference Paper, September 2018). www.researchgate.net/publication/327350438_Fake_Face_Detection_Methods_Can_They_Be_Generalized

Lago, F., C. Pasquini, R. Bohme, H. Dumont, V. Goffaux, and G. Boato. 2022. "More Real Than Real: A Study On Human Visual Perception Of Synthetic Faces." *IEEE Signal Processing Magazine* 20, no. 10: 23–40.

Meta AI. 2020. "Deepfake Detection Challenge Dataset." (Meta, June 25). https://ai.meta.com/datasets/dfdc

Nagle, John Copeland. 2008. "The Evangelical Debate over Climate Change." U. St. Thomas LJ 5: 53.

Pasquale, Frank. 2015. *The Black Box Society: The Secret Algorithms that Control Money and Information*. Cambridge, MA: Harvard University Press.

Rouvroy, Antoinette, and Thomas Berns. 2013. "Algorithmic Governmentality and Prospects of Emancipation: Disparateness as a Precondition for Individuation through Relationships?" Translated by Elizabeth Libbrecht. *Réseaux* 177, no. 1: 163–196.

Shane, Tommy, Emily Saltz, and Claire Leibowicz. 2021. "From Deepfakes to TikTok Filters: How Do We Label AI Content? *First Draft* (May 12).

Stiegler, Bernard. 2019. *The Age of Disruption: Technology and Madness in Computational Capitalism*. Translated by Daniel Ross. Cambridge: Polity Press.

Thompson, Stuart A., Tiffany Hsu, and Steven Lee Myers. 2023. "Conservatives Aim to Build a Chatbot of Their Own." *New York Times* (March 22). www.nytimes.com/2023/03/22/business/media/ai-chatbots-right-wing-conservative.html

Part I
Misinformation and Artificial Intelligence

Chapter One

It Is Artificial, But Is It Intelligent?

E. Bruce Pitman*

Forty-two

—Deep Thought, *Hitchhiker's Guide to the Galaxy*

The purpose of computation is insight, not numbers.

—Richard Hamming, *Numerical Methods for Scientists and Engineers*

Every few months, popular periodicals run a story with a title something like "AI's fabulous failures." Autopilot stories from 2021 include (Ravi 2021):

Tesla car runs off road when its AI autopilot fails to detect bend in the road.

Amazon AI recruiting tool biased against women.

Microsoft AI chatbot churns out sexist, racist tweets.

Amazon facial recognition software identifies 28 politicians as criminals.

---

*Research supported in part by NSF CDS&E award 2053874.

OK, some would contend that last one isn't a failure of AI . . . but they haven't been convicted. At least not yet.

My favorite: in the UK, an AI camera used for TV broadcast, to follow the ball and show the action on the field, mistakes the follicly challenged bald head of the lineman for the soccer ball.

Yet we continue to rely on AI systems to drive cars, to approve mortgage applications, to grant parole to prisoners, and to read the x-rays of cancer patients. Is this where we want to be?

This note is not intended to bash AI systems. There are some great successes. There are documented cases where an AI system detected tiny blobs in an image, a blob that a highly trained radiologist missed (Savage 2020). AI systems monitor my credit card purchases, and I am grateful when those systems flag a transaction that seems inconsistent with my usual behavior. Not long ago, an AI system generated the best guess of the unknown structure of large, complex protein molecules, structural knowledge that is important to biologists trying to understand how these molecules work (Callaway 2022).

Notice, however, that these successes all include a human-in-the-loop: a radiologist reviewing the findings of a machine-read x-ray; a representative checking with me whether I made a purchase from a store I haven't frequented; a biologist verifying the computer-generated structural information. The AI system is *not* being left on its own to make a decision without significant human impact.

To be clear about the systems and concepts we will refer to in talking about these systems, we should set some definitions. When we speak of artificial intelligence (AI), we are referring to the newest collection of algorithms and methodologies from computer science, dealing with agents that perceive and react to their environment and tackle problems of recognition and decision making—from robots to Watson playing chess to Siri's voice recognition. Machine learning, or ML, is a class of AI algorithms that postulate a model, and "learn," based on so-called "training data" in order to make predictions based on that model and training, about some "test" data. Finally, deep neural networks (DNNs) are a specific class of AI algorithms that attempt to mimic the human central nervous system, building a learning agent from a massive number of simple "neurons" arranged in layers, and connected according to a prescribed geometry. These DNNs classify the presence or absence of a signal; a signal could represent whether a specific pixel in an image is black or white, or if a piece of data satisfies a certain criterion. It is these massive neural networks that are used in big applications such as self-driving cars or facial recognition.

The basic neuron in a NN is a classifier, a switch, that takes the values of 1 or 0 depending on the presence or absence of a signal that satisfies a prescribed criterion. These networks can be huge—perhaps a million neurons connected in a geometry of ten or twenty layers, with differing numbers of connections among the many neurons. To train these networks requires massive amounts of data—Google's image recognition system requires millions of images. When it works, this system can identify me from my picture, and will distinguish my image from an image showing my wife's face.

And yet . . .

This 1-0, or on-off, character of each one of those millions of simple neurons is the ultimate source of potential failures of deep neural networks. Each neuron is forced to be 1 or 0—nothing in between, no partially on/partially off. This 1-0 character is replicated at each of the many layers of the NN, resulting in an output that is itself binary, and outputs that can be catastrophically incorrect (Heaven 2019).

Two principal deficiencies arise from this hard 1-0 classification.

First, deep neural networks are brittle. Change the training data a little bit and you come up with a very different output. There are classic examples in the CS world of image recognition failures: a DNN is trained and classifies a new image as a panda (Goodfellow et al. 2014). A second image of that same panda is altered by a tiny amount—an amount imperceptible to the human eye—but the DNN classifies the image as a gibbon; see figure 1.1. What is worse, the DNN classifier claims 57 percent confidence in its original "panda" classification and 99 percent confidence in its "gibbon" classification.

Figure 1.1. Panda misclassification under adversarial attack. The GoogLeNet classifier also reports a measure of confidence in the prediction (see Goodfellow et al. 2014). *Source:* Public domain.

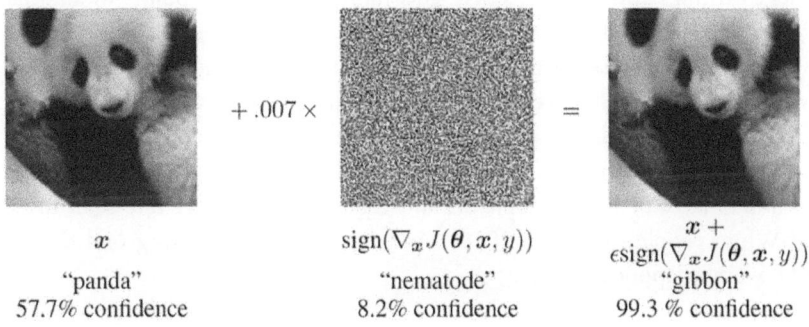

x
"panda"
57.7% confidence

$+ .007 \times$

$\text{sign}(\nabla_x J(\theta, x, y))$
"nematode"
8.2% confidence

$=$

$x + \epsilon\text{sign}(\nabla_x J(\theta, x, y))$
"gibbon"
99.3 % confidence

This occurs not only in these huge DNNs; one sees this brittleness in very small, very simple neural networks that can be used to gain intuition about the behavior of larger networks. The top plot in figure 1.2 shows five red o's and five blue x's arranged in the plane. Based on these ten training datapoints, a simple neural network with two inputs and two outputs and two interior layers with a total of five neurons has classified every point in the plane—every point in the plane is a test point, and is colored gray if that point is classified with the o's, and white if that point is classified with the x's (Higham and Higham 2019). The bottom plot shows a slightly different arrangement of the o's and x's, and a very different classification of all the test points in the plane. Can you spot the difference in the two arrangements of o's and x's?

Of course, there are fixes to the sensitivity of the classification in this simple x's and o's example. But those fixes add additional computing and complexity to the problem. The fixes don't really address the underlying brittleness of the algorithm itself.

Second, deep neural networks are non-explainable. Understanding the brittleness, and the failings, of neural networks is an active area of research. The panda figure is taken from a repository of images that computer scientists use to test out their algorithms. Yet there is no computer scientist who can say precisely why the first image was correctly identified as a panda and the second as a gibbon. Sure, a little noise was added—but where in the neural network did things start to go wrong? Nobody can tell. And no computer scientist is able to tell whether a third image of a panda, corrupted with slightly different noise, will be classified as a panda or as a gibbon. Or as a gorilla. This lack of interpretability can have significant consequences to humans who are caught in AI mistakes. For example, an AI system turns down a mortgage application; the banker can't tell exactly why the AI system said "No," and guesses at the reasons. But the banker also can't explain why the system said "Yes" to an applicant who has very similar employment earnings and credit history. This mortgage example points to another issue with DNNs that has profound social consequences—AI systems are (often) biased. These deep networks require enormous amounts of data on which to train and, so, very often, these training datasets, whether through inattention or a lack of care, are not comprehensive and tend to under-represent minority communities that are already disadvantaged in society. For example, faces of Black people are mis-classified at a higher rate than those of White people (Simonite 2019). And the Amazon recruiting tool doesn't like women applicants.

Figure 1.2. A very simple neural network classifier is trained on the five o's and five x's, and predicts the classes of all other points in the plane. The two arrangements of o's and x's are slightly different—try to spot the differences—but lead to very different classifications of the rest of the plane. *Source:* Created by the author.

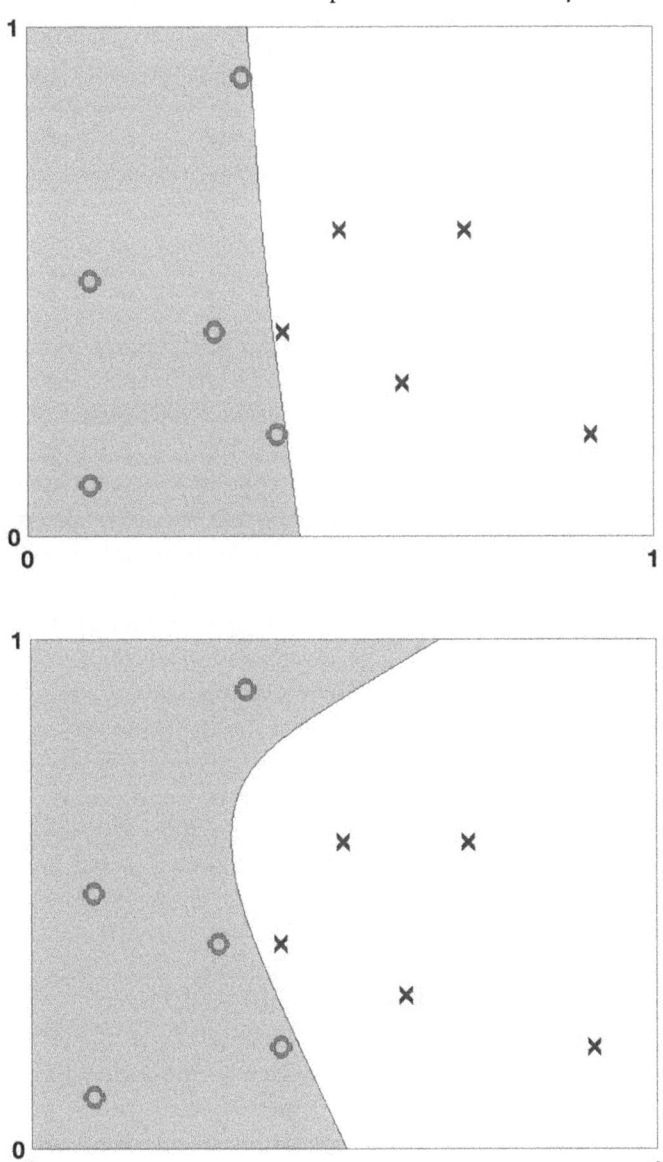

In a Rube Goldberg-esque turn, there have been attempts to dissect the output of a complicated neural network classification engine by building a second complicated network to "explain" the first. DARPA has supported just such a research thrust (Turek n.d.). Rudin (2019) argues that such "explaining" AI models are often not faithful to the calculations of the original model—for the simple reason that to construct an explanation, simplifications must be made. So, of course, the explaining model cannot be entirely faithful. Think about it for a minute—we are being asked to believe that the best way to explain a complex, non-interpretable neural network is by constructing a second complex network. One is justified in viewing all of this as a house of cards.

As noted, these networks require massive amounts of data to train on, and the network tends to fit the slight difference between images—fitting the noise—and not the overall trends and large-scale features. Moreover, it is virtually impossible to provide training data that thoroughly and accurately represents all the conditions in which the network will operate. Consider a NN trained to classify animals. Most of the images provided as training data will be of rabbits and dogs and birds and cats and whatever else, mostly in the daylight, in a reasonably clear and uncluttered image. But when deployed, this image classifier will be fed pictures of animals at dusk or under poor lighting conditions, from oblique angles, and in a picture frame with other objects. The classifier will be expected to extrapolate from all the relatively clean and clear images it knows, to a much more difficult setting. As any data scientist will tell you, extrapolation is always a tricky procedure.

The scientific method operates by postulating a hypothesis, performing several experiments to test the implications of that hypothesis, and modifying the hypothesis based on those experimental results. If, as a scientist, I hypothesized about the behavior of a physical system, and my hypothesis was proven not to hold true under many conditions, I would be forced to admit that my hypothesis was not true. Yet the computer science literature is filled with examples of DNNs that fail to correctly classify as they are supposed to, and yet they remain widely deployed. Such a poor predictive capability would never be tolerated as a scientific theory.

Yet another issue that hampers the real usefulness of DNNs is they have no ability to recognize something different from their training data and make an educated guess—and, importantly, to tell that it is a guess. That is, a DNN has no objective way of measuring its degree of confidence in the result it is reporting. In mathspeak, there is no objective error estimator external to the data. The confidence numbers claimed in the panda example are reports from the network, telling how well it thinks it did based on its training. That is, the system is trained on data, is tested against its training by an image of a panda, and reports a confidence number based on the very same training data. There are alternative approaches, different kinds of classification algorithms that can provide probabilistic estimates of whether a datum is closer to a 1 or a 0 . . . it can say "60 percent of me thinks this is a 1." See figure 1.3 for a plot of a probabilistic version of the classification of o's and x's used to generate figure 1.2. Here the o's are assigned a value of 1, and the x's a value of 0. The plot shows a surface that smoothly interpolates the 1-0 classes, and in fact looks much more like the bottom plot of figure 1.2. The two arrangements of x's and o's in figure 1.2 produce surfaces indistinguishable from one another, at any but the finest resolution. This probabilistic algorithm, called a Gaussian Process classifier, comes equipped with an estimate of likely variability—that is, a range of other potential interpolations and the probability associated with these other surfaces. A close study of this variability allows one to explore any uncertainty in the conclusions that may be drawn from the interpolation.

These probabilistic algorithms are harder to run, and more time consuming than DNNs (e.g., see Yu n.d.); at present, these alternatives cannot handle the huge volume of data needed for, say, a major deployment for

Figure 1.3. A smooth Gaussian Process classification of the o's, assigned a value of 1, and the x's, assigned a value of 0, from figure 1.2. *Source:* Created by the author.

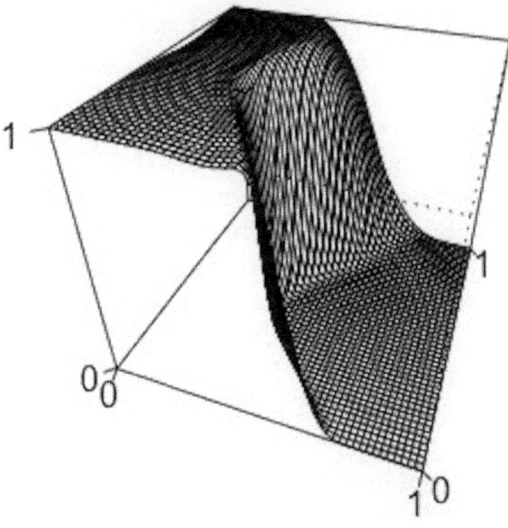

facial recognition. But these alternative approaches are not so brittle, and one can follow the decision process to interpret why a particular outcome was arrived at. (That said, there still may be training bias—an issue with all ML.) These probabilistic networks hold the promise of truly learning and of being more faithful to the data presented. Unfortunately, these methods are not being studied as actively as DNN ideas.

A cadre of scholars object to the current status of machine learning throughout the scientific community. Semenova et al. (2022) argue that finding complex models to fit data is rather easy, and finding simpler models can be difficult, but that simple models with comparable accuracy do exist in many important circumstances. The authors then provide a mechanism for checking whether such a simpler model does, in fact, exist.

As mentioned, Rudin (2019) writes that society should not use complex "black box" models for tasks with the potential for significant human impact—health care, provisioning of social services, and prison sentencing and parole, for example. The AI community sometimes poses a false dichotomy between accuracy and interpretability, arguing that greater accuracy precludes interpretability. Rudin offers alternative approaches with similar accuracy, which can be interpreted. I should make another distinction here: for AI systems, interpretability is a clear linking of cause and effect. Explainability, on the other hand, involves telling humans how the internal mechanisms of the AI system handle data input and output. These are different concepts, though closely related. I can interpret a science experiment by observing the several steps of the process. But explaining that experiment requires a deep dive into the chemistry and physics. Good AI should aim for both.

In fact, good AI ought to be interpretable, explainable, transparent, and robust. The data used to train the AI system ought not be biased in any way. The AI system ought to provide a measure of how uncertainty in inputs translates into uncertainty in outputs. There ought to be accountability if the system causes harm or injury. These are all characteristics of Trustworthy AI (Caltech n.d.). It is important to distinguish Trustworthy AI, and trust in AI systems. Trustworthy AI means AI that meets certain specifications of explainability, transparency, and robustness. Worthy of trust. It is reliable, like your car getting you to work every day. I might be disappointed in the AI system if it issued a decision inconsistent with past performance—just as I would be if my car transmission failed to engage. Trust in AI systems is a far more complex relationship—not only should the AI be trustworthy, but, as a user, I must be willing to place myself in a position of vulnerability by using this AI system. This AI system could do more than disappoint me; it could "hurt" me, by making a decision not consistent with my expectations (Chintada 2021). Riding as a passenger in a self-driving car as it flies down the highway requires a high level of trust, much more than being assured the vehicle is reliable and trustworthy.

This brings me back to this chapter's epigraph. After seven and a half million years of thinking and calculating, Deep Thought is ready to give the answer to the great question of life, the universe, and everything. An understanding of it all. Deep Thought's pronouncement: forty-two. No explanation. No insight as to why. No context in which to interpret the answer. Sounds familiar, eh? When I was in elementary school, my math teachers would say that a quiz problem would be marked incorrect if you wrote down an answer but didn't show your work. This is a lesson that should be applied to neural network research. With very different reasons for their insistence on showing your work, Deep Thought and my math teacher argue the case for explainability. The second epigraph is from Hamming's 1962 book on numerical methods. At the time, computing power was limited and scientists could not construct sufficiently fine grids on which to solve the problems of fluid dynamics or elasticity with much accuracy. Of course, the situation is much different today, where computers are powerful enough to determine the flow of air around the entire body of a jet airplane with high precision. Nevertheless, Hamming's dictum leads us to use computing to think about a challenging problem, to gain insight. The actual numbers are far less important. After all, no model is entirely perfect—no model incorporates every feature that might impact a result, so we shouldn't expect perfect answers. For us here—if you train a DNN for one particular problem, you will get a number as "the answer." If you change the problem a little, you must re-train the entire network before you can test it again. Insight, however, helps us understand why you arrive at the answer in the first case, and what the second answer might be without having to perform a large computational task. Insight helps us understand "Why." For science, Why is more important than any one number.

In spite of the tone of this exposition, I am not here to rant against AI systems and DNNs. But I do wish to rant against the uncritical, unsupervised, unchecked use of DNNs. If a network makes a prediction about the structure of a protein and sends this prediction to a scientist who is trying to verify protein structures computationally and experimentally, this DNN is providing great assistance to a structural biologist.

If a network reads an x-ray and sends its insights to a radiologist, who also reads the x-ray, the two analyses can be a whole lot better than if the radiologist was on her own.

But when an AI system decides to reject a bank mortgage application without a human reviewing the entire file and all the pertinent factors, that is unconscionable.

When an AI system makes parole decisions based on the likelihood of recidivism, without a human also reviewing that parole application, that is not serving justice.

Self-driving cars—there are lots and lots of miles that have been driven under fully autonomous mode, without incident. But self-driving vehicles have run into parked trucks, struck pedestrians, and driven off roads, even in lovely weather conditions. Thank you, but I'd rather take my chances with a New York City cabbie.

As a society we should not turn over important decisions to unsupervised and unchecked AIs. Some examples of critical sectors where decision making should not be left to AI without a human in the loop include

- the criminal justice system,
- financial systems,
- medical systems, and
- social services systems.

Foul-ups in these sectors can have very real consequences for very real people. AI should assist humans, not replace them. Interpretability of the models used to assist in these critical sectors should be a bare-minimum requirement (Rudin 2019).

More generally, we should not stand in thrall of AI systems. Just because a computer spits out an answer doesn't mean that answer is correct. AI systems are built by humans, are terribly fallible, and do not "learn," no matter how generously one defines "learn," from their experiences. Any veneer of intelligence that might appear around these systems is, indeed, artificial.

AI systems can provide insight valuable to human decision makers. But we should not have unwavering confidence in AI systems, on their own, to behave predictably and interpretably. I contend that humans must be in the loop, holding ultimate responsibility and ultimately being held accountable.

The argument in their favor is that AI systems save time and money and can do tasks that humans simply cannot. I suggest that we cannot afford to have unchecked and unsupervised AI systems making critical decisions. The cost to our social fabric is simply too large.

References

Callaway, E. 2022. "'The Entire Protein Universe': AI Predicts Shape of Nearly Every Protein." www.nature.com/articles/d41586-022-02083-2

Caltech. n.d. Caltech Science Exchange. Accessed November 25, 2022. https://scienceexchange.caltech.edu/topics/artificial-intelligence-research/trustworthy-ai

Chintada, S. 2021. "Forbes Addressing AI's Biggest Problem: Trust." Accessed November 25, 2022. www.forbes.com/sites/forbestechcouncil/2021/10/25/addressing-ais-biggest-problem-trust/?sh=6267322c257c

Goodfellow, I., J. Shlens, and C. Szegedy. 2014. "Explaining and Harnessing Adversarial Examples." arXiv:1412.6572

Heaven, D. 2019. "Why Deep Learning AIs Are So Easy to Fool." *Nature*. www.nature.com/articles/d41586-019-03013-5

Higham, C., and D. Higham. 2019. "Deep Learning: An Introduction for Applied Mathematicians." *SIAM Review*. https://doi.org/10.1137/18M1165748

Ravi, R. 2021. "AI Gone Wrong." Jumpstart. www.jumpstartmag.com/ai-gone-wrong-5-biggest-ai-failures-of-all-time

Rudin, C. 2019. "Stop Explaining Black Box Machine Learning Models for High Stakes Decisions and Use Interpretable Models Instead." Nature Machine Intelligence, 1:206–215. www.nature.com/articles/s42256-019-0048-x

Savage, N. 2020. "How AI Is Improving Cancer Diagnostics." *Nature* (March 2020). www.nature.com/articles/d41586-020-00847-2

Semenova, L., C. Rudin, and R. Parr. 2022. "On the Existence of Simpler Machine Learning Models." Proceedings FACCT'22. ACM. 1827–1858.

Simonite, T. 2019. "The Best Algorithms Struggle to Recognize Black Faces Equally." *Wired*. www.wired.com/story/best-algorithms-struggle-recognize-black-faces-equally

Sutrop, M. 2019. "Should We Trust Artificial Intelligence?" *Journal of Humanities and Social Sciences* 23: 499.

Turek, Matt. n.d. "Explainable Artificial Intelligence." Accessed November 25, 2022. www.darpa.mil/program/explainable-artificial-intelligence

Yu, J., E. Creager, D. Duvenaud, and J. Bettencourt. 2022. "Bayesian Neural Networks." October 30. www.cs.toronto.edu/~duvenaud/distill_bayes_net/public

Chapter Two

Disinformation, Power, and the Automation of Judgments

Notes on Algorithmic Harms to Democracy

Ewa Płonowska Ziarek

> When we rely exclusively on computation for answers to complex social issues, we are relying on artificial unintelligence.
>
> —Meredith Broussard, *Artificial Unintelligence: How Computers Misunderstand the World*

Information Integrity and Its Discontents

As more and more social relations and everyday human activities, from dating, driving, entertainment, and internet searches, to social services, hiring, health care, jurisprudence, and most recently, research itself, are mediated by algorithms rather than public decisions and debate, the far-reaching implications of these changes, especially for democracy as well as for gender, race, and economic equity, are hard to foresee. "Disinformation" is but one of the numerous symptoms of these irreversible computational transformations of everyday life (Ziarek 2020, 2022) and therefore cannot be treated in isolation or remedied primarily by technical and scientific solutions without a broader understanding of the consequences of the algorithmic technologies of power.

At first glance, a December 2022 report entitled "Roadmap for Researchers on Priorities Related to Information Integrity Research and Development," prepared by the National Science and Technology Council for the executive branch of the US government, seems to encourage such wider perspectives as it aims to comprehend whole "ecosystems" in which disinformation and its opposite—what the report calls "information integrity"—operate. Indeed, the assertion that such ecosystems are dynamic, complex, and unpredictable is a first step to any project attempting to remedy the harms of disinformation. At the same time, this roadmap significantly limits the analysis of sociotechnological and political interactions by prioritizing their measurable and formalizable dimensions. Consequently, while this document goes a long way toward recognizing uncertainty, gaps of knowledge, political polarization, and the complexities of AI-driven information technologies, its research agenda priorities fall short in three interrelated and predictable ways: first, this agenda delegates the task of understanding sociopolitical harms to quantitative sciences and technical solutions; second, it avoids a deeper analysis of power relations shaping AI/ML technologies; and third, it treats communities as objects of study or targets of literacy but not as equal participants or critical interlocutors, who might challenge expert knowledge of the sciences. To recall Foucault's famous formulation of the hierarchies of power/knowledge in Western modernity, algorithmic technologies continue to disqualify critical insights of a wider public as subjugated knowledge while privileging the knowledge of computational experts. Consequently, even though the "Roadmap" for information integrity research is concerned with new threats to democracy, national security, human rights, and disproportional harms inflicted by disinformation on the most vulnerable or underserved communities, such as the elderly, children, LGBTQ, or people of color, its research agenda is not driven by the priorities formulated by these communities but rather by "the science of information integrity."

"Roadmap" presents us therefore with three contradictions characteristic of a larger algorithmic culture. The first contradiction can be formulated as the acknowledgment of sociopolitical harms inflicted by AI/ML technologies and searching for remedies in the very technologies that produce those harms. As Kate Crawford argues, such focus not only refrains from the analysis of power relations "at the intersection of technology, capital, and governments" but in fact leaves them intact (2021, 9). The second contradiction lies in the assertion of the heterogeneity of sociopolitical and technological interactions and in the suppression of this unpredictable heterogeneity by measurable variety. And the third contradiction stems from the substitution of accurate measurement for what Hannah Arendt (1994) calls "difficulties of understanding" matters of common concern, which in our historical moment also include disinformation and algorithmic harms. In contrast to the science of information integrity, such understanding is relational, emerging from sharing and contesting intersubjective opinions and judgments with others who are mutually regarded as equal and distinct. The equation of critical understanding with measurement and "logical operations means to level the capacity for thought . . . to its lowest common denominator, where no differences in actual existence count any longer" (Arendt 1994, 318).

These three contradictions are evident in the formulation of the very first question that the research priorities are supposed to answer: "How do human, social, technical, and systemic elements of information ecosystems affect the integrity of information creation, exchange, and consumption, and how can modeling, measurement, and analysis enhance the understanding of the underlying mechanisms?" (US Government 2022, 3). Despite the grammatical conjunction "and" linking the two parts of this sentence, its meaning vacillates between an acknowledgment of the unpredictable complexity of sociopolitical/tech ecosystems and the assumption that this complexity can be measured by algorithmic "modeling." What enables such an unwarranted quantification of intersubjective, political, and technological interactions is the explicit economic, market-driven definition of communication in terms of its "production," "consumption," and exchange (5). Given this implicit approach to information as a market commodity, the task of research (which will determine what kind of projects will receive federal funding) is to develop better models, "including fundamental research on outcome metrics, algorithm design, and *the mechanistic relationship* between design choices, societal benefits, and forms related to manipulated information" (5, emphasis added). In this hegemonic framework, understanding, including an understanding of the "degradation of democratic processes" (5), is equivalent with the recurrent triple imperative—"analyze, model, and measure" (21). Even the insights into human attitudes toward "corrupted information," including memory, group affiliations, trust or distrust, are dependent on "reliable methodologies to measure persuasiveness of corrupted information and what causes it to affect cognition, beliefs, decision-making, and behavior" (24). It is hardly surprising, therefore, that the agents most equipped to comprehend sociopolitical dynamics, technological interactions, and even personhood itself are experts of computational and quantitative social sciences, ranging from sociology and linguistics to political science and behavioral psychology.

My discontent with "Roadmap for Researchers on Priorities Related to Information Integrity Research and Development" and its embrace of "mechanistic," quantitative solutions does not aim to downplay the role of the new technologies needed to reorganize the infrastructure of social interactions since many of the harms of disinformation—from racially biased face recognition algorithms to deep fakes—and algorithmic power are indeed perpetrated by the corporate tech designs aimed to increase profits and facilitate commercial competition for user attention at the planetary scale. However, technologies and qualitative social sciences alone cannot comprehend these harms, let alone design better infrastructures for more democratic and equitable interactions, without engagement with intersubjective understanding and without widespread political contestations of the corporate hegemony over AI infrastructures of information exchange (as the takeover of Twitter illustrates). Thus, if new technologies are needed to assist "communities to foster and maintain high integrity information ecosystems" (US Government 2002, 3, 24), they cannot be developed without regarding members of these communities as critical interlocutors and political agents capable of diagnosing and contesting algorithmic harms. By engaging in such wide-ranging public debates about disinformation and other forms of algorithmic harms, communities might develop their own "roadmaps" for priorities guiding further investigation, compensation, and development of directions for nonprofit technological platforms.

However, in "Roadmap" a proposed engagement with diverse communities is not based on such a participatory collaboration and understanding but rather driven by a top down, and at time patronizing approach, aiming to increase public and individual "literacy" (rather than political agency) and "assessment" of the "consumed information" (rather than critical judgments and evaluations of algorithmic infrastructures). It is not surprising therefore that in institutional agencies, discourse, and everyday language, common terms like "evaluation" and "judgment" have been so frequently replaced with measurable "assessment," as if its mathematical objectivity could transcend the unpredictability of social interactions. With only occasional references to community participation, cultivation of critical thinking, or the creation of counternarratives, this top-down education of communities about "information literacy" is also "mechanistic," dedicated primarily to technical solutions rather than to cultivation of political agency. Following

Hannah Arendt, I define such agency as deeply relational, that is, as created through intersubjective action and sharing of critical judgments among those who regard each other as equal and distinct.

This inadequate approach to understanding, power relations, and political agency in the governmental "Roadmap" is all the more troubling since power analysis and calls for wider public participation in algorithmic designs have been the focus of numerous scholars, mostly women and people of color, working on growing economic and racial disparities in computational technologies for at least the last ten years. Simone Browne's groundbreaking research on the perpetuation of the surveillance and profiling of Blackness by AI technology (2015); Safiya Umoja Noble's analysis of the intensification of racism in search engines (2018); and Ruha Benjamin's study of the "default racist and economic discrimination" in algorithmic systems (2019, 77–96) are some of the most notable examples. As this research shows, algorithmic technologies of power enact new forms of domination by automating and obfuscating racial, gender, and economic inequalities. Consequently, as the 2022 Mozilla Foundation report on power and AI demonstrates,[1] harms of disinformation require ongoing research not only on technical solutions but also on technologies of power, which automate historical dominations on the global scale and pose new threats to democracy.

Such an approach is deployed in Kate Crawford's 2021 book *Atlas of AI: Power, Politics, and the Planetary Costs of Artificial Intelligence*, in which she defines the infrastructure of artificial intelligence as "the massive industrial formation that includes politics, labor, culture, and capital" (9). Although not included in Crawford's *Atlas*, perhaps the most obvious technique of algorithmic power, which both limits political agency and increases harms of disinformation, operates through the obfuscation of proprietary algorithms of the big tech corporations that not only design platforms but also compete for dominance over information "production" and "consumption." Not merely an opposite of transparency, algorithmic secrecy is a technology of power intertwined with widely discussed digital surveillance driven by the economic logic of data extraction, which not only violates privacy but increases economic exploitation and undermines political agency. Because data collection and trading, user profiling, surveillance, and algorithmic predictions are not open to public scrutiny for legal, tech, and economic reasons, they transform democratic institutions and the public sphere into polarized "black box societies" (Pasquale 2015). As Ruha Benjamin demonstrates, such black boxing is intertwined with algorithmic racism, or what she calls a "new Jim Code" (2019). Since corporate obfuscation and surveillance technologies constitute the algorithmic infrastructures, is black boxing not strongly correlated with the spread of disinformation, distrust, and conspiracies, which are tolerated if not encouraged as long as they increase the number of clicks and generate profits?

Black boxing also shows systemic relations between the undermining of political agency and the global expansion of digital capitalism, also called data/racist capitalism (Milner and Traub 2021), computational (Stiegler 2019), or surveillance capitalism (Zuboff 2019). Hence it is not by accident that sociopolitical and technological interactions in the "information ecosystems" are so pervasively discussed in terms of information production and consumption, since on the "internet shopping mall" information is indeed a commodity. As all critics of digital capitalism concur, its logic of accumulation is driven by the imperative of accelerated data extraction from all computational operations and its conversion into profits through the production of prediction products, ranging from advertising to predictive policing. Since data is the dominant currency and "raw material," digital capitalism extracts more and more "collateral" data, the byproduct of the billions of users' interactions with social media, internet searches—for example, the information about frequencies, timing, wording of the search, spelling, pages visited, the number of clicks on the ads, and so forth—online transactions as well as on all "smart" devices. As Zuboff points out, this confiscated data about users' behavior is reinvested for the purposes of improving internet services. However, most of it constitutes lucrative "behavioral surplus" used not merely for matching advertising with user profile information (UPIs), but primarily for the fabrication of new, more accurate "prediction products" that anticipate our actions and which are in turn traded "in a new kind of marketplace for behavioral predictions" (Zuboff 2019, 8), a trade that undermines not only individual freedom but also political agency. As more and more scholars—Safiya Umoja Noble (2018), Yeshimabeit Milner and Amy Traub (2021), Bonnie Sheehey (2019), or Tressie McMillan Cottom (2020), among others—point out, the digital logic of capitalist accumulation is interconnected with racism, colonialism, and gender domination.

By undermining political agency, the synergy between algorithmic technologies of power and digital capitalism weakens democracy even further. These algorithmic threats to democracy have been an object of numerous interdisciplinary discussions initiated by, among others, O'Neil (2016), Noble (2018), Zuboff (2019), Benjamin (2019), Bernholz et al. (2021), Kuehn and Salter (2020), and Kate Crawford (2021). Indeed, the title of

Cathy O'Neil's book, *Weapons of Math Destruction: How Big Data Increases Inequality and Threatens Democracy*, conveys in a nutshell the main topics of these debates. What I want to add to this debate is the central claim that these technologies weaken political agency and understanding by the ever-increasing automation of judgments, debates, and decisions by algorithmic procedures. As we have seen, the 2022 "Roadmap" for information integrity with which I begin this chapter does not refer to judgments at all, privileging instead measurements, algorithmic predictions, and ultimately reinforcing the hegemony of computational and quantitative sciences. What are, therefore, the political, ethical, and epistemic consequences of such outsourcing the debates about matters of common concern to AI systems?

A Government by the People or a Government by Algorithm?

In her 2015 book *Undoing the Demos*, Wendy Brown succinctly summarizes the basic ideal of democracy as "a political form in which the whole of the people rule the polity and hence themselves" (178). Interpreted and historically implemented in a variety of ways, ranging from representative, participatory, and socialist, to liberal, capitalist, or neoliberal democracy, this form of governance from its inception is characterized by the contradiction between its professed ideals of equality and freedom for all, on the one hand, and white supremacy, gender domination, and economic inequalities, on the other. As Charles W. Mills (2005) powerfully argues, when Western democratic theory forgets this founding contradiction, or regards it an accidental aberration, then such theory turns into ideology. Although Brown herself limits her investigation of the foundational contradictions of democracy to the impact of neoliberalism, she rightly points out that democracy, at the very minimum, requires that "the people authorize their own laws and major political decisions, whether directly or through elected representatives," and that they have some means of participation in major institutions—public, legal, cultural, or economic—that govern their lives (Brown 2015, 178).

Because of the enduring contradiction between the ideal of democratic collective self-governance and the historical institutionalized practices of domination and exclusion, ranging from settler colonialism, economic exploitation, and white supremacy, many feminists, critical race theorists, and political critics of democracy point out that democratic politics and decision making are inseparable from dissent, contestation, and participation in new political struggles for equity and freedom. The politics of democracy is thus characterized by conflicts, struggles against exclusions and discriminations, and debates over interpretation of values; it involves challenges to discriminatory laws and their implementation.

Speaking indirectly to these contradictions, Brown lists the essential pre-conditions of democracy's existence, which at the very minimum include some redistribution of economic inequalities, political participation, and especially education oriented toward citizenship understood as "a practice of considering the public good" (2015, 179). Irreducible to literacy about information integrity, such education in both institutional settings and everyday contexts aims to enhance judgments about the ways "power, history, representation, and justice" operate in public lives (179). Indeed, as the intensity of the current conservative opposition to critical race theory in public schools demonstrates only too well, democratic education is by no means a neutral subject but—it is an extension of political struggles. All elements of this brief outline of democracy—self-governance, considerations of the public good, debate, discernment of justice, and I would stress, contestations of injustice and discriminations—explicitly foreground deliberation, judgment, and action.

For Brown, the politics of democracy is undone by neoliberal deregulation of the markets and further destruction of public institutions providing a very minimal framework for economic redistribution, public education, and political engagement. In 2023, the neoliberal threat to democracy is increased not only by growing populism, failures of democratic institutions, white supremacy and authoritarianism but also by digitally enhanced racial capitalism and AI technologies affecting all aspects of our daily lives. As Lucy Bernholz, Hélène Landemore, and Rob Reich rightly point out, these far-ranging effects of the ever-updated digital technologies and their applications on democratic institutions, human rights, economic equity, and citizenship have not yet been sufficiently addressed by democratic theorists, who tend to focus on the non-technological or low-tech reasons of the widespread crisis of democracy (2021, 3). Or, as we have seen, when these algorithmic technologies of power are confronted directly, their impact is all too frequently confined to an information/disinformation binary, or "assessments" of algorithmic bias. However, the fundamental reason why digital technologies of power radically exceed the information/disinformation divide or discussions of bias is because they signal the emergence of a new hybrid political formation, namely, government by algorithms. As I argue, one of the most characteristic features of this hybrid formation consists in the outsourcing of political judgments and high-stake decisions to computational systems. In other words, such automation of decision making and judgments not only poses a threat to democratic institutions and political activism but perhaps undermines them altogether.

I wish the phrase "government by algorithm" were either my clever concept or some attention-grabbing sensational headline, but unfortunately this is not the case. Echoing one of the most famous sentences in American political history, "government of the people by the people and for the people," "government by algorithm" is in fact part of the title of a report commissioned by the Administrative Conference of the United States and submitted by a large interdisciplinary group of lawyers, computer scientists, and social scientists from Stanford University and New York University in February 2020: "Government by Algorithm: Artificial Intelligence in Federal Administrative Agencies." Numerous aspects of this report are alarming: first, this report hopes to remedy ignorance and confusion—(the opposite of information integrity)—about the haphazard and often clandestine implementation of algorithms in numerous branches of government itself. The claim that "we know precious little about how government agencies themselves use AI" (Engstrom et al. 2020, 9) is especially disconcerting in the face of public calls for more legal regulation of AI developed by private tech corporations. How much trust can we have in legal regulation of AI and ML technologies if the government itself does not know what it is doing and therefore fails to examine whether its operations comply or violate institutional principles and rights, such as the right to due process? Second, the report tacitly admits that practices of black boxing and algorithmic secrecy in public institutions limit the findings of this powerful group of scholars, technology, and legal experts, who in their research must rely on publicly available sources, which "rarely provide sufficient technical detail on AI systems and offer little insight" on the process of gathering information in such cases (13). And if the expert knowledge concerning the role of algorithmic decisions in democratic governance is limited, what hope is there for ordinary citizens like me? Not only is there no coherent policy for the use of AI and machine learning in politics and public life but also no sufficient knowledge about governmental uses of these automated decisions. Consequently, the purpose of this report was to find out how wide the implementation of AI/ML in governmental agencies is and how these tools were obtained (that is, whether they were developed in house or designed by private contractors). By studying the 142 most significant federal departments, the report discovered that nearly half of them have already adopted AI, including the areas of law enforcement, health, financial regulation, adjudication, and perhaps most alarming for me, in communication with the public "about its rights and obligations as welfare beneficiaries, taxpayers, asylum-seekers, and business owners" (6). This "new algorithmic governance" is particularly prominent in the areas of law enforcement, immigration control, and distribution of benefits (otherwise known as the area of distributive justice).

Although the genealogy of these automated governmental practices can be traced to the 1990s, the report lists troubling new harms of such algorithmic governance. The first one is the inscrutability and lack of understanding of the complexity of algorithmic tools, such as the advanced neural networks, even by those who invented them (Engstrom et al. 2020, 11). Second, these automated decisions "operate according to rules that are so complex" that they not only defy practical interrogation, but more alarmingly "do not comport with any practical human belief about how the world works, or simply lie beyond human-scale reasoning" (11). Perhaps this is one of the main reasons why proposed research on information integrity (discussed in section 1) must rely on metrics to come to terms with algorithmic infrastructures exceeding human comprehension. And finally, as the report admits between the lines, these algorithmic practices undermine the very principle of deliberative, participatory democratic politics, namely, accountability for political decisions and judgments: "the growing sophistication and power of AI is nudging agencies toward fully automated decision-making, leaving progressively less to human discretion and judgment" (11). As the authors fully acknowledge, the automation of decision making and judgments raises new questions not only about fairness, transparency, and accountability for discrimination but undermines "reason giving," accountability, and justification of political judgments (13). It represents risks to rights, to distributive and restorative justice, as well as to due process. The basic question that the authors do not raise is whether government by algorithm is still compatible with participatory democracy. And if not, then what kind of political form is emerging from such government by algorithm? "The black box society?" "Algorithmic Leviathan?" Or "algorithmic governmentality"? Introduced by Rouvroy and Berns (2013) and referenced by Stiegler (2019), "algorithmic governmentality" is but one of several new concepts invented to name this new technology of power, which, in sharp contrast to deliberation or activism, aims to replace political decisions by algorithms.

On the Consequences of Automating Judgments

Any political theory regards sharing and giving reasons for political judgments and decisions as an indispensable feature of democratic politics. As Linda Zerilli points out in her 2018 "Toward a Democratic Theory of Judgment," such judgments are key characteristics of democracy (191) and, I would add, an indispensable part of any political practice aiming to contest the exclusionary character of democratic institutions. Because democratic institutions, politics, and activism are inconceivable without making, justifying, and contesting political judgments and decisions, democratic theory presupposes judgments even if it does not develop their role in depth. According to Zerilli, when democratic theory considers judgments directly, it focuses primarily on (1) contestable criteria of sound critical judgments (for example, should they be limited to rationality or should they take into account affectivity, cultural values, and embodiment?); (2) the difficulties of judging in multicultural societies, which lack unified norms, or, as critical race and feminist theorists of democracy would add, in which such norms are contested as legalized forms of discrimination; or (3) the difficulties of judging in the context of political conflicts (Zerilli 2018, 191). And conversely, suppression of judgments is regarded as synonymous with the crisis of democracy, ranging from the reduction of engagement in politics to the efficiency of an administrative apparatus or to the emergence of authoritarianism.

Why is the practice of political judgments inseparable from democratic politics? Whether epistemic, moral, political, or aesthetic, judgment connects general laws, concepts, and ideas with particular cases that might correspond to them, and vice versa. Even in the rational formulation of judgment by eighteenth-century philosopher Immanuel Kant, we find the claim that most ordinary judgments—"this is good," "this is a cat"—are far from being automatic, "mechanistic," or measurable. On the contrary, even the so-called determinate judgments based on the application of knowledge are for Kant a form of art, connecting sensible perceptions with general concepts thanks to imagination. This art of judging is especially conspicuous in the case of reflective or aesthetic judgments, which are made with no reference to concepts but formulated on the basis of pleasure and displeasure. Yet even these judgments (for example, "this is beautiful") are communicable to others and seek their agreement with no guarantee that such an agreement will occur. Kant calls this appeal to judgments of others "common sense" or "sensus communis," while Arendt calls it an "enlarged mentality" (Arendt 1982, 1994).

In her reinterpretation of Kant, Arendt regards judging as an eminently political practice. As Zerilli (2016, 2018) and Diprose and Ziarek (2018), among others, point out, for Arendt all judgments are political in two interrelated ways: first, the publicity of judgments means they must be communicated and justified to others. Second, for Arendt this appeal to others does not occur ex post facto but means that their potential and actual viewpoints must be taken into account already in the process of formulating judgments. As Zerilli puts it, the political significance of judgments means therefore that judging cannot occur in isolation: it "cannot begin without taking account of the viewpoints of others. The irreducible ground of judging is plurality—not the empirical existence of other people, but active taking into account of their points of view" (2018, 207). Consequently, making and sharing judgments is inseparable from democratic politics because judgment presupposes a common world that is shared with others, without whom we simply cannot think, act, or judge.

Perhaps paradoxically, this political appeal to judgments of others becomes most critical whenever we question or lack the accepted scientific, normative, or legal criteria of judgments. This occurs, first of all, whenever we are grappling with either catastrophic or unpredictable political events, which destroy or exceed our accepted norms and criteria of judging. Second, the appeal to the judgments of others sustains our critical ability to distinguish accepted norms from prejudices, often masquerading as sciences or laws, especially if these sociopolitical prejudices reflect systemic inequalities and domination. Such grappling with individual or collective biases is part of an ongoing political and ethical practice, which assumes that judging cannot transcend sociopolitical relations of power/knowledge by appealing to neutral criteria. Since an overcoming of prejudices and biases of the political and legal norms cannot occur on either an individual or scientific basis, it calls for a critical public practice of examining the very grounds of judging. As Arendt puts it, "to think critically applies not only . . . to the prejudices and traditions one inherits; it is precisely by applying critical standards to one's own thought that one learns the art of critical thought. And this application one cannot learn without publicity, without the testing that arises from contact with other people's thinking" (1982, 42). Based on the difficult education provided by others, such intersubjective practice, I argue, both presupposes and performs what Arendt calls an "enlarged mentality." That is why the publicity of judgments, their communication and justification to others who might refute them, is an indispensable feature of any political engagement. For Arendt, the public character of judgments, including their "testing" by others who can reject them, is a key element not only of political theory and practice but also constitutive of a public sphere, which, beyond its restricted institutionalization, comes into being whenever people come together to act, to argue, and to share their judgments.

Because of this publicity and the appeal to others, judgments are different from theoretical knowledge or empirical facts. For Kant, one implication of this difference between the art of judgment and knowledge means that highly educated persons might still lack the capacity of judging. Thus, despite being experts in their disciplines, doctors, lawyers, judges, scientists, or philosophers might fail to apply their judgments properly to specific situations. And conversely, persons can lack formal knowledge but excel in judging. Kant calls such deficiency of judgments "stupidity" and remarks that "it is not unusual to meet learned men who in the application of their scientific knowledge betray" a lack of judgment (Kant 1965, 178). Although the art of judgment cannot be taught directly, it, like every art, requires practice by the careful study of examples: "such sharpening of the judgment is indeed the one great benefit of examples" (178). In the case of the failure of judging, studying examples of judicious practices of others might be our best substitute. According to Kant, "Examples are thus the go-cart of judgments; and those who are lacking in the natural talent can never dispense with them" (178).

Reinterpreting Kant, Arendt analyzes a new and far more dangerous politics of stupidity in Western modernity (1994, 314–318). Writing in the aftermath of political catastrophes in the twentieth century, she argues that one of the main manifestations of such politics lies in the replacement of judging with others by calculation, or, to use a more contemporary expression, by metrics and assessments. Arendt calls this political substitution of calculation for judging "logicality" to distinguish it from a valid use of logic in the sciences. I would argue that such logicality also differs from those uses of statistics that aim to provide evidence, one among others, for further political testing and contestation. By contrast, logicality undermines or destroys deliberation because it assaults its very basis, namely, sensus communis performed by the sharing of judgments. As Arendt points out, logicality can become a substitute for sensus communis because of its paradoxical double quality: on the one hand, the capacity for logic, like communication of judgments, is common to all; on the other hand, its validity is utterly abstracted from the historical world, sensible phenomena, unpredictable events, and interactions with others: "all self-evidence from which logical reasoning proceeds can claim a reliability altogether independent of the world and the existence of other people. . . . Only under conditions where the common realm between men is destroyed and the only reliability left consists in the meaningless tautologies [of logic]," can people accept logicality—or in our historical moment, data and information—as the substitute for common understanding (318). Although in a less conspicuous way than direct violence, economic exploitation, racism, and homophobia, logicality also contributes to the destruction of the common world because of its indifference to the existence of others, their judgments, and their agency. As a detrimental technology of power, logicality undermines the formation of alternative public spheres, which come into being whenever people act together, argue, and share their judgments.

If democratic politics and any critical practice contesting inequalities and their legitimation by prejudicial sociopolitical norms depends on judging with and being judged by others, an algorithmic version of logicality has circumvented the difficulties of judging by outsourcing them to AI and ML. Or perhaps algorithmic technologies have finally invented what for Kant was inconceivable, namely, a substitute for the failure of judging. Why spend time and effort to practice judgments and justify them to others if it is more efficient and more profitable to delegate them to algorithmic procedures? Indeed, are not machine learning tools, such as the infamous COMPAS recidivism risk score, invented to disburden judges, doctors, lawyers, and we can add, teachers, hiring managers, college admission officers, government officials—from the public communicability and responsibility of judgment? Is everything around us—our gadgets, technologies, homes, and cities—becoming smarter and smarter in order to make us less reflective, more obsessed with metrics and targets, and (to paraphrase Kant) more prone to "algorithmic stupidity"?

In the aftermath of the wide-ranging debates about fairness of algorithmic predictions, critical data studies and computer science scholars also attempt to grapple with the consequences of outsourcing judgments to computational systems. The initial justification of such automation of judgments, namely, the claim that the mathematical neutrality of big data and ML could counter sociopolitical prejudices and inequalities, even if it were possible, is problematic because it repeats the hyper-rationalist dream of transcending human conflicts, desires, limitations, and embeddedness in the world. For Golumbia (2009), such justification is what constitutes an "ideology of computationalism." Indeed, as the subsequent work of O'Neil (2016), Noble (2018), Benjamin (2019), Eubanks (2018), Pasquale (2015), and Rouvroy and Berns (2013), demonstrates all too well, big data and AI reproduce harms and discriminations and make it more difficult to contest them. Numerous causes have been identified for this state of affairs: (a) technologies are never neutral tools but economic and sociopolitical operations of power; (b) social data used for machine training is shaped by the long-standing history of systemic racial, economic, and gender injustices (what Ruha Benjamin calls "double encoding"); and (c) the emergence of new hierarchies of power/knowledge between those who have the economic, political, and intellectual capital to extract data and design models, and communities subjected to unregulated algorithmic decisions. Following Arendt, I would add to this list algorithmic logicality, which not only erodes the political practice of judging but in fact remains indifferent to the existence of human beings and the world.

In the aftermath of the research of O'Neil (2016), Noble (2018), Benjamin (2019), Eubanks (2018), and Broussard (2018), among others, critical data and computer scientists have underscored the plethora of judgments and decisions encoded at each stage of the machine learning pipeline. As O'Neil argues, for example, "a model's blind spots reflect the judgments and priorities of its creators. . . . Here we see that models, despite their reputation for impartiality, reflect goals and ideology" (2016, 21). As she concludes, algorithmic "models are opinions embedded in mathematics" (21). Consequently, the problem of judgment does not disappear in machine learning but is obfuscated and stripped of its political character and accountability to the wider public. As a counterpart of the politics of black boxing, the machine learning pipeline optimizes priorities such as efficiency and profits of those who have power, the means of production, and capital, which are usually big tech private corporations. Since decisions, judgments, and priorities encoded in the machine learning pipeline are not open to the contestations of communities affected by the consequences of the algorithmic restructuring of the world, they abdicate political and moral responsibility for both history of domination, sociopolitical inequalities, and the new harms of an algorithmic regime. To redefine Golumbia's and O'Neil's notions of computational ideology specifically in the context of automating judgments, we could say that algorithmic technologies of power restrict and subordinate judgments and decisions to the demands of economic and intellectual capital.

However, in addition to such explicit power relations reflected in the formulation of problems to be solved by the machine learning pipeline, there's also implicit obfuscation of judgments in the procedural aspects of algorithmic functioning, which persists even if we can imagine a hypothetical and very desirable scenario in which a wider public obtains more control over the priorities and the uses of algorithms. What I have in mind are unacknowledged judgments involved in the transformation of qualitative concepts into measurable quantities amenable to machine learning. All too sparse considerations of the epistemic, political, and ethical consequences involved in the transformation of the qualitative features of human lives into computational measurements have been initiated by critical data, social, and computational sciences. In the aftermath of the wide-ranging debates about algorithmic harms, computer scientists themselves acknowledge that such questions cannot be adjudicated by the accuracy of measurement. As Jacobs and Wallach (2021) argue, any assessment of fairness in ML models is insufficient if it focuses only on reliable measurement (the so-called "operational" reliability) but fails to question the validity of transforming qualitative ideas—including their understanding, meaning, values, and interpretations—into qualitative proxies. Because questions of validity and reliable measurement are all too frequently treated as equivalents, in computer science the problems of fairness—a qualitative idea, with multiple and contestable meanings—like the problems of information integrity discussed in section 1, is approached primarily in terms of statistics, modeling, and data.

In the most general terms, measurement is deemed reliable if similar inputs to the model produce similar outputs. However, the question of validity is far more complicated, since it concerns the conversion of qualitative ideas, which cannot be measured directly—such as fairness, teaching effectiveness, or the one most frequently discussed in computer science literature, recidivism scores—into measurable proxies. As Jacobs and Wallach put it, "computational systems often involve unobservable theoretical constructs, such as socioeconomic status. . . . Such constructs cannot be measured directly but must be instead inferred from measurements of observable properties . . . thought to be related to them" (2021, 1). This process of the substitution of ideas by measurable proxies "necessarily involves making assumptions," and therefore introduces "the potential for mismatches between the theoretical understanding of the construct purported to be measured and its operationalization" in a measurement model (1). "Making assumptions" is not only inseparable from judging, but the very process of proximate substitution is also figurative—indeed, this is what literary scholars call metaphor.

Although the distinction between reliable measurement and validity is important, it nonetheless fails to question the legitimacy of the substitution of nonmeasurable values and ideas (abstract constructs, in Jacobs and

Wallach's parlance) into measurable proxies, for example, using income as a proxy for socioeconomic status, costs of care for patients' needs, or the most notorious in our discipline—test results as substitution for excellence in teaching. I would argue that this measurement by proxy is at the core of automation of judgments and its widespread consequences, such as the progressive replacement of moral, political, historical, and cultural values by scores—for example, using credit scores as indicators of individuals' reliability, popularity or "likes" in social media as a proxy for what is good, or profits as the indicator of truth (Broussard 2018, 11; Nopper 2019, 170–187; O'Neil 2016, 12). Despite these limitations of Jacobs and Wallach's analysis, the substitution of qualitative concepts into measurable proxies enables us a more substantial discussion of the validity of the numerous decisions and judgments—often made without reflection, as the term "assumptions" implies—in the process of automating judgments and their consequences for political and cultural life.

Out of the long list of various notions of validity provided by Jacobs and Wallach, I want to focus on its two types, namely, on the content and consequential validity, because these two concepts offer us insights into the high stakes of the automation of political judgments. Focused on the interpretation and meaning of the "constructs to be measured," content validity refers to the difficulties of measuring ("operationalizing") ideas, which have multiple and contested meanings: "[I]f a construct is essentially contested then it has multiple context-dependent, and sometimes even conflicting, theoretical understandings [. . .] Contentedness makes it inherently hard to assess content validity: [I]f a construct has multiple theoretical understandings, then it is unlikely that a single operationalization can wholly and fully capture its substantive nature in a meaningful fashion" (Jacobs and Wallach 2021, 5). I propose that "integrity" of information, or the unpredictability of political and technological interactions with which I began this chapter, belong to this class of contested and context-dependent notions, which are difficult to transform into measurable proxies. In fact, I would press these considerations of content validity even further, by arguing that most qualitative ideas and ordinary language expressions have context-dependent, multiple, and contestable significations in the areas of culture, politics, and justice. Multiple and contested meanings are neither exceptional nor hypothetical ("if"), but on the contrary a common state of affairs in public discourse. This is the case because cultural and sociopolitical significations of most of our values and aspirations—such as equality, fairness, racial and gender justice, and freedom—have been shaped by a long history of domination, multiple interpretations, and struggles for alternative significations. It is only by disregarding the history of contested meaning in politics, ordinary language, and culture that Jacobs and Wallach can consider the content validity of their examples, such as teaching effectiveness or risk of recidivism, as relatively uncontested notions.

The second type of validity, the so-called consequential validity that Jacobs and Wallach discuss, refers to difficulties of measuring social, political, and moral consequences, especially harmful consequences, of algorithmic procedures. As they admit, "assessing consequential validity often reveals fairness-related harms" (2021, 6), especially if such assessment is also automated, that is, conducted by predictive analytics. The most important but least developed insight of the article acknowledges in passing that different measurements do not merely reflect the world but in fact restructure it: "[A]ssessing consequential validity therefore means answering the following questions: How is the world shaped by using the measurements? What world do we wish to live in? If there are contexts in which the consequences of using measurements would cause us to compromise values that we wish to uphold, then the measurements should not be used in those contexts" (6).

These are profound questions, which exceed a narrow understanding of validity pertaining to the transformation of qualitative ideas into measurable proxies in social and computer sciences. To grapple with these questions, we need to reclaim multiple and contested meanings of validity itself in public discourse. As a quick look at any dictionary tells us, validity is intertwined with epistemic, moral, political, sociohistorical, and legal judgments. When we ask whether something is valid, we might be asking whether it is true or reasonable (epistemic judgments); just (moral judgments); lawful and constitutional (legal and political judgments); legitimate (judgments about political authority); useful (judgments about utilitarian values or common good); credible (judgments about explications and about public trust); or finally, whether its meaning is properly understood (judgments about interpretation). Consequently, any consideration of validity brings us back to a paradoxical difficulty in judging the algorithmic automation of judgments by wider and plural publics. Do we wish to live in a world in which acting, thinking, communicating, and judging with others are severely reduced or replaced by AI and ML? To paraphrase Arendt, we can say that this question reveals new difficulties of understanding in the age of algorithmic logicality. When the tasks of common understanding based on sharing judgments with others are "operationalized," or treated in mechanistic terms, then algorithmic logicality not only further exacerbates a crisis of democracy but also perpetuates dangerous indifference toward the existence of other people.

Note

1. Mozilla's 2022 "Internet Health Report" is focused on "the systems of power and human decisions that define how artificial intelligence is used and whom it impacts." For an excellent discussion of this report, see Larsen's informative lecture "Who Has Power over AI? Let's Discuss Mozilla's Latest Report on the Health of the Internet."

References

Arendt, Hannah. 1982. *Lectures on Kant's Political Philosophy*. Edited by Ronald Beiner. Chicago: Chicago University Press.
———. 1994. "Understanding and Politics (The Difficulties of Understanding)," in *Essays in Understanding 1930–1954: Formation, Exile, and Totalitarianism*, edited and introduction by Jerome Kohn, 307–327. New York: Schocken Books.
Benjamin, Ruha. 2019. *Race after Technology: Abolitionist Tools for the New Jim Code*. Cambridge: Polity Press.
Bernholz, Lucy, Hélène Landemore, and Rob Reich, eds. 2021. "Introduction," in *Digital Technology and Democratic Theory*. Chicago: University of Chicago Press.
Broussard, Meredith. 2018. *Artificial Unintelligence: How Computers Misunderstand the World*. Cambridge, MA: MIT Press.
Brown, Wendy. 2015. *Undoing the Demos*. New York: Zone Books.
Browne, Simone. 2015. *Dark Matters: On the Surveillance of Blackness*. Durham, NC: Duke University Press.
Crawford, Kate. 2021. *Atlas of AI: Power, Politics, and the Planetary Costs of Artificial Intelligence*. New Haven, CT: Yale University Press.
Diprose, Rosalyn, and Ewa Płonowska Ziarek. 2018. *Arendt, Natality and Biopolitics: Toward Democratic Plurality and Reproductive Justice*. Edinburgh: Edinburgh University Press.
Engstrom, David Freeman, Daniel E. Ho, Catherine M. Sharkey, and Mariano-Florentino Cuéllar. 2020. "Government by Algorithm: Artificial Intelligence in Federal Administrative Agencies." Report Submitted to the Administrative Conference of the United States. February 2020. www-cdn.law.stanford.edu/wp-content/uploads/2020/02/ACUS-AI-Report.pdf.
Eubanks, Virginia. 2018. *Automating Inequality: How High-Tech Tools Profile, Police, and Punish the Poor*. New York: St. Martin's Press.
Golumbia, David. 2009. *The Cultural Logic of Computation*. Cambridge, MA: Harvard University Press.
Jacobs, Abigail Z., and Hanna Wallach. 2021. "Measurement and Fairness." Conference on Fairness, Accountability, and Transparency. New York: ACM. https://doi.or/10. 1145/3442188.3445901

Kant, Immanuel. 1965. *Critique of Pure Reason*. Translated by Norman Kemp Smith. New York: St. Martin's Press.

Kuehn, Kathleen M., and Leon A. Salter. 2020. "Assessing Digital Threats to Democracy, and Workable Solutions: A Review of the Recent Literature." *International Journal of Communication* 14: 2589–2610.

Larsen, Solana. 2023. "Who Has Power over AI? Let's Discuss Mozilla's Latest Report on the Health of the Internet." Lecture. Stanford Institute for Human Centered Intelligence, January 18, 2023. hai.stanford.edu

McMillan Cottom, Tressie. 2020. "Where Platform Capitalism and Racial Capitalism Meet." *Sociology of Race and Ethnicity* 6, no. 4: 441–449.

Mills, Charles W. 2005. "'Ideal Theory' as Ideology." *Hypatia* 20, no. 3: 165–184.

Milner, Yeshimabeit, and Amy Traub. 2021. "Data Capitalism and Algorithmic Racism." Demos: Data for Black Lives, 2021. Accessed February 13, 2023. www.demos.org/sites/default/files/2021-05/Demos_%20D4BL_Data_Capitalism_Algorithmic_Racism.pdf

Mozilla Foundation. 2022. Internet Health Report. Accessed February 14, 2023. https://2022.internethealthreport.org

Noble, Safiya. 2018. *Algorithms of Oppression: How Search Engines Reinforce Racism*. New York: New York University Press.

Nopper, Tamara K. 2019. "Digital Character in 'The Scored Society': FICO, Social Networks, and Competing Measurements of Creditworthiness," in *Captivating Technology: Race, Carceral Technoscience, and Liberatory Imagination in Everyday Life*, ed. Ruha Benjamin, 170–187. Durham, NC: Duke University Press.

O'Neil, Cathy. 2016. *Weapons of Math Destruction*. New York: Crown Publishing.

Pasquale, Frank. *The Black Box Society*. Cambridge, MA: Harvard University Press, 2015.

Rouvroy, Antoinette. "Governing without Norms: Algorithmic Governmentality." *Psychoanalytical Notebooks* 32 (2018): 99–120.

Rouvroy, Antoinette, and Thomas Berns. 2013. "Algorithmic Governmentality and Prospects of Emancipation: Disparateness as a Precondition for Individuation through Relationships?" Translated by Elizabeth Libbrecht. *Réseaux* 177, no. 1: 163–196.

Sheehey, Bonnie. 2019. "Algorithmic Paranoia: The Temporal Governmentality of Predictive Policing." *Ethics and Information Technology* 21, no. 1: 49–58.

Stiegler, Bernard. 2019. *The Age of Disruption. Technology and Madness in Computational Capitalism*. Translated by Daniel Ross. Cambridge: Polity Press.

United States Government. 2022. "Roadmap for Researchers on Priorities Related to Information Integrity Research and Development: A Report by the Information Integrity Research and Development Interop Agency Working Group, Networking and Information Technology Research and Development Subcommittee of the National Science and Technology Council." (December 2022). www.whitehouse.gov/wp-content/uploads/2022/12/Roadmap-Information-Integrity-RD-2022.pdf

Zerilli, Linda. 2018. "Toward a Democratic Theory of Judgment," in *Judgment and Action*, ed. Vivasvan Soni and Thomas Pfau, 191–217. Evanston, IL: Northwestern University Press.

Zerilli, Linda M. G. 2016. *A Democratic Theory of Judgment*. Chicago: Chicago University Press.

Ziarek, Ewa Płonowska. 2020. "Triple Pandemics: COVID-19, Anti-Black Violence, and Digital Capitalism" *Philosophy Today* 64, no. 4 (Fall): 925–930.

———. 2022. "Against Digital Worldlessness: Arendt, Narrative, and the Onto-Politics of Big Data/AI Technologies." *Postmodern Culture* 32, no. 2. doi:10.1353/pmc.2022.0002

Zuboff, Shoshana. 2019. *The Age of Surveillance Capitalism*. New York: Public Affairs.

Part II
Science Communication, Cultivating Awareness

Chapter Three

Communicating Science in an Increasingly Politicized Environment

Yotam Ophir, Raphaela M. Velho, and Lilian Tzivian

For a long time, the assumption held by many science communicators and media scholars was that people's refusal to comply with science-consistent behaviors was the result of lack of knowledge—that is, ignorance (Kahan et al. 2012)—or at least the absence of accurate information, as often discussed in the context of the rise of misinformation (Hatcher 2020; Lewandowsky et al. 2012). Implied in this argument is the suggestion that if only the public were more educated and informed, support for science and compliance with its recommendations would improve. These assumptions would often be presented as part of the popular "Deficit Model" (Sturgis and Allum 2004).

Nevertheless, empirical work has demonstrated the limitation of the deficit hypothesis. First, some critics have argued that the conceptualization and measurement of knowledge exhibits inconsistencies across scholars and disciplines (Cappella, Ophir, and Sutton 2018). Others have pointed to difficulties in assessing the right or optimal set of facts (i.e., knowledge) needed for citizens to participate in public life in a democratic society (Delli Carpini and Keeter 1993; Lupia 2015). Moreover, the predictive power of knowledge was found to be limited when it comes to science-consistent behaviors. In fact, not only does knowledge not always predict support for or compliance with science, but under some circumstances the more educated and knowledgeable exhibit increased resistance to scientific conclusions, as in the case of conservatives and climate action (Kahan 2015). Following recent developments in the science of science communication, and motivated by the findings from studies by the likes of Dan Kahan (2012, 2015), we argue here that to make sense of resistance and lack of compliance with science, as was evident, for example, around the globe during COVID-19, one should look at the growing politicization of science, and its effect on trust (Bolsen and Druckman 2015; Walter, Ophir, and Jamieson 2020; Walter et al. 2022).

The aim of this chapter is thus to explore the role of politicization of science in rejection of and inadequate compliance with science-consistent behaviors and policy. To that end, we first discuss a traditional model that attempted to explain lack of compliance with science by pointing to problems of ignorance, namely the Deficit Model (Sturgis and Allum 2004). Second, we explain why such an approach failed to explain citizens' compliance with and support of science and scientists, particularly in light of the growing partisan politicization of science (Kahan et al. 2012). Instead, we point to the key role played by trust in science and scientists (Fiske and Dupree 2014; Gauchat 2011; Ophir and Jamieson 2021). Third, we demonstrate how politically motivated distrust hampered the global effort to slow down the COVID-19 epidemic, bringing an international perspective from multiple countries across three continents. Finally, we discuss ways to improve science communication by restoring trust through more accurate explanations of its scientific values (Jamieson 2017; Ophir and Jamieson 2021; Oreskes 2021); bolstering scientific literacy with a particular attention to how science works; and designing messages that take into account the audiences' needs and motivations (Bolsen and Druckman 2015; Ophir et al. 2022; Walter, Ophir, and Jamieson 2020; Walter et al. 2022).

The Rise and Fall of the Deficit Model

Since 2016, the American Food and Drug Administration (FDA) has been implementing new nutrition facts labels on packaged food. According to the FDA, the "updated label makes it easier for consumers to make better informed food choices" (FDA 2022a). Changes include, for example, a larger font for calories, more detailed information on added sugars, and nutritional information per serving size. At the bottom of new labels, a footnote was added to explain the way daily values are calculated. Behind such a regulatory move is the theoretical assumption that people fail to act in healthy or science-consistent ways due to their lack of accurate knowledge, hence the theory's name—Deficit Model (Sturgis and Allum 2004). By that approach, technical solutions like increasing the font size to emphasize added sugars or providing informative footnotes are seen as capable of encouraging better, healthier, more pro-social behaviors.

The Deficit Model, also known as the Gap Model among scholars of science communication, is based on the idea that science is inherently too complex for the general public to understand. Therefore, the argument goes, science should be mediated to laypersons, scientifically literate professionals specialized in knowledge translation, including science educators and journalists (Bucchi 2008). This perspective, which dominated the discussions around the public understanding of science until the 1990s (Bauer, Allum, and Miller 2007), considered the public ignorant about science and its achievements. Such ignorance was seen as explanatory of the public hostility toward scientific innovations, science itself, and scientists (Turney 1998). Congruently, popular and influential definitions and measurements of science literacy, such as Miller's (Miller 1983), included knowledge about scientific facts, methods, positive outcomes of science, and the rejection of superstitious beliefs. These factors were used, for example, in the biannual surveys deployed by the National Science Board, measuring Americans' scientific literacy for decades (Bauer et al. 2007). The consistently low scores Americans received in these literacy tests were interpreted by scientists, educators, and policymakers as proof of the general population's lack of understanding of science. Following the Deficit Model, the proposed solution to these low scores was often science communication in the form of a unidirectional knowledge transfer from experts—scientists—to the public, mediated by the media (Bucchi 2008).

However, the effectiveness of this approach proved limited at best, and potentially even detrimental. First, decades of science communication efforts have led to only minor changes in science literacy levels (Ziman 1991). For example, a series of reports published by the Royal Society Committee, including the influential Bodmer Report (The Royal Society 1985), showed that people's scientific knowledge was the result of not only expert-based mediated communications but also interpersonal interactions. In other words, as in other domains such as fashion and politics (Katz and Lazarsfeld 1966), knowledge and perceptions about science were highly circumstantial and socially construed (The Royal Society 1985). Second, these early British studies demonstrated that people do not passively accept knowledge coming from scientific experts; rather, they tend to judge the experts' credibility and choose to believe in or reject their claims accordingly. These insights led to the development and implementation of new approaches to science communication, aimed at increasing engagement with science (Bauer et al. 2007), assuming that such factors as enjoyment could yield more science-consistent attitudes and behaviors (Miller 2003).

One such strategy to improve attitudes toward science was to move from a focus on descriptive facts to more emotional, engaging, narrative-type messaging (Kreuter et al. 2007). The theoretical reasoning behind such effort is that engaging messages could reduce resistance, increase involvement, and make individuals more accepting of counter-attitudinal positions (Moyer-Gusé 2008). For example, studies demonstrated the effectiveness of graphic warning labels for tobacco products (Brennan et al. 2018). These labels, which replace the informative text warning about the dangers of smoke with a visual representation, for example of a damaged lung, or in more recent iterations, the personal story of smoking victims (Ophir et al. 2017), have already been implemented in many countries, including Australia and Canada (Brennan et al., 2018). While empirically effective (Nabi 2010), such emotional persuasion may face regulatory and legal challenges, especially in the United States (CBS News 2012). The representation of often complicated and nuanced statistical scientific information in the format of a personal narrative also raises some ethical concerns among science communicators, as narratives may fail to fully and accurately represent such phenomena (Dahlstrom and Ho 2012).

As the role of attitudes and social factors in the acceptance or rejection of science became more apparent, at the beginning of the twenty-first century, evidence began to point toward common gaps between one's scientific knowledge and support for science (Kahan et al. 2012; Sturgis and Allum 2004). Take, for example, the context of evolution. According to some estimations, about 45 percent of Americans reject the notion that human beings evolved from another species (Kahan 2015). It is tempting to conclude that Americans are ignorant, that they did not learn or internalize the facts. Nevertheless, the empirical evidence doesn't add up. As explained by Kahan: "Numerous studies have found that profession of 'belief in' evolution has no correlation with an understanding of basic evolutionary science. Individuals who say they 'believe' are no more likely than those who say they 'don't' to give the correct responses to questions pertaining to natural selection, random mutation, and genetic variance" (2015, 3). It is not the case that knowledge doesn't matter at all, but rather that knowledge interacts with attitudes and values (Sturgis and Allum 2004). In fact, the impact of values could be so large that in some cases those higher on scientific literacy actually score lower on support for science-consistent policy (Kahan et al. 2012).

Instead of trying to follow a tradition that aims to improve upon the persuasiveness of messages by tinkering with its characteristics, trying to make it more engaging on average (Kreuter et al. 2007), we argue that a more adequate response to resistance to comply with science would aim to understand the psychological mechanisms that serve as obstacles for cooperation. Specifically, following empirical research, for example in the context of climate change (Kahan et al. 2012) and epidemics (Ophir and Jamieson 2021), we focus on the decline in trust in science and scientists, particularly in light of the alarming rise in science politicization and polarization (Motta, Stecula, and Farhart 2020).

The Polarized Politicization of COVID-19

Many were caught unprepared for the politicized nature of the response to the COVID-19 outbreak. Yet we should not have been surprised. One can think of many examples from recent memory where the public's reaction to and compliance with science was driven by waves, and at times floods, of distrust. In areas such as climate change (Supran and Oreskes 2021) and tobacco control (Cappella et al. 2015), science deniers have attempted for decades to sow discord among the public, to exaggerate the level of uncertainty around scientific findings, and to undermine the scientific community as unreliable and untrustworthy (Oreskes and Conway 2011). In the context of vaccines, a semi-organized coalition of fringe doctors, political figures, enthusiastic media, and anxious parents have been spreading lies and conspiracy theories about alleged coordinated plots by scientists and health organizations to deceive the public and promote unsafe vaccines for the sake of greed and financial gains (Kata 2010; Offit 2010b). While doing so, some have abused the distrust they themselves cultivated toward mainstream science to promote alternative treatments, most unhelpful, some extremely dangerous (Offit 2010a).

The public health crisis around the COVID-19 pandemic demonstrated the risks associated with growing distrust in science. Across the world, misinformation and intentional disinformation led many to reject public health interventions, and hampered compliance with measures aimed at curbing the spread of the virus, from masking, to social distancing, to vaccination (Brennen et al. 2020; Romer and Jamieson 2020). Distrust was not spread symmetrically across the population and was tied to politicians and political ideologies. Case in point, while distrust in scientists was on the rise among Republicans in the United States, some surveys demonstrated an increase in trust among Democrats during the same period (Borenstein and Fingerhut 2022). The disproportional distrust in science among the American conservative Right was fueled in part by the waves of misinformation disseminated through right-wing media (Motta, Stecula, and Farhart 2020) and conservative and Republican elites (Pink et al. 2021). Further complicating the situation was the cooptation of COVID-19 misinformation into the dangerous and violent Q-Anon conspiracy, which attempted to connect misinformation about the disease, containment efforts, and the vaccine to broader "deep state" conspiracy theories (Bodner, Welch, and Brodie 2020). The partisan polarization in trust in science translated into action, as Republicans, and particularly Trump voters and supporters, were dramatically less likely to get vaccinated than Democrats (Pink et al. 2021; Relman 2021).

In Latin America, citizens of multiple countries exhibited low levels of trust in health authorities and health care professionals during the pandemic (Rodriguez-Morales and Franco 2021). As was the case in the United States, distrust in South America was also driven to a degree by political polarization and populist leaders who belittled the severity and spread of the virus. In Brazil, for example, President Jair Bolsonaro, who sowed doubts and confusion around COVID-19 from its early days, spread misinformation about the COVID-19 vaccines, questioning their effectiveness and implying that they were dangerous, and "could turn one into a crocodile" (Kirby 2022). Throughout the crisis, Bolsonaro ridiculed protective measures (Kirby 2022), failed to impose effective quarantine programs, and delayed the order of available vaccines (Reuters 2021, while continuing to spread misinformation about the origins of the disease using the national media and his own social media platforms (Phillips 2022). Although most of the Brazilian population has historically been pro-vaccine (Hochman 2011), Bolsonaro's words and policies resulted in an enormous and preventable number of deaths and infections and contributed to a deep divide within the country around support and trust in science. Just as in the United States, the data suggest that some waves of COVID-19 cases and deaths were substantially higher in municipalities were Bolsonaro won the election than in the rest of the country (Xavier et al. 2022).

In Mexico, scholars have accused president Andrés Manuel López Obrador of mismanaging the pandemic from its very beginning, while also using the crisis to attack political opponents (Rocha-Quintero 2020). According to critics, Obrador constantly appealed to superstitions when talking about the virus—for example, when claiming that his amulets would protect him from any disease, including COVID-19 (Stott 2020). During the entire first year of the pandemic, his officials reported misleadingly low numbers of deaths and infections, as a product of few tests being performed (García 2021), resulting in little efforts to restrict people's mobility to prevent the spread of the virus (Ahmed 2020). Similarly, and going against recommendations by scientists around the globe, tests were limited only to those showing COVID-19 symptoms, which resulted in the late diagnosis of thousands of people (Cattan and Silver 2021). That, and the lack of implementation of meaningful stay-at-home policies, such as financial aid to the needy, contributed to the collapse of the health system and to the preventable infections and deaths of thousands. Unsurprisingly, in light of these developments and lack of governmental support in science, vaccine hesitancy and refusal served as a major barrier for containing the disease in Mexico throughout the pandemic (Ramonfaur et al. 2021).

Similar patterns during the COVID-19 pandemic could be seen around Western and Eastern Europe as well, influenced by the lack of consistent messaging across the European Union on one hand, and the flow of misinformation from Russia on the other. Eastern European countries, particularly those once part of the Soviet Union, have long been struggling with distrust in government (McKee et al. 2013). Countries such as Latvia, a former Soviet country that borders Russia and Belarus, found themselves unprepared for the pandemic following decades of political corruption that resulted in inadequate health systems, often led by people lacking the appropriate medical or epidemiological education and experience needed to orchestrate a crisis response. Case in point, Latvian media accused both the Latvian Minister of Health and the Head of the Vaccination Bureau of not having proper epidemiological or medical degrees, with their prior public service experience dedicated mostly to the arts and the organization of song and dance festivals (Rozenberga and Anstrate 2021). Epidemiologists and virologists with expertise in pandemics claimed that their recommendations were largely neglected by colleagues at the Association of Physicians, and some have argued that officials were spreading misinformation that minimized the severity of the disease (Berzina and Purina 2020; Purina 2021). Public trust was also negatively affected by ineffective and disorganized procedures by the state to obtain masks and vaccines, both of which were described as scandals and instances of corruption by Latvian media (LETA 2021; Zvejnieks 2022). The lack of consensus among public officials, the growing media criticism of the public health system, and the flood of disinformation on Russian news media (Nisbet and Kamenchuk 2021), consumed by many Russian-speaking Latvians, have all worked together to erode Latvians' trust in the public health system's ability to cope with COVID-19. As was the case in the United States and elsewhere, political beliefs corresponded to COVID-19 attitudes and behaviors, and reports from Latvia indicated that four of every five patients hospitalized with COVID-19 in Latvia were Russian-speakers, a group that represents less than 40 percent of the Latvian population (Janus.Lv 2021). Similarly, resistance to Western vaccines was higher among Russian-speakers, who were fed Russian misinformation that promoted the Russian vaccines at the expense of the Pfizer and Moderna vaccines (TVNET 2021).

Distrust in public health authorities was a cause for concern among Western European countries as well, particularly those suffering from higher levels of COVID-19–related deaths (Oksanen et al. 2020). Once again, part of the skepticism around COVID-19 and its treatment came from scientists. A case in point was the so-called Great Barrington Declaration, an open letter published in October 2020, authored by Swedish epidemiologist Martin Kulldorff, Stanford University professor Jayanta Bhattacharya, and British infection epidemiologist Sunetra Gupta. The three called for the replacement of lockdowns with "focused protection" of the most vulnerable (Lenzer 2020). Those supporting this position, later to be called "the Swedish approach," heavily criticized European governments who opted to protect the public via stricter policy and regulations. As a result of the Swedish approach, which was fueled by public pressures to maintain "normalcy" in the face of the pandemic, Sweden had one of the highest infection rates in western Europe, including in comparison to its neighbors Denmark, Finland, and Norway, which led to a high number of casualties in the country (Claeson and Hanson 2021). The Swedish government eventually apologized for its mishandling of the epidemic at its early stages (DW 2020). While the Swedish case remains a relative outlier among European countries, resistance to public health regulations and mandates prevailed across many countries, often fueled by politicians and partisan media, including in the United Kingdom (Drury 2020), Germany (Hill 2022), and Spain (BBC News 2020), among others. In most cases, political polarization played a key role in dividing citizens around COVID-19 (Krastev and Leonard 2021).

The Growing Partisan Politicization of Science

COVID-19 served as a painful reminder of the state of politically motivated public distrust in science, scientists, and the institutions that translate their work into policy. As demonstrated above, the politicization of science was not limited to a specific country, leader, or political party, but rather proved to be a global challenge. Perhaps more than any epidemic before, COVID-19 was politicized along partisan lines across the globe. Alarmingly, no evidence suggests that the polarization of science would extend beyond COVID-19 to areas where it was once absent (Harry 2021). For example, in the United States, the politicization and polarization of science is now so embedded in our culture, that it is easy to forget that the phenomenon, at least in its current breadth and intensity, is relatively new. At the first half of the twentieth century, and particularly after its contribution to achievements in the two World Wars, science enjoyed bipartisan support, and scientists and their innovations were often celebrated (Oreskes 2021). Challenges to science began to appear in the form of Rachel Carson's criticism of the pesticides industry and its impact on the environment in her famous 1962 book *Silent Spring*. While the book shed light on the need to balance scientific benefits and risks, its argument was not partisan in nature. The Republican administration under Richard Nixon established the Environmental Protection Agency in 1970 (Train 1996).

Nevertheless, the Nixon presidency also began exhibiting a growing tension between Republican leaders and scientific advisors, tensions that only grew larger during the Ronald Raegan presidency in light of the rise of the Religious, Conservative New Right, and its resistance to evolution and abortion rights (Fitzgerald 2017; Ophir et al. 2022). Misrepresentation of and conflict with scientists dramatically increased during the George W. Bush administration (Mooney 2007), and the spread of scientific misinformation became a staple of the Donald Trump presidency (Yamey and Gonsalves 2020). While many scientific subjects were put under politicized scrutiny during these decades, perhaps none received as much attention as climate change, where the growing scientific evidence for human-based destruction of the planet's climate faced resistance from conservatives, who saw it as an attack on capitalism and neoliberalism (Oreskes and Conway 2011) and Christians, who perceived it to be an attack on their beliefs (Goldberg et al. 2019). For example, in 2000, a conservative Christian group published a document signed by more than 1,500 clergy and theologians, denying manmade global warming. Importantly, their resistance was not led by the lack of scientific literacy. The authors of the Cornwall Declaration on Environmental Stewardship were not ignorant of the scientists' positions and consensus around climate change and humans' role in it. Instead, they rejected the scientific conclusions as speculation, arguing that as humans operate under God's design, they could not be thought of as consumers and polluters who exhaust the Earth of its resources, but rather only as producers and stewards whose impact is inevitably and inherently positive (McCammack 2007).

Understanding the partisan politicization of science, as we have attempted to do in this chapter, could provide critical insight for moving forward and reclaiming the epistemological authority of science. The disputes around COVID-19, and particularly around climate change provide striking evidence against the deficit models of scientific distrust. Not only were conservatives, Republicans and Christians, not driven by ignorance (that is, by not knowing what scientists are saying), at times the more scientifically literate they were, the less supportive they were of the scientific community's consensus and conclusions (Kahan et al. 2012). Instead, we believe that the phenomenon should be understood as a crisis of asymmetric politically motivated distrust in organizations of knowledge, such as academia, the media, and the government, and particularly in science (Borenstein and Fingerhut 2022; Fletcher and Park 2017; Ophir and Jamieson 2021).

In recent years, scientists have warned about the community's reluctance to engage in public science communication. Scientists often avoid communicating publicly due to myriad reasons, from lack of incentives to do so (in terms of professional promotion and prestige), to fears that the public or the media won't fully understand their messages, to the fact that very few academic institutions provide their researchers with science communication skills (Harris 2017; Jamieson 2017). But even among the few scientists who are willing or wanting to communicate with the public, we need to sharpen our arguments in favor of trusting science. We conclude our chapter by discussing misconceptions about how science works, and how its epistemic authoritative role should be communicated.

SCIENCE AS A CANDLE IN THE DARK

Starting with the scientific revolution, different scholars came up with different reasonings in support of trust in science as our most reliable way of knowing. Many of these explanations, while still being used to this day, betray the values of science and portray its process and products in inaccurate, even misleading fashion (Jamieson 2017; Oreskes 2021). These include, for example, the false claims that we should trust science because "it works," because scientists are brilliant, well educated, and bring experience and expertise, and the idea that science should be trusted because it is based on the systematic (methodological) act of observation. Each of these explanations, while compelling, doesn't hold up to epistemological scrutiny, as we briefly discuss below. Attempts to communicate trust in science based on these notions is thus misleading and detrimental.

First, science cannot be trusted because "it works." True—if it wasn't for science, we would not have trains, microwaves, smartphones, or vaccines. However, just because something seems to work doesn't mean the knowledge on which it is based is reliable. The Ptolemaic star system was able to produce quite a lot of accurate predictions, even though its assumptions in regard to the Earth's location in the universe were wrong (Oreskes 2021). Moreover, at times, things we thought we knew to be working will prove useless, or even dangerous, as new data are collected, requiring new knowledge and understanding. A prominent example could be seen in the emotional and cognitive rollercoaster that was the science of trans fats, cholesterol, and heart diseases, on which the scientific consensus kept changing over the years, leading to inconsistent dietary recommendations regarding products such as butter and margarine (Offit 2017).

Second, science should not be trusted due to the intellectual superiority, brilliance, or educational credentials of scientists. Such misunderstanding is based on the wrong perception that science is an individualistic pursuit. From a young age, children are exposed to scientific narratives of eureka moments, where falling apples (in the case of Isaac Newton) or boat trips (in the case of Charles Darwin) resulted in a miraculous eureka moment, discernable only to uniquely bright, often eccentric men (Avraamidou 2013). The misperception is supported by the way news media tend to cover scientific stories, as linear discovery narratives (Ophir and Jamieson 2021). Similarly, our entertainment media are full of depictions of hyperindividualistic mavericks, often swimming against the stream of society who experience revolutionary moments of (mostly unethical and dangerous, as is the case with Frankenstein's monster or the DNA experiments of Jurassic Park) revelation (Weingart, Muhl, and Pansegrau 2003). Yet, science doesn't work that way. Charles Darwin did not invent the theory of evolution from scratch, but instead built upon decades of scientific work across multiple fields. It was therefore plausible that the theory would be co-discovered by another British naturalist at around the same time, Alfred Russel Wallace (Rogers 1997). Critically, a blind reliance on the great men of science could fail us. Andrew Wakefield, the British physician who promoted the erroneous hypothesis that autism results from the Measles, Mumps, and Rubella (MMR) vaccine (Gerber and Offit 2009), received an excellent education, worked in a leading hospital and school of medicine, and published his fraudulent study in one of the most prestigious scientific journals, *The Lancet*. Credentials and competence don't guarantee that one is right or trustworthy (Ophir et al. 2023).

The third explanation for why we should trust science that is worth debunking here is that science is a unique way of knowing due to its reliance on methods of systematic observation. Such an approach was at the heart of the positivist movement, first born in the eighteenth century, and championed by the likes of David Hume and Auguste Comte. Positivism relied on the principles of observation, induction, and verification, and these tasks were entrusted to the scientific method (Oreskes 2021). While it is tempting to believe that science's superiority over dogma and belief lies in its ability to verify realities based on observations, this assumption is doomed to logical fallacies. In short, as argued by Austrian philosopher of science Karl Popper, no matter how many observations one collects, they would never be able to make valid inductive conclusions (Popper 2005). Following Popper's own example, no matter how many white swans scientists could observe, they would not be able to conclude that all swans are white.

So why should we trust science? While criticizing positivism, Popper began to provide the answer in his justified insistence that what separates science from non-science, or what he called elsewhere pseudo-science (Popper 2012), is the principle of falsifiability. In essence, according to Popper and his followers, science is the collective project (Kuhn 2012) of skeptically assessing evidence. According to falsifiability, a theory could be considered scientific only if it could be tested and rejected empirically. For these reasons, Popper vehemently attacked the work of thinkers like Sigmund Freud and Karl Marx, whose arguments he claimed could not be falsified (Popper 2012). So in the post-positivistic sense, science should earn our trust thanks to its reliance on collective healthy skepticism. As opposed to other belief systems that reach a set of accepted beliefs that are not meant to be challenged by new scholars (e.g., religions), science encourages the establishment of collective institutions that eternally scrutinize, criticize, and develop old knowledge in an endless search for new discoveries (Oreskes 2021).

Which brings us back to COVID-19. Part of the challenge scientists and science communicators faced during the COVID-19 pandemic was the result of the epidemic's erratic and unexpected nature. Scientific knowledge is never finite, and the pace of changes and developments can dramatically accelerate during public health crises (Coombs 1999). In such conditions, scientists find themselves between a rock and a hard place. While crises yield an urgent need for timely and novel information (Ophir 2018), scientific data take time to collect and analyze, and diseases like COVID-19 mutate and change over time, making early predictions and recommendations obsolete (Liu, Ophir, and Walter, forthcoming). During the COVID-19 pandemic, the views of public health experts on the effectiveness of and need for masks, for example, consistently changed. At first, public health experts, like Dr. Anthony Fauci, told Americans not to wear masks, before changing his message as more data became available about the scope and transmission of the disease (Roche 2021).

But the commitment to self-correction among scientists and science as an epistemological ideology is exactly what makes it a reliable way of knowing to begin with. While other ways of knowing begin with dogma and assumptions that cannot and in some cases, must never, be questioned, science acknowledges that knowledge is always evolving, and scientists continue to put existing knowledge to the test, even after it was supported empirically. A case in point, after the Johnson & Johnson vaccine was approved for public use during the COVID-19 pandemic, concerns around potential side effects led to a temporary limit on its distribution, until more data could be obtained regarding its safety. After additional tests supported its safety, the vaccine was redeployed (FDA 2022b).

Conclusion

In this chapter we have discussed the challenges facing scientists and governmental agencies that translate scientific work into policy and recommendations. We demonstrate how science communication has evolved in light of a growing politicization and accumulated evidence for motivated reasoning and trust serving as a barrier to compliance. We argue that the global challenges of science communicators during the COVID-19 pandemic demonstrate the need to better explain the values of science (Jamieson 2017). Crises such as epidemics emphasize the ever-developing nature of science, and scientists' need to continue to explore questions and revise their conclusions as new data and evidence are gathered and analyzed. These moments of revision are often misinterpreted by politicians and the news media as indications that science is broken or in crisis (Jamieson 2018), a discourse that could lead to distrust and harm compliance with the recommendations of scientists and public health experts (Ophir and Jamieson 2021).

Yet, science communication could be vastly improved if we could accurately convey to the public that such setbacks, including the reexamination of data and the coming to new conclusions, are all part of a healthy scientific process. Simply put, science's tendency to self-correct is not a bug but rather its most essential feature. Finally, we acknowledge that even improved science communication could not guarantee a full acceptance or compliance with science and the recommendations of the scientific community. More research is needed to fully understand the components of and mechanisms underlying distrust in science, and particularly potential interactions between beliefs, attitudes, and political ideology (Ophir, Walter, Jamieson, and Jamieson, forthcoming).

Recent studies point to promising potential avenues, from more accurate communication of the scientific process and its self-correcting nature (Ophir and Jamieson 2021), to identifying facets of scientific literacy that actually matter for support of science (focusing on how science works, not on scientific facts, see Kahan et al. 2012), to communicating science compassionately, in ways that account for the motivated reasoning of skeptics, ideology, and values (McIntyre 2021). Importantly, understanding the role played by motivated reasoning in the rejection of science in the face of scientific facts can open doors to more effective science communication (Bisgaard 2019). Groups such as the Evangelical Climate Initiative (Nagle 2008), whose messages explain how protecting the Earth and fighting climate change could be understood through Christian values and perspective, provide an example for effective science communication targeting value-motivated groups and individuals. As we have stressed in this chapter, building a more robust scientific literacy through education programs that focus on how science works (even at the expense of scientific facts and findings) could help us take stock of the challenges we face in the polarized environment of the twenty-first century, so as not to abandon hope.

References

Ahmed, Azam. 2020. "Cifras occulta: México desatiende ola de muertes en la capital." *The New York Times*, May 8. sec. en Español. www.nytimes.com/es/2020/05/08/espanol/america-latina/mexico-coronavirus.html

Avraamidou, Lucy. 2013. "Superheroes and Supervillains: Reconstructing the Mad-Scientist Stereotype in School Science." *Research in Science & Technological Education* 31, no. 1: 90–115. https://doi.org/10.1080/02635143.2012.761605

Bauer, Martin W., Nick Allum, and Steve Miller. 2007. "What Can We Learn from 25 Years of PUS Survey Research? Liberating and Expanding the Agenda." *Public Understanding of Science* 16, no. 1: 79–95. https://doi.org/10.1177/0963662506071287

BBC News. 2020. "Hundreds Gather in Madrid for Anti-Mask Protest." BBC News. www.bbc.com/news/av/world-europe-53802226

Berzina, Sabine, and Evita Purina. 2020. "Ko Ārstu biedrības valdes loceklis Apinis tev nestāsta par Covid-19? | Re:Baltica." https://rebaltica.lv/2020/10/ko-arstu-biedribas-valdes-loceklis-apinis-tev-nestasta-par-covid-19

Bisgaard, Martin. 2019. "How Getting the Facts Right Can Fuel Partisan-Motivated Reasoning." *American Journal of Political Science* 63, no. 4: 824–839. https://doi.org/10.1111/ajps.12432

Bodner, John, Wendy Welch, and Ian Brodie. 2020. *COVID-19 Conspiracy Theories: QAnon, 5G, the New World Order and Other Viral Ideas.* Jefferson, NC: McFarland.

Bolsen, Toby, and James N. Druckman. 2015. "Counteracting the Politicization of Science." *Journal of Communication* 65, no. 5: 745–769. https://doi.org/10.1111/jcom.12171

Borenstein, Seth, and Hannah Fingerhut. 2022. "Americans' Trust in Science Now Deeply Polarized, Poll Shows." AP NEWS, January 26, sec. Coronavirus pandemic. https://apnews.com/article/coronavirus-pandemic-science-health-covid-19-pandemic-4e99139d995581319dffab4107627a5e

Brennan, Emily, Erin Maloney, Yotam Ophir, and Joseph N. Cappella. 2018. "Designing Effective Testimonial Pictorial Warning Labels for Tobacco Products." *Health Communication* 34, no. 12): 539–546. https://doi.org/10.1080/10410236.2018.1493417

Brennen, J. Scott, Felix M. Simon, Philip N. Howard, and Rasmus Kleis Nielsen. 2020. Types, Sources, and Claims of COVID-19 Misinformation (RISJ Factsheets). Reuters Institute for the Study of Journalism. https://ora.ox.ac.uk/objects/uuid:178db677-fa8b-491d-beda-4bacdc9d7069

Bucchi, Massimiano. 2008. "Of Deficits, Deviations and Dialogues: Theories of Public Communication of Science," in *Handbook of Public Communication of Science and Technology*, ed. Massimiano Bucchi and B. Trench. New York: Routledge.

Cappella, Joseph N., Erin Maloney, Yotam Ophir, and Emily Brennan. 2015. "Interventions to Correct Misinformation about Tobacco Products." *Tobacco Regulatory Science* 1, no. 2: 186–197. http://dx.doi.org/10.18001/TRS.1.2.8

Cappella, Joseph N., Yotam Ophir, and Jazmyne Sutton. 2018. "The Importance of Measuring Knowledge in the Age of Misinformation and Challenges in the Tobacco Domain," in *Misinformation and Mass Audiences*, ed. Brian G.

Southwell, Emily A. Thorson, and Laura Sheble, 51–70. Austin: University of Texas Press.

Cattan, Nacha, and Vernon Silver. 2021. "Mexico Covid Crisis: AMLO, Government's Response Ahead of Delta Variant—Bloomberg." Bloomberg. www.bloomberg.com/news/features/2021-07-15/mexico-covid-crisis-amlo-government-s-response-ahead-of-delta-variant

CBS News. 2012. "Judge Blocks FDA Requirement for Graphic Tobacco Warning Labels." www.cbsnews.com/news/judge-blocks-fda-requirement-for-graphic-tobacco-warning-labels

Claeson, Mariam, and Stefan Hanson. 2021. "The Swedish COVID-19 Strategy Revisited." *The Lancet* 397, no. 10285: 1619. https://doi.org/10.1016/S0140-6736(21)00885-0

Coombs, Timothy W. 1999. *Ongoing Crisis Communication: Planning, Managing, and Responding*. Thousand Oaks, CA: Sage Publications.

Dahlstrom, Michael F., and Shirley S. Ho. 2012. "Ethical Considerations of Using Narrative to Communicate Science." *Science Communication*, September, 1075547012454597. https://doi.org/10.1177/1075547012454597

Delli Carpini, Michael X., and Scott Keeter. 1993. "Measuring Political Knowledge: Putting First Things First." *American Journal of Political Science* 37, no. 4: 1179–1206. https://doi.org/10.2307/2111549

Drury, Colin. 2020. "NHS Worker Punched and Thrown from Tube Train after Confronting Passengers for Not Wearing Masks." *The Independent*. October 28. www.independent.co.uk/news/uk/crime/london-underground-tube-mask-nhs-attack-high-street-kensington-coronavirus-b1391500.html

DW. 2020. "Architect of Sweden's Coronavirus Approach Admits Shortcoming," DW, June 3, 2020. DW.COM. www.dw.com/en/architect-of-swedens-coronavirus-approach-admits-shortcoming/a-53672606

FDA. 2022a. "Changes to the Nutrition Facts Label." FDA, March. www.fda.gov/food/food-labeling-nutrition/changes-nutrition-facts-label

———. 2022b. "Coronavirus (COVID-19) Update: FDA Limits Use of Janssen COVID-19 Vaccine to Certain Individuals." FDA, May 6. www.fda.gov/news-events/press-announcements/coronavirus-covid-19-update-fda-limits-use-janssen-covid-19-vaccine-certain-individuals

Fiske, Susan T., and Cydney Dupree. 2014. "Gaining Trust as Well as Respect in Communicating to Motivated Audiences about Science Topics." *Proceedings of the National Academy of Sciences* 111 (Supplement 4): 13593–13597. https://doi.org/10.1073/pnas.1317505111

Fitzgerald, Frances. 2017. *The Evangelicals: The Struggle to Shape America*. New York: Simon and Schuster.

Fletcher, Richard, and Sora Park. 2017. "The Impact of Trust in the News Media on Online News Consumption and Participation." *Digital Journalism* 5, no. 10: 1281–1299. https://doi.org/10.1080/21670811.2017.1279979

García, Jacobo. 2021. "México admite que la cifra de fallecidos por la covid es al menos un 60% más alta." El País México, March 28. https://elpais.com/mexico/2021-03-28/mexico-ademite-que-la-cifra-de-fallecidos-por-la-covid-puede-ser-al-menos-un-60-mas-alta.html

Gauchat, Gordon. 2011. "The Cultural Authority of Science: Public Trust and Acceptance of Organized Science." *Public Understanding of Science* 20, no. 6: 751–770. https://doi.org/10.1177/0963662510365246

Gerber, Jeffrey S., and Paul A. Offit. 2009. "Vaccines and Autism: A Tale of Shifting Hypotheses." *Clinical Infectious Diseases* 48, no. 4: 456–461. https://doi.org/10.1086/596476

Goldberg, Matthew H., Abel Gustafson, Matthew T. Ballew, Seth A. Rosenthal, and Anthony Leiserowitz. 2019. "A Social Identity Approach to Engaging Christians in the Issue of Climate Change." *Science Communication* 41, no. 4: 442–463. https://doi.org/10.1177/1075547019860847

Harris, Richard. 2017. *Rigor Mortis: How Sloppy Science Creates Worthless Cures, Crushes Hope, and Wastes Billions*. New York: Basic Books.

Harry, Enten. 2021. "Flu Shots Uptake Is Now Partisan. It Didn't Use to Be." CNNPolitics. www.cnn.com/2021/11/14/politics/flu-partisan-divide-analysis/index.html

Hatcher, William. 2020. "A Failure of Political Communication Not a Failure of Bureaucracy: The Danger of Presidential Misinformation During the COVID-19 Pandemic." *The American Review of Public Administration* 50, no. 6–7: 614–620. https://doi.org/10.1177/0275074020941734

Hill, Jenny. 2022. "German Covid Protests Turn Nasty in Row over Rules and Vaccinations." BBC News, January 24, sec. Europe. www.bbc.com/news/world-europe-60059543

Jamieson, Kathleen Hall. 2017. "The Need for a Science of Science Communication: Communicating Science's Values and Norms," in *The Oxford Handbook of the Science of Science Communication*, ed. Kathleen Hall Jamieson, Dan Kahan, and Dietram A. Scheufele, 15–24. New York: Oxford University Press.

———. 2018. "Crisis or Self-Correction: Rethinking Media Narratives about the Well-Being of Science." *Proceedings of the National Academy of Sciences* 115 (March): 2620–2627. https://doi.org/10.1073/pnas.1708276114

Janus, Lv. 2021. "Četri no pieciem Covid-19 pacientiem krieviski runājošie? Komentē Stradiņa slimnīcas pārstāve." Jauns.lv. https://jauns.lv/raksts/zinas/467656-cetri-no-pieciem-covid-19-pacientiem-krieviski-runajosie-komente-stradina-slimnicas-parstave

Kahan, Dan M. 2015. "Climate-Science Communication and the Measurement Problem." *Political Psychology* 36, no. S1: 1–43. https://doi.org/10.1111/pops.12244

Kahan, Dan M., Ellen Peters, Maggie Wittlin, Paul Slovic, Lisa Larrimore Ouellette, Donald Braman, and Gregory Mandel. 2012. "The Polarizing Impact of

Science Literacy and Numeracy on Perceived Climate Change Risks." *Nature Climate Change* 2, no. 10: 732–735. https://doi.org/10.1038/nclimate1547

Kata, Anna. 2010. "A Postmodern Pandora's Box: Anti-Vaccination Misinformation on the Internet." *Vaccine* 28, no. 7: 1709–1716. https://doi.org/10.1016/j.vaccine.2009.12.022

Katz, Elihu, and Paul Felix Lazarsfeld. 1966. "Personal Influence, the Part Played by People in the Flow of Mass Communications." New Brunswick, NJ: Transaction Publishers.

Krastev, Ivan, and Mark Leonard. 2021. "Europe's Invisible Divides: How Covid-19 Is Polarising European Politics—European Council on Foreign Relations." ECFR (blog), September 1. https://ecfr.eu/publication/europes-invisible-divides-how-covid-19-is-polarising-european-politics

Kreuter, Matthew W., Melanie C. Green, Joseph N. Cappella, Michael D. Slater, Meg E. Wise, Doug Storey, Eddie M. Clark, et al. 2007. "Narrative Communication in Cancer Prevention and Control: A Framework to Guide Research and Application." *Annals of Behavioral Medicine* 33, no. 3: 221–235. https://doi.org/10.1007/BF02879904

Kuhn, Thomas S. 2012. *The Structure of Scientific Revolutions*. 50th anniversary edition. Chicago: University of Chicago Press.

Lenzer, Jeanne. 2020. "Covid-19: Group of UK and US Experts Argues for 'Focused Protection' Instead of Lockdowns." *BMJ* 371 (October): m3908. https://doi.org/10.1136/bmj.m3908

LETA. 2021. "Vakcīnu iepirkumu skandāls: epidemiologi mudinājuši iepirkt visu pieejamo 'Pfizer' apjomu." https://nra.lv/latvija/348374-vakcinu-iepirkumu-skandals-epidemiologi-mudinajusi-iepirkt-visu-pieejamo-pfizer-apjomu.htm

Lewandowsky, Stephan, Ullrich K. H. Ecker, Colleen M. Seifert, Norbert Schwarz, and John Cook. 2012. "Misinformation and Its Correction: Continued Influence and Successful Debiasing." *Psychological Science in the Public Interest* 13, no. 3: 106–131. https://doi.org/10.1177/1529100612451018

Lupia, Arthur. 2015. *Uninformed: Why People Seem to Know So Little about Politics and What We Can Do about It*. New York: Oxford University Press.

McCammack, Brian. 2007. "Hot Damned America: Evangelicalism and the Climate Change Policy Debate." *American Quarterly* 59, no. 3: 645–668.

McIntyre, Lee. 2021. "Talking to Science Deniers and Sceptics Is Not Hopeless." *Nature* 596, no. 165. https://doi.org/10.1038/d41586-021-02152-y

McKee, Rebecca, Adrianna Murphy, Erica Richardson, Bayard Roberts, Christian Haerpfer, and Martin McKee. 2013. "Do Citizens of the Former Soviet Union Trust State Institutions, and Why?" *East European Politics* 29, no. 4: 377–396. https://doi.org/10.1080/21599165.2013.821981.

Miller, Jon D. 1983. "Scientific Literacy: A Conceptual and Empirical Review." *Daedalus* 112, no. 2: 29–48.

Mooney, Chris. 2007. *The Republican War on Science.* New York: Basic Books.
Motta, Matt, Dominik Stecula, and Christina Farhart. 2020. "How Right-Leaning Media Coverage of COVID-19 Facilitated the Spread of Misinformation in the Early Stages of the Pandemic in the U.S." *Canadian Journal of Political Science* 53, no. 2: 335–342. https://doi.org/10.1017/S0008423920000396
Moyer-Gusé, Emily. 2008. "Toward a Theory of Entertainment Persuasion: Explaining the Persuasive Effects of Entertainment-Education Messages." *Communication Theory* 18, no. 3: 407–425. https://doi.org/10.1111/j.1468-2885.2008.00328.x
Nabi, Robin L. 2010. "The Case for Emphasizing Discrete Emotions in Communication Research." *Communication Monographs* 77, no. 2: 153–159. https://doi.org/10.1080/03637751003790444
Nagle, John Copeland. 2008. "The Evangelical Debate over Climate Change." *University of St. Thomas Law Journal* 5, no. 1: 53–86.
Nisbet, Erik C., and Olga Kamenchuk. 2021. "Russian News Media, Digital Media, Informational Learned Helplessness, and Belief in COVID-19 Misinformation." *International Journal of Public Opinion Research* 33, no. 3: 571–590. https://doi.org/10.1093/ijpor/edab011
Offit, Paul A. 2010a. *Autism's False Prophets: Bad Science, Risky Medicine, and the Search for a Cure.* New York: Columbia University Press.
———. 2010b. *Deadly Choices: How the Anti-Vaccine Movement Threatens Us All.* New York: Basic Books.
———. 2017. *Pandora's Lab: Seven Stories of Science Gone Wrong.* Washington, DC: National Geographic Books.
Oksanen, Atte, Markus Kaakinen, Rita Latikka, Iina Savolainen, Nina Savela, and Aki Koivula. 2020. "Regulation and Trust: 3-Month Follow-up Study on COVID-19 Mortality in 25 European Countries." *JMIR Public Health and Surveillance* 6, no. 2: e19218. https://doi.org/10.2196/19218
Ophir, Yotam. 2018. "Spreading News: The Coverage of Epidemics by American Newspapers and Its Effects on Audiences—A Crisis Communication Approach." https://repository.upenn.edu/entities/publication/fb442f21-bf48-4712-b4e8-3194fd16d85a
Ophir, Yotam, Emily Brennan, Erin K. Maloney, and Joseph N. Cappella. 2017. "The Effects of Graphic Warning Labels' Vividness on Message Engagement and Intentions to Quit Smoking." *Communication Research* 46, no. 5: 619–638. https://doi.org/10.1177/0093650217700226
Ophir, Yotam, and Kathleen Hall Jamieson. 2021. "The Effects of Media Narratives about Failures and Discoveries in Science on Beliefs about and Support for Science." *Public Understanding of Science* 30, no. 8: 1008–1023. https://doi.org/10.1177/09636625211012630
Ophir, Yotam, Meredith L. Pruden, Dror Walter, Ayse D. Lokmanoglu, Catherine Tebaldi, and Rui Wang. 2022. "Weaponizing Reproductive Rights: A Mixed-

Method Analysis of White Nationalists' Discussion of Abortions Online." *Information, Communication & Society*, June: 1–26. https://doi.org/10.1080/1369118X.2022.2077654

Ophir, Yotam, Dror Walter, Patrick E. Jamieson, and Kathleen Hall Jamieson. 2023. Factors assessing science's self-presentation model and their effect on conservatives' and liberals' support for funding science. *Proceedings of the National Academy of Sciences*, 120, no. 38, e2213838120. 10.1073/pnas.2213838120

Oreskes, Naomi. 2021. *Why Trust Science?* Princeton, NJ: Princeton University Press.

Oreskes, Naomi, and Erik M. Conway. 2011. *Merchants of Doubt: How a Handful of Scientists Obscured the Truth on Issues from Tobacco Smoke to Global Warming*. New York: Bloomsbury Press.

Phillips, T. 2022. Police call for Bolsonaro to be charged for spreading Covid misinformation. https://www.theguardian.com/world/2022/aug/18/jair-bolsonaro-covid-misinformation-charge-brazil-police

Pink, Sophia L., James Chu, James N. Druckman, David G. Rand, and Robb Willer. 2021. "Elite Party Cues Increase Vaccination Intentions among Republicans." *Proceedings of the National Academy of Sciences* 118, no. 32: e2106559118. https://doi.org/10.1073/pnas.2106559118

Popper, Karl. 2005. *The Logic of Scientific Discovery*. London: Routledge.

———. 2012. *The Open Society and Its Enemies*. London: Routledge.

Purina, Evita. 2021. "Analīzes Covid-19 gaitas prognozēšanai—vai Aizsilniecei taisnība? | Re:Baltica." https://rebaltica.lv/2021/11/analizes-covid-19-gaitas-prognozesanai-vai-aizsilniecei-taisniba

Ramonfaur, Diego, David Eugenio Hinojosa-González, Gloria Paulina Rodriguez-Gomez, David Alejandro Iruegas-Nuñez, and Eduardo Flores-Villalba. 2021. "COVID-19 Vaccine Hesitancy and Acceptance in Mexico: A Web-Based Nationwide Survey." *Revista Panamericana de Salud Pública* 45 (October): e133. https://doi.org/10.26633/RPSP.2021.133

Relman, Eliza. 2021. "94% of Republicans Believe or Are Unsure of at Least 1 Falsehood about COVID-19 or the Vaccines." *Business Insider*. www.businessinsider.com/94-republicans-believe-are-unsure-of-covid-19-vaccine-falsehoods-2021-11

Reuters. 2021. Pfizer got no response to offers to supply vaccine to Brazil last year, exec says. https://www.reuters.com/business/healthcare-pharmaceuticals/pfizer-got-no-response-offers-supply-vaccine-brazil-last-year-exec-says-2021-05-13/

Rocha-Quintero, Jorge E. 2020. "La pandemia de covid–19 en México, entre la polarización política y las tendencias electorales," July. https://rei.iteso.mx/handle/11117/6426

Roche, Darragh. 2021. "Fauci Said Masks 'Not Really Effective,' Email Reveals." *Newsweek*, June 2. www.newsweek.com/fauci-said-masks-not-really-effective-keeping-out-virus-email-reveals-1596703

Rogers, Everett M. 1997. *History of Communication Study*. New York: Free Press.

Romer, Daniel, and Kathleen Hall Jamieson. 2020. "Conspiracy Theories as Barriers to Controlling the Spread of COVID-19 in the U.S." *Social Science & Medicine* 264 (September): 113356. https://doi.org/10.1016/j.socscimed.2020.113356

Rozenberga, Mara, and Vita Anstrate. 2021. "Vakcinācijas biroju vadīs bijusī Dziesmu svētku izpilddirektore Eva Juhņēviča." LSM. www.lsm.lv/raksts/zinas/latvija/vakcinacijas-biroju-vadis-bijusi-dziesmu-svetku-izpilddirektore-eva-juhnevica.a389956

The Royal Society. 1985. "The Public Understanding of Science." https://royalsociety.org/news-resources/publications/1985/public-understanding-science

Stott, Michael. 2020. "Pandemic Politics: The Rebound of Latin America's Populists." *Financial Times*, September 23.

Sturgis, Patrick, and Nick Allum. 2004. "Science in Society: Re-Evaluating the Deficit Model of Public Attitudes." *Public Understanding of Science* 13, no. 1: 55–74. https://doi.org/10.1177/0963662504042690

Supran, Geoffrey, and Naomi Oreskes. 2021. "Rhetoric and Frame Analysis of ExxonMobil's Climate Change Communications." *One Earth* (May): S2590332221002335. https://doi.org/10.1016/j.oneear.2021.04.014

Train, Russell E. 1996. "The Environmental Record of the Nixon Administration." *Presidential Studies Quarterly* 26, no. 1: 185–96.

Turney, J. 1998. "To Know Science Is to Love It? Observations from Public Understanding of Science Research." www.communicatingastronomy.org/repository/guides/toknowscience.pdf

TVNET. 2021. "Kuros Rīgas Rajonos Vakcinācijas Aptvere Ievērojami Pārsniedz Vidējo Rādītāju?" Latvijā. September 9. www.tvnet.lv/7334224/kuros-rigas-rajonos-vakcinacijas-aptvere-ieverojami-parsniedz-videjo-raditaju

Walter, Dror, Yotam Ophir, and Kathleen Hall Jamieson. 2020. "Russian Twitter Accounts and the Partisan Polarization of Vaccine Discourse, 2015–2017." *American Journal of Public Health* 110, no. 5: 718–724. https://doi.org/10.2105/AJPH.2019.305564

Walter, Dror, Yotam Ophir, Ayse D. Lokmanoglu, and Meredith L. Pruden. 2022. "Vaccine Discourse in White Nationalist Online Communication: A Mixed-Methods Computational Approach." *Social Science & Medicine* 298 (April): 114859. https://doi.org/10.1016/j.socscimed.2022.114859

Weingart, Peter, Claudia Muhl, and Petra Pansegrau. 2003. "Of Power Maniacs and Unethical Geniuses: Science and Scientists in Fiction Film." *Public Understanding of Science* 12, no. 3: 279–287. https://doi.org/10.1177/0963662503123006

Xavier, Diego Ricardo,. Eliane Lima e Silva, Flávio Alves Lara, Gabriel R. R. e Silva, Marcus F. Oliveira, Helen Grugel, and Christovam Barcellos. 2022. Involvement of political and socio-economic factors in the spatial and temporal dynamics of COVID-19 outcomes in Brazil: A population-based study. *The Lancet Regional Health Americas*, 10, 1-16. https://doi.org/10.1016/j.lana.2022.100221

Yamey, Gavin, and Gregg Gonsalves. 2020. "Donald Trump: A Political Determinant of Covid-19." BMJ, April, m1643. https://doi.org/10.1136/bmj.m1643

Ziman, John. 1991. "Public Understanding of Science." *Science, Technology, & Human Values* 16, no. 1: 99–105. https://doi.org/10.1177/016224399101600106

Zvejnieks, Olafs. 2022. "Korupcija vai nekompetence? Štelmahers atklāj patiesību par daudzkārt lietojamo higiēnisko masku iepirkumu." LA.LV. 2022. www.la.lv/stelmahers-korupcija-vai-nekompetence

Chapter Four

Generative Media and Our Collective Response to the Ecological Crisis

JOHN FIEGE

A Lion used to prowl about a field in which Four Oxen used to dwell. Many a time he tried to attack them; but whenever he came near they turned their tails to one another, so that whichever way he approached them he was met by the horns of one of them. At last, however, they fell a-quarrelling among themselves, and each went off to pasture alone in a separate corner of the field. Then the Lion attacked them one by one and soon made an end of all four.
United we stand, divided we fall.

—Aesop, "The Four Oxen and the Lion"

The myth does not point to a fact; the myth points beyond facts to something that informs the fact.

—Joseph Campbell

Within communities that share a concern about climate change and ecological crisis, a particular myth has carried great power: the myth that climate change denial is at the heart of our inability to effectively address climate change. First, this myth leads many to counter denialism with ever more facts and science: if they knew more, then they would change. Second, this myth gives enormous responsibility and power to the deniers: if they change, then all is won. Like most myths, there is some truth embedded in it, but it is not the whole truth. This myth of denial has, like a magician's hand, taken our eyes off of the other hand: the actions of those who seek to change or overcome the deniers. If we want to solve the mystery of how to make progress on climate change, I believe we need to look much more closely at this other hand.

Effectively addressing ecological destruction and human impacts on the climate is not just about being right, or having a solution, or being in power—it is about cooperation on a grand scale. Cooperation requires communication, and we communicate with large numbers of people through media. When environmental media pushes away audiences, it fails to communicate effectively or build cooperation among diverse audiences. This repulsion can come from an excessive focus on disaster or fear. It can come from being perceived as boring or overly technical. It can come from associations with particular politics or cultures. It can come from impressions of arrogance, elitism, condescension, or dogmatism. Without cooperation, without media that brings people together rather than pushing them apart, we cannot change our societies and ways of living quickly enough. Carbon emissions continue to rise. Global temperatures continue to climb. Species extinctions continue to accelerate. Divided we fall.

This chapter chronicles my search for an alternative way to communicate and make media about ecological crisis—and what I've learned more broadly about how to communicate about challenging societal issues. I am a filmmaker focused on confronting environmental problems through the stories of communities on the front lines of environmental calamity. To increase the number of stories I can address, the speed of production, and the frequency of my engagement with audiences, I recently launched a podcast, called Chrysalis, as a way to confront our ecological predicament through conversations with a broad diversity of environmental thinkers. As the title intimates, Chrysalis is a podcast about transformation—the transformation of the podcast guests, the audience, our collective relationship to the rest of nature, and me personally as I engage deeply in conversation. As my guests and I discuss the ecological crisis in its many forms, I center the process of transformation and an attitude of curiosity and openness to change.

In my assessment of the media landscape we inhabit and the work I've done so far with the podcast, I ask how we can change the way we make media about vital societal issues, such as climate change and the extinction crisis, in order to build stronger coalitions and transform our societies to effectively confront these crises. The conclusions I come to are as much about changing ourselves as they are about changing others. We must start by looking in the mirror.

Our Responses to Misinformation

> The chief task in life is simply this: to identify and separate matters so that I can say clearly to myself which are externals not under my control, and which have to do with the choices I actually control. Where then do I look for good and evil? Not to uncontrollable externals, but within myself to the choices that are my own . . .
>
> —Epictetus, *Discourses*, 2.5.4–5

Epictetus was born a slave in the Roman Empire in the first century CE before winning his freedom and becoming a renowned Stoic philosopher and teacher. His words regarding the "chief task in life" resonate today as we ask ourselves what in the world we can change. Changing others is often difficult, if not impossible, or worse: they might turn against us with renewed ferocity. In contrast, changing ourselves is an option with every decision we make. Regarding climate denialism or other types of misinformation, we have a difficult time controlling that misinformation in the world, but we can control our own reactions and responses to it.

Sally Kohn, who has described herself as a "liberal lesbian commentator at Fox News" (Kohn 2018), gave a TED talk in 2013 entitled "Let's Try Emotional Correctness," which explores this question of what we can control and what we cannot, using her concept of "emotional correctness." In the talk, Kohn lays out her experience working at Fox News, where her "biggest takeaway is that for decades, we've been focused on political correctness, but what matters more is emotional correctness . . . political persuasion doesn't begin with ideas or facts or data. Political persuasion begins with being emotionally correct." She defines emotional correctness as "the compassion for others that we want them to have for us," and she was surprised to find that the conservatives on Fox News, like Sean Hannity, were genuinely nice to her and had "impressive" levels of emotional correctness, despite their profound political disagreements. In contrast, she says, "liberals on my side, we can be self-righteous, we can be condescending, we can be dismissive of anyone who doesn't agree with us. In other words, we can be politically right but emotionally wrong. And incidentally, that means that people don't like us" (Kohn 2013).

It is not difficult to find examples of the self-righteous, condescending, and dismissive tone that Kohn references. A particularly egregious example was published on Gawker in November of 2015, not long before Trump clinched the Republican presidential nomination. This was the time of the Syrian refugee crisis and a hot political debate in the United States over whether or not to accept Syrian refugees. The essay was titled, not-so-subtly, "Dumb Hicks Are America's Greatest Threat." After recounting several examples of conservative politicians who cited misinformation and made racist, xenophobic, or Islamophobic comments to justify their refusal to accept the refugees, author Hamilton Nolan writes, "you, our elected officials, are embarrassing us. All of us, except your fellow dumb hicks, who voted for you in large numbers. You—our racist, xenophobic, knuckle-dragging ignorant leaders—are making us look bad in front of the guests (the whole world). You are the bad cousin in the family who always ruins Thanksgiving. Go in the back room and drink a can of beer alone please." Nolan then names a litany of offenses he blames on "dumbass hicks," from slavery, to lynchings, to the Iraq War, before claiming authority from his own identity: "I was born and raised down south and I can testify that it is full of dumb hicks, running things" (Nolan 2015).

Over the next year, Hillary Clinton began referring to half of Trump's supporters as a "basket of deplorables," describing them as "the racist, sexist, homophobic, xenophobic, Islamaphobic—you name it. And unfortunately there are people like that. And he has lifted them up" (Reilly 2016) Like "dumb hick," "deplorable" was a slur—a mean, condescending way of referring to white Americans who live outside of cities, who often don't have college degrees, and who probably go to church. These are exactly the folks who most enthusiastically put Trump in the White House (Pew Research Center 2018).

Just after Trump lost the 2020 presidential race, *Politico* published an autopsy of his presidency and what it revealed about America, according to thirty-five commentators. One recurrent theme is liberal elites, how they're out of touch with the rest of America, and how Trump supporters resented their attitudes. Mark Bauerlein, a professor emeritus at Emory University, writes,

> Ordinary Americans looked at the elite zones of academia, Hollywood, Silicon Valley, Wall Street and Washington itself, and saw a bunch of self-serving, not very competent individuals sitting

pretty, who had enriched themselves and let the rest of America slide. Remember when Trump told crowds at his rallies to turn around and "Look at 'em!"—at the media with their cameras and notepads? The audience complied, stared back at the Fourth Estate, raised their phones and put them on camera—a turnabout that delighted Americans sick of these strutting egos who had been putting the rank and file down for years. (*Politico* 2020)

Trump's call to "Look at 'em!" resonates surprisingly well with Sally Kohn's directive, which I might call, "Look at us!"

Kohn ends her talk with a story about the letters she gets, including one she received from a Fox viewer who didn't agree with her political views. On the TED stage, Kohn says,

> I'm not perfect, but what I am is optimistic. Because I don't just get hate mail. I get a lot of really nice letters, lots of them. And one of my all-time favorites begins: "I am not a big fan of your political leanings or your sometimes tortured logic, but I'm a big fan of you as a person." Now this guy doesn't agree with me—yet. But he's listening—not because of what I said, but because of how I said it. And somehow, even though we've never met, we've managed to form a connection. That's emotional correctness, and that's how we start the conversations that really lead to change. (Kohn 2013)

Considering the imperative from Epictetus to determine what we can control, this is one of the key things we can control: how we say something. Even if our words are in opposition to someone else's beliefs, we can say them in a way that makes it easier for that person to listen and respond. We can say them in a way that is not accusatory. We can say them in a way that doesn't make us sound elitist, self-righteous, condescending, dismissive, or superior. This is an essential lesson I am attempting to bring into the environmental conversation with my podcast.

Forging Generative Media

In 2018, Sally Kohn was a guest on the podcast "On Being," hosted by Krista Tippett, who is a skilled practitioner of emotional correctness, in the way Kohn described it, and who is one of the main people who inspired me to start a podcast. I began listening to "On Being" years ago and found it to be nourishing, while I found the news and other media I was consuming to be largely depleting. The show exposed me to a great number of new ideas, people, and stories, and it made me feel good in a way that I wasn't finding with any other sources of media. In addition to her dexterity with emotional correctness, Tippett is remarkably adept at deep listening—but the power of her work goes beyond both of these concepts.

In the fall of 2022, Tippett released a short series of podcast episodes that explored some of the lessons and values she had garnered in producing the show for over two decades. The first episode is called "Seeing the Generative Story of Our Time," and she explains what she means by "generative stories":

> We are fluent in the story of our time marked by catastrophe and dysfunction. That is real, and it is grave—but it's not the whole story of us. Here's what this phrase—the generative story, the generative narrative of our time—is insisting on: that there is also an ordinary and abundant reality of learning and growth that is happening, of dignity and care and social creativity and evolution.
>
> The great challenges of this century call us to rise to our highest human capacities. They need the landscape of generative people and projects to act like an ecosystem: sharing what we are learning, joining our vulnerabilities, and joining our flourishing. (Tippett 2022)

I find Krista Tippett's concept of generative stories to be a complement to Sally Kohn's emotional correctness. In both cases, they are imploring us to find the good in the midst of the bad—however we define those values.

After I listened to this episode, I put a name to what I had been responding to in Krista Tippett's show for so many years and what I was trying to do myself with conversations and stories about our ecological predicament: these were generative stories, and I wanted to make generative media. I wanted to find the good in the midst of the bad, as I saw it, and I had faith in the idea that finding the good can help us build more powerful coalitions with a greater diversity of ideas that will allow us to confront issues as vital and existentially terrifying as the climate crisis and ecological catastrophe.

In a similar vein, Makoto Fujimura urges us to practice "culture care" and "generative creativity" as a way to resist the culture wars. Fujimura is both a renowned contemporary painter and a devout Christian—identities that place him in two different camps traditionally opposed to one another in the culture wars. He doesn't want to choose sides. Instead, he wants to dissolve the conflict: "Culture is not a territory to be won or lost but a resource we are called to steward with care. Culture is a garden to be cultivated" (Fujimura 2017). Back in 1995, fellow artist Robert Kushner described Fujimura's art this way: "The idea of forging a new kind of art, about hope, healing, redemption, refuge, while maintaining visual sophistication and intellectual integrity is a growing movement, one which finds Makoto Fujimura's work at the vanguard" (Kushner 1995).

Both Krista Tippett's generative stories and Makoto Fujimura's generative art are about building up rather than tearing down, but they also share a distinctively slow, contemplative rhythm. Krista Tippett's shows are an hour long, and she also releases the unedited shows, which can exceed two hours. This length of time allows her to have a genuine conversation and provides ample space both for her and her guest to follow tangents and related ideas and for the listener to contemplate the conversation that emerges. Makoto Fujimura is associated with the "slow art" movement. He uses materials that are sometimes difficult and slow to work with, such as pulverized oyster shells, but he also paints large abstract canvases that invite viewers to slow down, sit with the art, and contemplate (Brara 2019). The pace and rhythm of both Krista Tippett's show and Makoto Fujimura's work stand in marked contrast to the hurried, frenetic character of our contemporary digital world. Their work is generative not just because of its content or subject matter but because of its form.

Form is essential, and some recent books reveal how various information technologies can change our cognition and brain structures. Both Maryanne Wolf's *Reader, Come Home: The Reading Brain in a Digital World* and Nicholas Carr's *The Shallows: What the Internet Is Doing to Our Brains* argue that digital reading and other internet habits are changing the structures of our brains and denying us the cognitive benefits of sustained, focused reading with a traditional paper book (Wolf 2018; Carr 2010). Their work underscores how form, not just content, changes our experience of consuming information. In a recent interview on Ezra Klein's podcast, Wolf invoked Marcel Proust, who wrote eloquently about the importance of the act of reading. Wolf said:

Imperceptibly we are developing a mind-set or habit of reading in a particular way that, by and large, is based on a kind of skimming reading. Again, because of all the information we have to process in any given day. So the habit or mind-set is now so largely influenced by us reading on screens that we take that mind-set, even back to print. We can build habits of mind, a kind of reading that's after the innermost landscape of our thinking, whether we call it a sanctuary of reading, Proust always had something amazing to say about everything. He saw the heart of reading as the place where we go beyond the wisdom of the author to discover our own.

Wolf also invoked Aristotle and his thoughts on a good society: "he said there are three lives to a good society. The first life is the life of productivity and knowledge and accrual of information. The second life is, and in the Greek sense, leisure, entertainment. One has to have that. But he said the third life that is essential is the life of reflection. He used the word contemplation." In the digital age, she argues, we've retained Aristotle's first two lives—you might say in overabundance—but we've largely lost Aristotle's third life: "the contemplative is going missing and we don't realize how important it is to insight" (The Ezra Klein Show 2022). Part of our resistance to misinformation must be a resistance to the form in which much of that misinformation is delivered: the frenetic, lightning-fast, short attention span world of the internet, infused with the twenty-four-hour news cycle. We need more media that is generative: more books, podcasts, films, and art that allow us to go deep, see the complexity of situations, slow down, reflect, contemplate, discover ourselves, and generate new ideas and opinions.

Even within the twenty-four-hour news cycle world of journalism, there are echoes of this generative work in a movement to shift the tone and the focus of the news. An American organization called the Solutions Journalism Network works with news organizations and journalists all over the world to shift coverage away from problems and toward solutions—what they call "solutions journalism" (Solutions Journalism Network 2023). Similarly, the Denmark-based Constructive Institute defines "constructive journalism" as "a response to increasing tabloidization, sensationalism and negativity bias of the news media today. It is an approach that aims to provide audiences with a fair, accurate and contextualized picture of the world, without overemphasizing the negative and what is going wrong" (Constructive Institute 2021).

The story of a seasoned NPR environmental reporter, Ashley Ahearn, reveals how podcasts, as a medium, lend themselves well to "solutions journalism," "constructive journalism," and generative stories. In 2020, Ahearn launched a podcast series called Grouse, which told the story of the Greater Sage-Grouse—"the most controversial bird in the West"—and its imperiled and contentious status in Western sage brush country. In the opening episode, she shares her story of why she wanted to go into environmental reporting:

> I operated from the belief that if people knew more about what we were doing to the planet, then they'd change their behavior or elect better leaders to make better policy. So I threw myself into stories about climate change, melting glaciers, toxic algal blooms, dying orcas, drought, wildfire, salmon, die offs, coal mining, oil spills. The news on the environment beat is never, or at least very rarely, good. But I felt like I was doing some good in the world, and I was winning awards and climbing the NPR career ladder.

But the higher she climbed at NPR, the more she felt like her stories were just "depressing and hopeless," and she was frustrated that she was continually forced to "explain some super complex problems" in stories that were only a few minutes long and getting shorter all the time. (Ahearn 2020) After Trump was elected president, Ahearn covered the pipeline protests at Standing Rock in North Dakota, before she saw Trump come into office and push the pipeline through despite the historic protests. She felt even more hopeless and realized that "living in the liberal echo chamber that is Seattle" was distorting her understanding of what was happening in the country:

> I felt like I didn't know my own country. I didn't understand how Trump had won. For a journalist, there is nothing worse than feeling like you're in the dark or you're not getting the whole story. And that's how I felt after the election. I was covering the environment, so natural resources, wild things, salmon, livestock, logging, wildfire. But I was doing it from a city for city listeners. I think I just had this feeling of hopelessness that my journalism or any journalism really wasn't making a difference in this post-truth era we live in. (2020)

She quit her job with NPR and moved to the Methow Valley, one of the poorest, most conservative areas in rural Washington state. She didn't know what she was going to find, but she knew she had to meet and understand people who were very different from her. Over eight podcast episodes, she explores in depth the precarious ecological state of the Greater Sage-Grouse and how this bird brings out strong emotions in all kinds of people for different reasons. The story reveals the complexity and contentiousness of environmental issues, but it also reveals the humanity in all of those involved. It's an attempt to see the situation from other people's perspectives and try to find space for alignment and cooperation. It's a generative podcast.

I had already begun production on my podcast before I heard Grouse; but after I heard it, Ahearn's work helped me conceptualize what I was trying to do in terms of highlighting perspectives underrepresented in the media, countering the endless stream of terrifying and depressing climate stories in the media, and assembling a fuller picture of the complexities and opportunities we face with the climate crisis. Rather than focusing on counter-arguments to rampant climate misinformation in the media, I wanted to transform the way we engage with environmental stories in the media and the way we represent and relate to people who appear to be anti environmental or vulnerable to environmental misinformation. I, too, was trying to create a generative ecological podcast.

Generative Ecological Conversations

I began recording interviews for the Chrysalis podcast in the summer of 2020, and I launched the podcast in the fall of 2021. The interviews spanned anywhere from an hour and a half to three hours. I covered the span of the guests' lives, from their relationships to nature growing up, to the work they did over the course of their lives, to what they've learned along the way. In the spring of 2022, I began developing several new series for the podcast, with a slightly different format, titled Poets, Artists, Kitchen, and Projects, respectively, each addressing a different mode of engagement with ecological issues. As of this writing, I have recorded forty shows, although I've only released a few. With my guests, I strive for depth and diversity. I dive into complicated issues, often with unexpected, contradictory, or confounding elements. I prepare intensively and leave room for spontaneity. I am searching for the ecological conversations that are too infrequent. I am shining a light on the perspectives we don't hear often enough in the media.

I am hoping to generate new ideas, new actions, new ways of being. I want the audience to be nourished, to be transformed, and to find themselves in the conversations.

One of my guiding concepts in this podcast has been to highlight the climate crisis as a cultural crisis. Environmental discourse is often dominated by science, policy, and economics, which are all vitally important to the conversation, but without a strong cultural understanding of environmental problems it is very difficult to find meaningful solutions that align with people's values and move them to act. One of the first guests I had on Chrysalis was Heather Houser, who writes about the environmental humanities and is a professor of English at the University of Texas at Austin. In her work, I found theoretical frameworks for my sense that culture was all too neglected in the environmental conversation.

For many years, one of the main strategies of proponents of climate action has been to combat bad information with good information—exhaustively researched, exceptionally rational, scientifically sound, peer-reviewed information, often delivered by prominent politicians, passionate activists, or esteemed scientific panels with Nobel Prizes. In my interview with Houser, I asked about the deficit model of climate communication, which she describes in her book *Infowhelm* as a model that identifies the public's lack of information and comprehension as the primary obstacle to environmental action (Houser 2020). She points out that the abundance of environmental information the public now has access to has not led to an abundance of environmental action. The deficit model is common in many scientific and policy communities, but Houser posits that it is flawed to assume that "people are vessels, and you just fill them with information, and the outcome will be predictable" (Fiege 2022a).

The deficit model doesn't take culture into account. Here's how Houser describes the importance of culture: "We need to understand the emotional factors, issues of race and class; and economics and geography; and sex, sexuality, gender; all of these things that really play such an important role when people are responding to that information. And I think that's where the arts and different forms of cultural representation are so important." Much of what I'm doing on the podcast is highlighting a diversity of forms of cultural and artistic expression and asking what each perspective, each example, can offer our understanding of ecological problems and how to approach them.

In addition to the stories of artists, poets, playwrights, and filmmakers, I highlight stories of culture as tradition, ways of being, and various forms of identity, including religion, race, class, and gender. One story that has stuck with me is from Rev. Kyle Meyaard-Schaap, who is an evangelical Christian climate activist—not a combination of descriptors we often hear. He tells the story about his conversion from someone who didn't think much about the environment to someone who devoted his life to caring for it. His older brother, who he describes as "my hero for much of my life," did a college semester abroad program in New Zealand and came back a vegetarian. Here's how he describes his reaction to his brother's news upon return:

> For my Midwestern, pretty conservative meat-and-potatoes family, that was pretty shocking . . . as a junior in high school, I didn't know anybody like me who had ever made that choice. And I had the caricature in my mind of the hemp friendship bracelet-weaving, vegan pizza-eating, throw-paint-on-fur-coats-on-the-weekends vegetarian, and I was forced to either keep that caricature and then put my brother in that camp along with them, which was painful, or to suspend my assumptions and hear him out. And he was gracious and patient, and kind of laid out for me all of his rationale for the decision. And most importantly, he helped me see why that decision to become a vegetarian was not a jettisoning of the values that we had been taught by our community. It was, in fact, a deepening of those values. It was a way for him to live more fully into those values, like loving our neighbor, loving God, caring for God's creation. All of the values that we had been instilled with, it was another opportunity to express those values more deeply. And that was, that was a real lightbulb moment for me. (Fiege 2021a)

Meyaard-Schaap was able to hear his brother and not just dismiss his vegetarian turn because he admired and trusted him and because they shared the same cultural background and values. It's not just about the message; it's about the messenger. And the reason the messenger matters is that culture matters—it affects how we see the situation, how we see ourselves in that situation, and how we see the truth.

Now that Meyaard-Schaap is a leader himself, it's interesting to see how he interacts and communicates with young evangelicals, many from conservative communities, just like the one he's from. Most importantly, he speaks their language—he's a native speaker himself. For example, he almost never uses the words "nature" or "environment." Instead, he frequently uses "creation" and "creation care." I asked him about his use of language and its ability to unite or divide us. Here's how he answered:

> It's central to the work of anybody who's trying to organize a community around a particular issue or toward a particular action. First and foremost, you have to understand who you're trying to reach; you have to understand your community; you have to understand what they care about; you have to understand how they perceive their identity; you have to understand what values drive their actions and then find the language that will connect to those identities, to those values . . . And in many ways, the messenger is almost more important than the message itself too. Who is delivering that message? Are they an outsider or do they get us? Do they understand who we are? Do they share important values? And do they share our identity or not? All of that goes into whether or not anyone is receptive to any kind of message. And just like my brother gave me permission to lean more deeply into who I was, and the values that I held dear in my action on this, that's what we try to do with the people we're talking to: give them permission to recognize how their existing identity and the values that already drive them are exactly the identity and the values that the movement needs and that they can bring to bear on this issue.

For countless young evangelicals, Meyaard-Schaap is playing the role that his brother played for him. That essential relationship is completely lost on many people from outside of the evangelical community—often people from big cities, with lots of education and not much interest in religion or understanding of religious communities—who would also like to see evangelicals support environmental action. He continues,

> A lot of people in the Evangelical church, a lot of folks right of the political center, hear a lot of environmental language. And a lot of times they hear it communicated as essentially saying here are all of the ways that you and the community you love are wrong. Here are all of the ways that you need to change the life that you love to be more like us. Doing so will alienate you from people you love. But don't worry, because it'll make you more like us and the world way more like we want it to

be instead of hearing: here are all of the things about you and the community you love that are great. Here are other people who share your values that are taking action, as a way to deepen those values. When you take action to join them, you become more connected to them, you become more connected to your community. And the world becomes more like you want it to be.

Meyaard-Schaap is a very effective climate evangelist for the evangelical community. Like him, if we are more sensitive to the importance of culture, we can find ways to communicate with a wide diversity of people in ways that bring them in rather than push them away. And that is exactly what the climate movement needs more of.

Our understanding of culture is essential, but culture also must change. Our dominant cultural ways of being around the world have created the climate crisis and continue to fuel it. Another guest on the show, Layel Camargo, uses culture as strategy in their climate organizing work—"strategizing around what are the cultural shifts that are needed in order for us to be able to be in right relationship with the planet." Camargo is a transgender and gender non-conforming person who is of Indigenous descendant of the Yaqui and Mayo tribes of the Sonoran Desert, and they identify cultural diversity—the opposite of what they call monoculture—as a key element in addressing the climate crisis. Just as an agricultural monoculture lacks "the reciprocal relationships that it needs from other crops," so too, Camargo argues, does the monoculture of dominant human culture need a variety of different cultures to thrive. As a consequence, the dominant culture must shift to find new ways of relating to life on Earth (Camargo 2021).

The wildfires that have been ravaging the American West over recent years are good examples of the perils of our current dominant culture. European colonists and their descendants took over the control of most Western forests from Indigenous peoples and began implementing forest management practices that combined fire suppression with logging, abandoning centuries of the Indigenous practice of using fire to manage the forests. These European forest management practices, over time and combined with climate change, have led to extremely hot, massive, and devastating wildfires, unlike the milder wildfires that have been an essential feature of Western forests for millennia (Avitt 2021). On the show, Camargo speaks of their most recent project, the Shelterwood Collective, a nonprofit organization that has acquired land in Northern California to steward and build resiliency to wildfire within the forest by combining both Western and Indigenous conservation practices.

This work does not choose one culture over another; it combines the best of both and demonstrates how cultures can shift.

Questions of culture require a delicate balance. We must be sensitive to the culture of others to communicate more effectively but, at the same time, allow cultures to be malleable in order to change for the better. These are not easy contradictions or questions to confront or discuss, but they are essential—and a key focus on the podcast. The environmental movement has its own culture, which can sometimes feel like a checklist of dos and don'ts: eat this, not that; do this, not that; say this, not that. While those behaviors, actions, and ways of speaking can be important, a focus on them can lead to the pursuit of purity, which is both impossible to obtain and alienating to anyone who is not seeking the same sort of purity. Through many of the podcast conversations, I've found that complexity is far more important than purity, and I have found that questioning dogmas can reveal more profound understandings of our ecological challenges and how to tackle them.

Jacqui Patterson is a prominent environmental justice organizer and, at the time of my interview with her, directed the Environmental and Climate Justice Program at NAACP, the National Association for the Advancement of Colored People. On the show, she told the story of a time when a funder asked her to give a talk to a group of solar industry folks: "And when I gave my slides, the funder was like, 'Yeah, we just want you to focus on solar, you know, and on energy.'" Rather than strip her talk of content about race and justice—the main issues she focuses on—she said she wasn't going to use slides after all and was renaming the talk "Black Lives Matter: Energy Democracy and the NAACP Civil Rights Agenda" (Fiege 2021).

Patterson's talk was received extremely well. She was asked to "just talk about solar," but she complicated it. She showed them that you can't think about this one thing without considering another. Rather than her audience becoming frustrated with the added complexity, she helped them understand more profoundly how addressing climate change required addressing racism simultaneously, giving new purpose and meaning to the work they were already doing. Complexity strengthened her argument and her impact.

Complexity of a different kind undergirded one of the most striking moments in my conversation with Adam Rome, an environmental historian at the University at Buffalo, where I teach as well. In his book, *The Genius of Earth Day: How a 1970 Teach-In Unexpectedly Made the First Green Generation*, Rome describes the remarkable institutional achievements in the wake of the first Earth Day: the formation of the Environmental

Protection Agency and the passage of the Clean Air Act in 1970, the Clean Water Act of 1972, and the Endangered Species Act of 1973, all under a Republican administration, no less. He also writes about the twentieth anniversary celebration of Earth Day in 1990, just after climate change became a widely publicized environmental concern. Like the first Earth Day, it was a huge event—with more professional planning, better funding, and a more focused message than in 1970—but it did not lead to an environmental decade that confronted climate change or any other environmental issues in a significant way, as the first Earth Day had (Rome 2013). When I asked Rome what accounted for the stark differences between the two events and their outcomes, he answered:

> Mobilizing isn't organizing. And mobilizing isn't empowering. It doesn't take people new places . . . advertising isn't about teaching you anything. It's about getting you to buy, you know, something. Political messaging isn't about educating you. It's about getting you to vote for this guy or woman rather than that person. So, it's yes or no . . . Earth Day, the original Earth Day was so much more complicated than that. It left it up to millions of individuals to say, what does this mean to me, what am I going to do? It didn't try to marshal them all in one direction, or to enlist them into a preexisting cause. (Fiege 2022)

The first Earth Day was messy. It was complicated. With 12,000 events across the country and more than 35,000 speakers from every walk of life—young and old, scientists and preachers, liberals and conservatives—the transformative power of the first Earth Day, conceived as a teach-in rather than a rally or a protest, is hard for us to imagine in our contemporary era of stark political polarization, social media activism, and climate denial politics. It was a generative event. Participants learned about a wide array of issues, met new people from all walks of life, and spent time—sometimes months in planning—thinking about who they were and how they were going to respond to the ecological situation. It changed countless people's lives and the course of history. The twentieth anniversary of Earth Day in 1990 seemed like a mere marketing event in contrast.

Just like the original Earth Day, I want the Chrysalis podcast to be messy and complicated. I aspire to assemble guests with wide-ranging identities and perspectives and provide a space to engage deeply in nuanced discussion about the state of our world and how to respond. For the new

Poets series on the podcast, I interviewed poet Forrest Gander, who remarked that addressing the environmental crisis will require "a chorus of not just scientists and biologists but a chorus of artists and priests and poets," and that's how he described what I'm doing with the podcast: "that's what you've been doing is putting together this other chorus of responses to our crisis. And I think it's going to take the voices of a lot of people from a lot of different trajectories to effect any kind of change" (Gander 2022). I think he's right.

The original Earth Day had a chorus of voices, and I believe our contemporary world would greatly benefit from revisiting, reimagining, and expanding the idea of an ecological chorus—even if, today, it doesn't take the form of a teach-in. A chorus requires trust in its participants—plus flexibility, creativity, cooperation. As I build my own chorus of voices with the podcast, I intend for there to be ever more diversity of perspectives, identities, and nationalities represented. I expect it to be cacophonous at times, but at other times melodious, even harmonious. Like life itself.

As humans, we are good at adaptation, innovation, and building connections. We can apply these talents to changing our behaviors and ways of being. Time is short, and we must act quickly to stem the damage of ecological destruction and begin to build societies that allow ecosystems around the planet to thrive rather than collapse. There will be an endless diversity of beliefs, cultural traditions, and value systems behind these behavioral changes. Environmental media must make space for as much of that diversity as possible and find ways to effectively communicate and cooperate. Making media more generative is an action we can take right away that can help us bring more people together to make these changes. We need everyone.

Like Aesop's oxen, we must put our tails together and keep our horns out. If we continue "a-quarrelling" among ourselves, the lion will certainly get us all.

A Proclamation of Generative Media

To be generative is to reproduce, procreate, produce offspring, create someone or something new. Media is generative when it produces something new, creates new ideas, grows the mind, inspires creative thinking, leads to learning, invites deep engagement, embraces complexity, finds commonality, encourages community, sees through the eyes of others, reveals the magic of the world, revels in the mystery of the universe, envisions symbiosis between humanity and the rest of nature, has patience for slow change, and dreams of a world that more closely resembles our boldest and most hopeful dreams. Generative media finds the good in the midst of the bad, finds joy in a world containing good and evil, and finds the good and the bad in all things.

I believe generative media can unleash the forces of creativity to imagine the world we want to inhabit, to build this world more quickly, and to heal fractures in ecology, in society, in ourselves. Not all media must aspire to be generative, but I feel strongly that the planet needs more media that is generative—and so do our souls.

References

Ahearn, Ashley. 2020. "Episode 1: Stranger In A Strange Land." Grouse, Boise State Public Radio, September 15. www.boisestatepublicradio.org/podcast/grouse/2020-09-15/episode-1-stranger-in-a-strange-land

Avitt, Andrew. 2021. "Tribal and Indigenous Fire Tradition." Forest Service, United States Department of Agriculture, November 16. www.fs.usda.gov/features/tribal-and-indigenous-heritage

Brara, Noor. 2019. "'Art-Making Is an Act of Hope': How Japanese Artist Makoto Fujimura's Paintings Became an Homage to His Recently Deceased Mother." Artnet News. June 5. https://news.artnet.com/partner-content/waterfall-makoto-fujimura

Camargo, Layel. 2021. Interview with the author for a forthcoming episode of the Chrysalis with John Fiege podcast. Recorded August 17, 2021.

Carr, Nicholas. 2010. *The Shallows: What the Internet Is Doing to Our Brains.* New York: W. W. Norton.

Constructive Institute. 2021. "Welcome." Accessed January 31, 2021. https://constructiveinstitute.org

The Ezra Klein Show. 2022. "Transcript: Ezra Klein Interviews Maryanne Wolf." New York Times, November 22. www.nytimes.com/2022/11/22/opinion/transcript-ezra-klein-interviews-maryanne-wolf.html

Fiege John. 2022. "Adam Rome—An Historical Perspective on Our Environmental Future." Chrysalis with John Fiege April 14, 2022. https://johnfiege.substack.com/p/adamrome#details

———. 2022a. "Heather Houser—Deluged by Data in the Climate Crisis." Chrysalis with John Fiege June 14. https://johnfiege.substack.com/p/heatherhouser#details

———. 2021. "Jacqui Patterson—Envisioning Eco-Communities amidst Toxic Legacies." Chrysalis with John Fiege October 21. https://johnfiege.substack.com/p/jacquipatterson#details

———. 2021a. "Rev. Kyle Meyaard-Schaap—The Biblical Call for Ecological Care." Chrysalis with John Fiege November 18, 2021. https://johnfiege.substack.com/p/kylemeyaard#details

Fujimura, Makoto. 2017. *Culture Care: Reconnecting with Beauty for Our Common Life*. Grand Rapids, MI: IVPress.

Gander, Forrest. 2022. Interview with the author for a forthcoming episode of the Chrysalis with John Fiege podcast. Recorded October 4, 2022.

Houser, Heather. 2020. *Infowhelm: Environmental Art and Literature in an Age of Data*. New York: Columbia University Press.

Kohn, Sally. 2013. "Let's Try Emotional Correctness." Filmed December 4, 2013, at TED@NYC. Video, 5:46. www.ted.com/talks/sally_kohn_let_s_try_emotional_correctness?

———. 2018. "What I Learned as a Liberal Lesbian at Fox News." Fast Company, April 10. www.fastcompany.com/40554388/what-i-learned-as-a-liberal-lesbian-at-fox-news

Kushner, Robert. 1995. "Hiroshi Senju and Makoto Fujimora at Dillon." Art in America, December. https://imagejournal.org/article/culture-war-culture-care

Nolan, Hamilton. 2015. "Dumb Hicks Are America's Greatest Threat." Gawker, November 19. www.gawker.com/dumb-hicks-are-americas-greatest-threat-1743373893

Pew Research Center. 2018. "An Examination of the 2016 Electorate, Based on Validated Voters."August 9. www.pewresearch.org/politics/2018/08/09/an-examination-of-the-2016-electorate-based-on-validated-voters

Politico Magazine. 2020. "What Trump Showed Us about America." *Politico*, November 19. www.politico.com/news/magazine/2020/11/19/roundup-what-trump-showed-us-about-america-435762

Reilly, Katie. 2016. "Read Hillary Clinton's 'Basket of Deplorables' Remarks about Donald Trump Supporters." *Time*, September 10. https://time.com/4486502/hillary-clinton-basket-of-deplorables-transcript/

Roberts, Roxanne. 2021. "Hillary Clinton's 'deplorables' Speech Shocked Voters Five Years Ago—But Some Feel It Was Prescient." *Washington Post*, August 31. www.washingtonpost.com/lifestyle/2021/08/31/deplorables-basket-hillary-clinton/

Rome, Adam. 2013. *The Genius of Earth Day: How a 1970 Teach-In Unexpectedly Made the First Green Generation*. New York: Hill and Wang.

Solutions Journalism Network. 2023. "What Is Solutions Journalism?" Accessed January 31, 2023. www.solutionsjournalism.org

Tippett, Krista. 2022. "On Being Foundations." On Being, accessed January 31, 2023. https://onbeing.org/on-being-foundations

Wolf, Maryanne. 2018. *Reader, Come Home: The Reading Brain in a Digital World*. New York: Harper.

Chapter Five

SWAMP (Studies of Work Atmospheres and Mass Production)

Matt Kenyon

With the rise of social media and the internet, it's become easier than ever to disseminate false information, and many people find themselves struggling to separate fact from fiction. Again and again, I am reminded of the song "Crosseyed and Painless" by the American rock band Talking Heads, released in 1980 on their album "Remain in Light." I always found the lyrics of the song somewhat cryptic, but to my ears they seem to suggest a narrator struggling to make sense of the world quickly changing around them. The line "Facts all come with points of view" reminds us that truth is not always objective and that even our fleeting understanding of reality is shaped by our perspective. This theme of the subjectivity of facts within a quickly changing world is particularly relevant today, where misinformation and fake news are rampant. Truth is often more complex than it appears.

SWAMP

In the world of punk rock and activism, a quote by Jello Biafra has always resonated with me: "Don't hate the media, become the media." As an artist, I have a love–hate relationship with media and technology. I am fascinated by the power they hold, but also deeply wary of it. For over twenty years,

I have been running a studio called SWAMP (Studies of Work Atmospheres and Mass Production), which focuses on critical themes addressing the effects of global corporate operations, mass media and communication, military-industrial complexes, and general meditations on the liminal area between life and artificial life. During the COVID-19 pandemic, I found myself watching and rewatching the classic film "The Invisible Man."

This film's narrative centers on the work of a pioneering scientist, Dr. Jack Griffin, who concocts a potion that grants him the power of invisibility. Rather than using his newfound capabilities for benevolent purposes, he embarks on a sinister path, robbing a bank, killing police officers, causing a train derailment that results in hundreds of deaths. This sci-fi storyline forces us to ponder—are there societal checks in place on how invisible power operates?

Like the film, my work aims to bring attention to the invisible and elusive influence that frequently pervades our society, especially in matters of wealth and authority. In my artistic practice, I have consistently examined the intricacies of this intangible power, challenging and questioning its forces.

As the Invisible Man uses his powers to cause chaos, the film's innovative special effects are powerful metaphors for the unseen and harmful ways power can be misused, a theme I often explore in my work. In this chapter, I'll discuss several of my artworks that tackle this theme, and share the methods I've used to do so.

Spore

In the early days of my artistic career, I created an artwork called "Spore." The project was a self-contained ecosystem for a rubber tree plant, purchased from Home Depot, a popular home improvement store. To outcompete local independent retailers, Home Depot, much like other large anti-market retail chains, implemented an all-encompassing return policy for their plants. If a plant died for any reason, one could bring its carcass back with the receipt and receive a replacement plant at no charge.

Back in 2002, when wireless internet or Wi-Fi was considered cutting-edge technology, I started working on "Spore" with my collaborator Doug Easterly. We devised a unique enclosure using custom electronics, connecting the watering system of a plant to the stock value of the home improvement store. The concept behind this work was simple: if the company's stock performed well, the plant would receive water; if not, the plant would

Figure 5.1. Spore 1.1 (2002). *Source:* Artwork and photo by the author.

go without. In my mind, I envisioned a symbiotic relationship where the plant would flourish alongside the success of the company, while potentially withering during times of decline.

What fascinated me most about integrating living organisms with data-driven systems is the element of surprise they can bring. And true enough, the plant kept dying repeatedly. Despite the soaring stock value of the home improvement store, or rather because of it, the plant's roots were waterlogged and rotting. This paradoxical situation arose because we were amidst a housing bubble, with people mortgaging their homes to splurge on lavish items like granite countertops. While the home improvement store reaped record-setting profits, the unfortunate plant bore the brunt of this disconnect.

"Spore" taught me a valuable lesson: living organisms cannot be reduced to a single data stream, such as profit. The intricacies of life and growth extend far beyond mere numbers. It served as a humbling reminder of the profound intricacies of nature and the necessity of comprehending the complexity of life itself. Through this project, I came to appreciate that countless factors contribute to the well-being of a living organism. It's not solely about financial success or a single indicator of prosperity. The rubber tree operated on its own intricate rhythm, defying simple quantification. It reminded me of the inherent limitations of markets relying solely on quantitative metrics to gauge the vitality of a living entity—even if that entity is a corporation. Just as a plant requires a harmonious blend of sunlight, water, and nutrients to thrive, our complex society cannot be encapsulated within the single data point defined as growth.

Cloud

"Cloud" is an examination of the 2008 housing crisis, its aftermath, and its lingering repercussions. With the utilization of a custom-made cloud-making machine, the narrative of a neighborhood's real estate boom and bust over the preceding ten years is distilled into a potent ten-minute spectacle. This wheeled device can be set to function within the confines of an art gallery, where it builds a floating housing estate on the ceiling, creating a surreal

Figure 5.2. Cloud, 2021. Mobile cart, helium, compressed air, housing data, water and surfactant. *Source:* Artwork and photo by the author.

tableau. Alternatively, it can be positioned on neighborhood streets, where it serves as a beacon, signaling the historical shifts in housing dynamics. The resulting floating house clouds are visible for miles.

This artwork utilizes clouds shaped like houses, crafted out of a unique blend of lighter-than-air foam, to dissect the intricacies of the 2008 mortgage crisis and the home-front turmoil sparked by volatile financial markets. Each cloud house is meticulously shaped from a special foam, crafted from a surfactant blend, and aerated with a mixture of helium and compressed air. The foam undergoes an extrusion process through a data-driven motorized die, which expands and contracts to form the cookie-cutter silhouette of a house. A mechanized arm then deftly slices away each cloud house, setting it free to soar into the gallery space. Viewers of the piece witness the common house ownership dreams disappear as quickly as they materialize, just as many of us saw the false promises of our homes disappear during the period of this epidemic of foreclosure.

This artwork, "Cloud," invites viewers to reflect on their pattern-finding tendencies and how these relate to global market dynamics. As we view cloud houses, we're led to question whether the patterns we see are real or imagined. We might recall looking at clouds as a child and discovering a dragon, a castle, or a galloping horse out of mere puffs of water vapor. Finding patterns in clouds taps into pareidolia, a psychological phenomenon driven by our brain's tendency to perceive familiar shapes in random stimuli. It's a testament to the intricate neural networks engaged in visual recognition and interpretation, demonstrating how our minds continuously strive to make sense of randomness.

This becomes all the more pertinent as we navigate the choppy waters of a bear market, where the raw, untamed forces of the market seem omnipotent and omnipresent. "Cloud" is an interpretation of the 2008 housing crisis, urging us to consider how our view of markets shapes our understanding of the world.

Giant Pool of Money

Staying within the deranged world of global finance, the next artwork bears the title "Giant Pool of Money." As I began my research for this project, I was struck by an intriguing discovery: a coin minted by the Knights of Malta in the 1630s, when popular belief held that the value of coins was directly tied to the amount of precious metals they contained. The Knights,

Figure 5.3. Giant Pool of Money, 2015. Champagne glass pyramid, gallium coins, Bitcoin miner, custom electronics. *Source:* Artwork and photo by the author.

facing a shortage of such metals, had a stroke of genius: they imprinted the coin with an inscription that its value was not in the metal itself but in the trust placed in it.

NON AES SED FIDES' (Not Money But Trust)

—Inscription on a Knights of Malta coin (1636)

What are the ways we visualize our understanding of money's value? Take, for instance, the English system of tally-sticks. In the days before the invention of double-entry bookkeeping, the empire's financial records were kept on notched wooden sticks, known as tally-sticks. These sticks were used well into the sixteenth century to record debts and pay taxes. However, as double-entry bookkeeping emerged, it became clear that one could not keep two sets of books, and tally-sticks were phased out.

The tale goes that, to dispose of six centuries of tally-sticks, workers were instructed to burn them in the furnace of the basement of the House of Commons. Legend has it that they were a bit too enthusiastic in their efforts, and the resulting fire nearly destroyed the entire building. This moment of transition from one system of record keeping to another is immortalized in J. M. W. Turner's famous painting, "The Burning of the House of Commons." This episode highlights the explosive effects that change in systems of value measurement can have. The accidental incineration of the House of Commons due to discarded tally sticks points to the paradox of a system that was at once structured yet vulnerable, similar to a house of cards or a pyramid of champagne glasses. Such a pyramid, a recognized symbol of affluence and finance, can subtly critique the flawed concept of trickle-down economics, revealing a system that's simultaneously hierarchical, flawed, and fragile. In the ever-evolving world of global finance, it is essential to remember the power these symbols and systems hold in shaping our perceptions of wealth.

My installation "Giant Pool of Money" delves into the mindset and convictions that sparked the 2008 global financial crisis and the ensuing significant erosion of confidence in markets. At the center of the work stands a fifteen-foot pyramid of champagne glasses, which is linked to a change machine that transforms dollar bills into "quarters." These coins, however, are not what they seem. They're minted from gallium, a metal that melts at human body temperature. A complex network of conveyor belts carries these gallium coins to the top of the pyramid, dropping them into the highest champagne glass, where a heater harnessing the hot air from a Bitcoin "miner" melts them. A Bitcoin miner is a powerful computer used to validate transactions and secure the Bitcoin blockchain network. The mining process generates a lot of heat, so miners use cooling systems to prevent overheating, resulting in the blowing of hot air. As the coins melt, they flow down the pyramid, creating a surreal representation of trickle-down economics.

Visitors feed their own paper money into the machine, prompting them to connect their personal experiences with the overwhelmingly complex, media-fueled representation of our global economy. What once felt like solid, familiar currency dissolves right before our eyes, threatening to topple the delicate system—a tangible embodiment of our wavering faith in our globally interconnected economy.

As the world went into lockdown during the COVID-19 pandemic, I returned to reflect on the symbolism of the pyramid and the role of money in our society. Champagne, a drink often associated with celebrations and the wealthy, also plays a role in this project. I should note that contrary to popular belief, champagne was not invented by Dom Perignon, but rather gained its status as a symbol of wealth and power through careful marketing.

The "Giant Pool of Money" installation encourages viewers to ponder the influence of mass media marketing in our lives and how it molds our understanding of power and wealth. Once the gallium covers the interior of each champagne glass, they transform into mirrors. This incorporates the reflections of gallery viewers within the installation. Observing the coins liquefy and creating intricate patterns, we are reminded that money, much like the champagne symbolized in the pyramid, is a manufactured symbol and doesn't inherently represent true value.

Tide

In 2016, a devastating flood hit Baton Rouge, Louisiana, dumping over thirty inches of water in just two days. The resulting flash flood inundated 50,075 houses and claimed the lives of thirteen people. As a native of Baton Rouge, the event hit particularly close to home for me. My own family, including my father and stepmother, were evacuated by a massive military HEMTT (Heavy Expanded Mobility Tactical Truck), and my brother had to carry his one-month-old son through neck-deep floodwaters.

This event, like many others in recent years, begs the question: how frequent are these "once in 500 years" events becoming? The answer, unfortunately, is not reassuring. Climate change is making such extreme weather

Figure 5.4. Tide, 2022. Champagne glass pyramid, casts of houses, custom electronics. *Source:* Artwork and photo by the author.

events more frequent and more severe, and it's not just coastal communities that are at risk. Baton Rouge, an inland city, is but one example of a community impacted by the effects of climate change.

In my latest sculpture, "Tide," the coupe glass again takes center stage in a massive pyramid of champagne glasses. Each champagne glass in the installation houses a tiny sculpture of an actual home, crafted from a special polymer material I've developed that possesses the same refractive index as water. When submerged, these houses become invisible. A pump in the ceiling of the gallery drips water down onto the pyramid, feeding on climate and foreclosure data, simulating the effects of flooding on housing values. As the glasses fill up with water, the houses become nearly invisible, and as the water trickles down the pyramid, the houses are reduced to tiny rooflines before disappearing entirely.

"Tide" draws a poignant contrast between the grand imagery of a champagne glass pyramid and the imminent crisis of climate change and escalating flood risks, creating a visual metaphor for the hidden fragility within today's housing market. This crisis has already made its way into our common vernacular, with the term "underwater mortgage" indicating a property's value being less than the loan owed on it. Over time, a gradual drip will fill the pyramid, flooding the interlinked glasses and rendering the houses invisible. This oscillation of visibility aims to bring attention to how climate change continues to inject uncertainty into communities, persisting long after the media has shifted their focus away, moving on to other news and other extreme weather incidents.

"Tide" was inspired by an obscure and fascinating piece of technology from the past: the Phillips hydraulic computer, also known as the monetary national income analog computer, or MONIAC. The MONIAC was a revolutionary machine that sought to simulate the complexities of the economy using a combination of water tanks and valves. Developed in the late 1940s by economist Bill Phillips, the MONIAC was a true marvel of engineering. The MONIAC was a complex machine, with its network of tanks, tubes, and valves each representing the various components of the economy. Each tank might represent a different economic sector, such as agriculture or industry, and the valves controlled the flow of water between them, simulating the interactions of these sectors.

Although the MONIAC was a highly intricate system, it excelled in producing a distinctive form of economic simulation. It was able to demonstrate how changes in one sector could ripple through the rest of the economy, and how government policies could impact economic growth. In fact, it was so effective that it was used by governments and central banks around the world to help inform economic policy decisions. However, the MONIAC was not without its limitations. For one, it was incredibly large and unwieldy, making it difficult to transport and set up. Additionally, its reliance on water as a medium for computation made it prone to leaks and other mechanical issues.

Despite these limitations, the MONIAC was an important step forward in the field of economic modeling. Its creation marked the beginning of a new era in which computers could be used to simulate and understand the intricacies of the economy. And while the MONIAC may no longer be in use, its legacy lives on in the many economic models and simulations that continue to inform and misinform policy decisions to the present day. While researching "Tide," I was lucky enough to visit one of the only remaining functional examples of this machine in New Zealand. The machine was an ambitious attempt to use fluid dynamics to understand the complex interactions of households, businesses, government, and international trade. Years later, it would be used by economists to test popular economic theories about fiscal and monetary policy, such as the "trickle-down" theory, which posits that cutting taxes for the wealthy will ultimately benefit everyone.

The theory of trickle-down economics, also known as "supply-side economics" or encapsulated in the phrase "a rising tide lifts all boats," gained popularity in the 1970s. This economic ideology posits that tax cuts for the affluent will eventually result in societal benefits across the board. However, an earlier metaphor offers a more fitting perspective on this theory. This alternative story is often illustrated through the "horse and sparrow" analogy. It suggests that if a horse is fed enough oats, some will inevitably pass through undigested, falling to the ground within the horse shit and thereby providing sustenance for the sparrows.

It all started with a drawing on a napkin. One of the key figures in the history of trickle-down economics is Arthur Laffer, an economist who at dinner in 1974 with Donald Rumsfeld and Dick Cheney sketched out an important idea that would have long-lasting effects. The dinner took place at the Two Continents Restaurant in Washington, DC, which is also, oddly enough, the site of a crucial scene in the film *The Godfather, Part II*. At this dinner, Laffer reportedly picked up a napkin and drew a curve, now known as the Laffer Curve, which illustrates the theory that cutting tax rates can increase tax revenues. This idea, though debunked by many economists, has played a starring role in Republican campaigns for tax cuts, including under President Ronald Reagan in 1981, President George W. Bush in 2001, and President Donald Trump in 2017. As a visual artist, it is interesting to me that this false theory of economics, which has had such a significant negative impact on society, began with a simple napkin drawing at a dinner between political figures and an economist.

"Tide" appropriates the concept of employing water to illustrate invisible economic currents and references a past era of pre-digital computing, reminiscent of the Phillips Machine. It serves as a commentary on the futility of trying to simulate something as multifaceted and unpredictable as an economy, highlighting the constraints of overly simplistic, reductionist thinking. Through this piece, I aim to evoke a sense of wonder and stimulate curiosity about the elaborate, and at times destructive, systems that form the foundation of our economic world. The installation serves not only as a reminder of the devastating effects of climate change on communities like Baton Rouge but also as a call to action for individuals and policymakers to take the necessary steps to address this crisis before it's too late.

Supermajor

The whale skeleton that hangs suspended in the New Bedford Whaling Museum in Massachusetts is a haunting reminder of the destructive impact

Figure 5.5. Supermajor, 2013. Vintage oil cans, custom electronics, custom lighting. *Source:* Artwork and photo by the author.

of human industry on the natural world. The museum acquired the skeleton in the early 2000s, but it wasn't long before a dark secret was revealed: the bones were oozing oil.

For over twenty years, the whale skeleton has been slowly seeping a dark, viscous liquid, staining the floor and filling the air with the pungent smell of whale oil. The source of the oil was traced back to the whaling industry of the nineteenth century when the bones were stripped of their blubber and processed for oil. The residual oil, trapped within the bones for over a century, is now slowly dripping out. For me, the sight of the oil-soaked whale skeleton is a stark reminder of the brutal and wasteful practices of the whaling industry, which decimated whale populations and left a toxic legacy that continues to this day. It is a poignant symbol of the destructive impact of human greed and carelessness.

While the museum staff has been unable to halt the seepage of oil, they've implemented measures to manage the situation. They've arranged a series of interconnected funnels and tubes to capture the escaping droplets, channeling them into a special sort of glass decanting jar. A plastic barrier, reminiscent of a sneeze guard, has been placed around the skeleton to catch any escaping droplets of oil and prevent them from spreading, and the area is regularly cleaned and ventilated to reduce the smell.

Despite or perhaps because of the museum's efforts to contain the oil, the sight of the whale skeleton, grand and haunting in its stillness, can't help but draw a parallel to the modern-day practice of oil mining. Just as the once vibrant whale has been reduced to bones floating in mid-air, the relentless extraction of oil depletes and scars the Earth, leaving behind environmental skeletons of ecosystems that were once thriving. The bones tell a simple yet powerful story: our past actions matter; unless something changes, we'll leave behind a harmful legacy.

The world of fluid flows and extractive economies leads to my next artwork, "Supermajor." This piece explores the limits between seeing and believing. The illusion in Supermajor is perpetuated by the perceptual structures of the human brain, which enable individuals to see the world around them as stable, although the sensory information may be incomplete and rapidly varying. These perceptual structures are highly susceptible to manipulation by specially controlling the lighting conditions and the flow of oil—viewers' eyes can be tricked into seeing something that ought to be impossible.

The work's title, "Supermajor," is often used as a term to describe the world's seven largest publicly owned oil companies, which dominated the global petroleum industry from the mid-1940s to the 1970s. These seven companies are

- Exxon (formerly Standard Oil Company of New Jersey)
- Mobil (formerly Standard Oil Company of New York)
- Chevron (formerly Standard Oil Company of California)
- Gulf Oil
- Texaco
- BP (formerly Anglo-Iranian Oil Company)
- Shell

Collectively, these companies were also known as the "Seven Sisters." They controlled about 85 percent of the world's petroleum reserves at their peak.

"Supermajor" presents a collection of vintage labeled oil cans, with a conspicuous hole in the can at the center. Unusually, instead of oil leaking out of the hole, it appears to be trickling back in. This illusion of oil defying gravity and time's arrow creates a spectacle, challenging our ingrained belief that what goes up must inevitably come down. In gallery talks, I often introduce this work as using a simple cheap illusion meant to draw attention to the larger and more expensive illusion that oil companies are constantly advertising—that oil is endless, and that our global energy economy must be built on fossil fuels.

Tap

The water is on fire. As a founding civil servant in the Environmental Protection Agency (EPA), my grandfather once shared with me a powerful moment from 1969. It was an image published by *Time* magazine, capturing the Cuyahoga River in an unusual state—not flowing with water, but engulfed in flames. The river, polluted from years of industrial waste, caught fire on a Sunday morning in June. However, this was not the first time the river burned. Over a dozen fires have been recorded on the Cuyahoga River, with the first dating back to 1868. The burning river photo *Time* published was not even from 1969; it was in fact a photo of the river burning seventeen years earlier in 1952. The media attention in 1969 helped

Figure 5.6. Tap, 2021. Vintage sink, plasma speaker, audio recordings, electronics, custom lighting. *Source:* Artwork and photo by the author.

galvanize public support for a series of ambitious pollution control activities eventually resulting in the Clean Water Act, and later on, the establishment of the federal Environmental Protection Agency.

In 1969, the same year as the Cuyahoga fire, Dr. A. G. Cattaneo, the manager of United Technology's Physical Sciences Laboratory, invented what is known as a plasma speaker. While attempting to replicate the jet-flame exhaust of rocket motors, Dr. Cattaneo inadvertently discovered that a specialized high-voltage electrical arc could distort a high-temperature plasma flame. As the flame expanded and contracted, it produced a sound akin to a conventional speaker's surface, giving birth to the flame speaker's unique mechanism. This accidental invention opened strange new possibilities for generating audio through the manipulation of plasma flames. In the end, however, plasma speakers proved impractical for wide-scale public use for obvious safety reasons.

To this day, a dual sentiment persists among people: a hope and a fear that our era of material abundance, fueled by fossil resources, will never end. Back in 2010, I was living and teaching in Central Pennsylvania, a region that had become ground zero for hydraulic fracturing, commonly referred to as fracking. This region found itself in the crosshairs of an energy industry eager to tap into the rich deposits of natural gas that lay buried deep underground, locked in shale formations. Fracking is a process that involves drilling deep into the Earth, typically using a vertical well that then extends horizontally for several thousand feet into the rock layer containing the oil or gas. A high-pressure fluid, usually a proprietary mix of water, sand, and chemicals, is then injected into the well. This fluid fractures the rock, creating fissures through which oil or gas can flow more freely, making it easier to extract. This process has sparked a significant boom in oil and gas production, and has also become the center of controversy, due to its wide-ranging negative impacts on the environment and public health.

In "Tap," visitors to the gallery are presented with a vintage sink installed vertically on the wall, with eerie black flames pouring from the faucet. As the flame spills out, a faint voice can be heard, which is actually a plasma speaker. The voice is a dynamic amalgamation of media coverage and personal narratives. This ever-changing collection of stories encompasses a wide spectrum of perspectives and experiences related to fracking. From property owners engaged in deliberations about the advantages and disadvantages of allowing their land to be utilized for mining operations, to truck drivers employed to transport the massive quantities of water required to fracture a single well, the discourse surrounding fracking is multifaceted and diverse. These narratives shed light on the complex considerations, debates, and individuals involved in the practice, painting a nuanced picture of the various dimensions and devastating impacts of fracking.

The image of a domestic kitchen sink spouting forth flames has since become synonymous with "Fracking." This striking visual symbolizes the concerns and consequences related to fracking, particularly the wide-scale contamination of groundwater with fracking chemicals and methane leakage. The surreal phenomenon of flaming faucets, where tap water becomes combustible due to methane contamination, has been documented in areas near fracking sites, raising significant environmental and safety concerns.

Alternative Rule

Both safety concerns and the spread of disinformation and misinformation have infiltrated our schools, intensifying the ongoing political crisis and fostering deep divisions within communities. As a middle school student, I witnessed a shooting. It was the mid-1990s. I was attending class at Westdale, an inner-city public middle school located in my childhood hometown of

Figure 5.7. Alternative Rule, 2020 (ongoing). Ink on paper, microprinted alternate-rule paper. *Source:* Artwork and photo by the author.

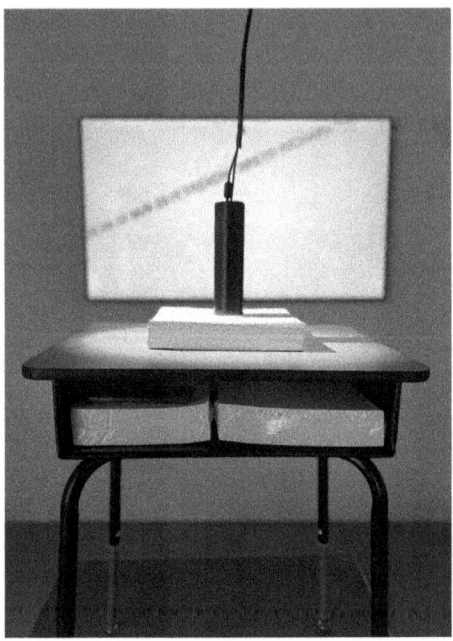

Baton Rouge, Louisiana. I remember the announcement over the intercom to shelter in our classroom and our teacher in a hushed voice telling us to lay down on the floor. I remember the police jogging down the hallway with their guns and the subsequent shootout in the field behind the school. Stray bullets punched neat little holes high up in the windows of the classroom.

That event left an impression on me that I have revisited each time I learn about another school shooting. I recall that memory, and contrast it with the present. At Westdale, it was a failed bank robbery that led to the shootout, not a targeting of the school. Luckily, no students were injured in the panic. At the time, like so many, I struggled to make sense of that violence and to process it with my friends and family—just as we struggle today with what we can do to prevent such events, and how it might ever be possible to recover.

In 2020, I created "Alternative Rule," a circulating memorial and protest tool to commemorate the lives of schoolchildren who have been injured or killed by school shootings. "Alternative Rule" looks just like the blue- and red-lined paper we all used as students to learn penmanship, but in Alternative Rule, the lines on the paper are made up of thousands of micro-printed names and dates of children who have been victims of gun violence since the 1999 Columbine High School shooting. Microprinting is a security feature normally reserved for use in banknotes and other official documents to deter counterfeiting. This technique involves printing minute, almost microscopic text onto the material, often so small that it appears as a solid line or pattern to the naked eye. It's only under magnification that the text becomes legible.

I've spent the last three years giving out the paper to people of all ages—inviting them to take a sheet and use it as stationary to write a letter to members of government and people in power, to advocate for gun control in America. I want these names to become part of the living archive of correspondence—so that as long as letters on this paper are received and archived, the names of the victims will continue to demand the justice they deserve.

We face a lot of challenges in the wake of such events, but I have hope that many people want to demand change—that after so much violence, something must change. Politics feels entrenched and unwilling to take action or to do much more than offer the over-used platitudes of thoughts and prayers. Alex Jones, who established the media platform known as InfoWars, has been involved in intentionally disseminating disinformation and spreading false narratives regarding school shootings. Through his platform, Jones has promoted dangerous conspiracy theories and unfounded claims, often asserting that various tragic events, such as the Sandy Hook school shooting, were staged or fabricated. Jones has not only propagated disinformation about school shootings but has also profited from these misleading assertions. His antisocial delusional behavior has resulted in confusion and distress among the public, while simultaneously undermining genuine efforts to address the critical issue of school violence. By distorting the true nature of these incidents, Jones has hindered the public's understanding and created further obstacles in finding effective solutions. In order to combat this disinformation, we must acknowledge that the history of gun violence cuts deep into our country, and that gun laws in the United States are intertwined with structural racism and white supremacy.

In response to the tragic shootings in Buffalo and Uvalde, I have organized a series of letter-writing events where participants use the paper to write letters, demanding a change in America's gun policies, which have harmed so many (figure 5.8). These gatherings function as opportunities to come together as a community to read the names and commemorate the

Figure 5.8. A young student writes their U.S. Senator using Alternative Rule during a June 2022 letter-writing event organized by the artist in Buffalo, New York. *Source:* Photo by the author.

lives of loved ones lost in the last weeks and years, as well as to take direct action now to call for change.

Near the end of the film "The Invisible Man," after wreaking havoc, Dr. Jack Griffin finds refuge in a barn during a snowstorm. The climax of the story unfolds against a stark snow-laden landscape, which strikingly contrasts the invisible protagonist. The film ends when a farmer stumbles upon Griffin by sheer luck. The police surround the barn and set it on fire. Forced to flee, Griffin's footprints in the freshly fallen snow expose his location. This visual juxtaposition emphasizes that despite Griffin's invisibility, his disruptive actions leave a profound and visible impact on his surroundings. In a final confrontation, the chief detective brings an end to Griffin's reign of terror.

Through my artwork, I aim to make the unseen visible, much like the way the fresh snow in "The Invisible Man" reveals the hidden protagonist. I strive to highlight the often-unseen influence of power and wealth, bringing these forces into focus by creating works that might catch the footprints left in the snow.

Part III
Building Trust

Chapter Six

Trust and Confidence in Medicine among Americans

JESSIE POON AND LAURENE TUMIEL BERHALTER

The United States' fully vaccinated population (66.4%) is among the lowest in developed countries. One reason is the low level of trust in medical scientists. Only 29 percent of Americans report that they are highly confident that medical scientists will act in the public's interest (Kennedy, Tyson and Funk, 2022). In a survey of twenty-eight countries, the market research company Ipsos (2021) found the medical profession to be the most trustworthy profession. Other studies show Americans to be satisfied with the medical services provided by their doctors. Yet, Americans are less likely than other countries to trust their doctors (Benson et al., 2014). The American Association of Medical College's Center for Health Justice recognizes the importance of trust in the delivery of quality health care for all and the reduction of health inequity by establishing Principles of Trustworthiness as a guide for health care and public health.[1] Trust has been identified in a burgeoning literature as an important mechanism for combating vaccine hesitancy and misinformation (Franic 2022). Understanding the influences that explain trust and leveraging existing resources can help inform public policy regarding how trust may be improved to mitigate against misinformation at a time of public health crisis. This chapter examines the influence of socioeconomic, demographic, and institutional factors on trust in medicine based on data from the General Social Survey (GSS). We compare trust influences over two time periods from 2006 to 2021.

Medicine and Hesitancy

Lack of trust in medicine and research has impacted the quality of care for individuals and overall population health. It has contributed to health disparities. This distrust is derived, in part, from misinformation that is prevalent in our communities and is shared widely today through social media. Several outbreaks were driven on fear propagated by misinformation (Sell 2020) and enhanced stigma in various underrepresented groups driving health disparities (Poos 2020). Distrust has been found to be prominent in groups that are more likely to experience health disparities such as those with lower education and African Americans (Rajakumar et al. 2009; Nguyen et al. 2021; Viswanath et al. 2021; Willis et al. 2021). These groups are also vulnerable to disinformation and misinformation that contribute to vaccine hesitancy (Frenkel 2021).

Vaccine hesitancy is associated with a history of misinformation (College of Physicians in Philadelphia 2022). As early as the 1300s, misinformation was reported claiming that Jewish communities poisoned well water, causing the bubonic plague. This was also the first time the government enacted quarantine rules (Poos 2020). The smallpox vaccine in the late 1800s was viewed as unchristian because it was derived from animals and this view resulted in an anti-vaccination movement (College of Physicians in Philadelphia 2022). Misinformation regarding the influenza pandemic of 1918 included rumors of espionage and bio-warfare (Poos 2020). From the 1970s to 1990s, misconceptions and hesitancy existed regarding the measles, mumps, and rubella vaccine when the vaccine was linked to increased risk of autism and other conditions (College of Physicians in Philadelphia, 2022). This saw a resurgence of the anti-vaccine movement, which was accompanied by advocacy efforts. The spread of misinformation surrounding Ebola in 2006 was propagated through social media where jokes and memes were thought to be real (Sell et al. 2020). In 2006, the HPV vaccine became available and was met with hesitancy due to stigma and concern regarding side effects (Bednarczyk 2019). As late as 2019, 23 percent of US parents remained hesitant of vaccinating their children (Szilagyi 2020).

Mistrust has had a direct impact on vaccine hesitancy over time but has reached a new level with the COVID-19 pandemic. Ever-changing information and the speed of vaccine development were at the forefront of public discourse like never before. The public demanded more information on the scientific process, and questioned research findings and health care guidance. Public health officials were faced with unprecedented demands to communicate science and its direct impact on health care. The confluence of the pandemic and dissemination of information on social media by bad actors provided a fertile ground for conspiracy theories and rumors, for example that COVID-19 was a hoax or that the virus was deliberately released for sinister reasons.

Health care providers play a pivotal role in increasing vaccine uptake. It has been shown that people who receive information on vaccines from their providers have fewer concerns with vaccines than those who get their information from other sources. Variations exist in the promotion of vaccines among providers. For example, providers' likelihood for recommending HPV vaccination were impacted by patient, provider, and system level variables such as if they perceived their patients to be low risk or vaccine hesitant, if they were uncomfortable discussing sexual health, or if they were unclear of policy guidelines such as school requirement (Gilkey and McRee 2016). However, providers need to be better educated to explain science and dispel misinformation surrounding vaccination. Resources are available to assist in this area, recognizing ongoing changes and the prevalence of misinformation (Shen and Dubey 2019).

Factors Influencing Trust and Confidence

Messengers of misinformation rely on trust to spread their messages. In their book on misinformation, Stephens, Poon, and Tan (2023) show that epistemic communities, that is, experts from institutions ranging from the Central Bank to the Center for Disease Control and Prevention (CDC), depend on trust to legitimize their authority in specific expertise. Destabilizing trust is one mechanism through which misinformation operates. Societies have become more complex, and division of labor has meant that individuals often lack information in making decisions from financial matters to health. Trust increases tolerance for uncertainty when individuals are confronted with a knowledge gap. Social scientists thus see the act of trusting as a mechanism for managing uncertainty and risk (Sztompka 1999). Placing one's trust in a physician's treatment, for example, is to commit to some expectation that the physician will act in the patient's best interest, thereby minimizing uncertainty about an illness. In the context of missing information or information deficit, trust may be used to reduce uncertainty by setting norms and expectations of behavior. Patients expect physicians to provide effective treatments, and trust offers some security in extracting cooperation between patient and physician. Reasonable functioning of public institutions such as health institutions depends on trust between citizens and medical practitioners. Trusting medical officers and health officials facilitates navigation of decisions when individuals are faced with uncertainty about diagnoses and treatments. In turn, public officials rely on citizens and residents' trust when delivering health care guidance, including the recommendation of COVID-19 vaccines.

Yet trust has been declining in the United States for many years. According to the Pew Research Center (2022), three-quarters of Americans trusted the federal government to do the right thing in 1958. Today, that share is about 20 percent. A recent survey commissioned by the national news network NBC shows that only 44 percent of respondents trusted information from the CDC, compared to 57 percent who trusted information from their employers (Hart Research Associates 2022). One bright spot, however, is the medical system. A recent Gallup poll found that trust in the medical system ranks fourth (44%) compared to bottom-ranked Congress (12%). But even here, the share has declined to 38 percent in 2022 (Jones 2022). Moreover, as we suggested earlier, Americans generally trust their medical treatments but are less trusting of doctors compared to other developed countries.

While trust has dominated polls and surveys, the General Social Survey (the principal source of data for this chapter) measures trust in medicine in the context of Americans' confidence in medicine. Many studies appear to use the two terms interchangeably (Cook and Gronke 2005; Croker et al. 2013), with Rowe and Calnan (2006) suggesting that trust is related to an individual's confidence in the competence of medical practitioners.[2] To explore the influences of trust and confidence, we draw on two sets of literature, namely, extant scholarship on doctor–patient relationship as well as studies identifying the determinants of vaccine hesitancy. The latter can be instructive as they point to certain behavior related to trust. Both sets of literature are consulted.

Demographic factors such as age, education, and race/ethnicity have been found to be relevant determinants. In a study that examines factors determining patients' trust in doctors, Croker et al. (2013) show that trust and confidence in doctors increase with age and among white patients. Lin, Tu, and Beitsch's (2021) systematic review of the literature on receptivity to the COVID-19 vaccine indicates that those over sixty-five tend to be the most receptive while the results for the younger population between eighteen and thirty-four tend to be more mixed. Konstantinou et al. (2021) found, for instance, that younger individuals are more vaccine-hesitant, exhibiting lower trust, but other studies suggest the opposite (Bowman and Goldstein 2020). Education level matters. A recent study exploring the science confidence gap theorized and empirically confirmed that education works through the "malady of modernization." Less-educated individuals distrust science and its institutions because institutions project a level of abstraction and impersonality in relationships that accompany the modernization of societies. For these individuals, there is a sense of loss of control in dealing with changes brought about by modern institutions and their demands. On the other hand, the more educated are open to scientific methods but are ostensibly critical of the more institutional dimensions of scientific organization (Achterberg, de Koster and van der Waal 2017). Examining 3,142 US counties, Khairat, Zou, and Adler-Milstein (2022) report that those without a high school education are more hesitant of the COVID-19 vaccine. Furthermore, the hesitant are less likely to trust the vaccine, as the previous section suggests. Like age, the role of sex appears to be mixed. Cao et al. (2021) report that women are more hesitant about vaccines. Actual turnout for the COVID-19 vaccine in the United States, however, surprised researchers. The CDC reported that as of June 2021, 9.5 million more women had been vaccinated than men (Puzio 2021). One explanation is occupation. Many women are in the child-care, education, and health care sectors, which required workers to be vaccinated. Another explanation is that men view themselves to be masculine and thus less vulnerable to COVID-19.

Black Americans tend to mistrust the medical system more than white Americans do (Freimuth et al. 2017; Cao, Ramirez and Alvarez 2021). In a study of COVID-19 vaccine hesitancy, interviews with Black adults reveal considerable mistrust of government and health care systems (Sekimitsu et al. 2022). Respondents point to a history of mistreatment, as demonstrated by the 1932 Tuskegee syphilis experiment that withheld effective treatment on poorly educated rural African American males by the US Public Health Service. But Sekimitsu et al's survey also shows that while Black Americans worry about being used as guinea pigs, increased medical advice from doctors on COVID-19 vaccine could increase rates of acceptance. Similar mistrust of the medical institution by Black Americans has been reported by Peteet et al. (2022), who attribute their mistrust to a lower quality of health care.

Next, income is relevant because socioeconomic status influences access to health care. Low-income communities tend to be more hesitant about vaccines, expressing lower trust. Examining vaccine hesitancy in the state of Texas, Lee and Huang (2022) found lower-income rural areas to be under-vaccinated. A major reason is that they are less likely to be insured and face lower access to health care. But the authors also suggest that members of these communities tend to be less trusting of government. Similarly, a survey of influenza vaccine acceptance among low-income adults in Central New York indicates that lack of access contributes to low uptake, leading the authors to recommend an increase of vaccine services in places such as local supermarkets (Suryadevara et al. 2014).

Finally, institutional factors are examined. As mentioned earlier, recent surveys indicate that trust in government and institutions such as the CDC has declined. Wroe's (2016) work suggests that economic security and trust in government are correlated. Americans with a low level of economic security are more likely to distrust government. Health risks such as worries about losing health coverage and being unable to get medical treatment are important dimensions of Wroe's economic security measure. They contribute to distrust by reinforcing the belief that the government is not functioning. Wroe argues that risks are increasingly shifted to the individual under an increasingly popular view that well-being such as health is an individual's rather than government's responsibility. Notably, he maintains that Americans are ideologically conservative and operationally liberal. In this sense, political affiliations and associations matter. We adopt a sociological interpretation of institutions as social structures with normative and behavioral elements. Institutions are not just a system of rules but are embedded in social interactions. Putnam (2000) for instance views trust as being embedded in individuals' associations and affiliations in a club, voluntary organization, or church. Individuals go about socializing with one another in these institutions on the assumption that they can trust one another and not be taken advantage of. Trust here operates as a resource in the development of social capital. Akin to the idea of human capital, social capital refers to resources that become available to individuals from their social interactions. Trust encourages cooperation and this, in turn, strengthens social capital (Herreros 2004).

Two institutions may be identified, namely, political and religious institutions. Following Wroe's argument about the shift of risks to the individual, we expect that Republicans and Conservatives are more likely to distrust health and medical information and their institutions. Lin et al.'s (2020) system review of confidence of COVID-19 vaccine also reveals a sharp partisan difference in confidence, with Republicans reporting lower confidence. Stephens, Poon, and Tan (2023) found that those who are more religious tend to be less informed (e.g., they believe scientific evidence for global warming is lacking). Similar belief regarding the safety of COVID-19 vaccine has also been found; in this case, those who are religious tend to be misinformed about the science behind the vaccine's safety. According to Corcoran et al. (2021), Christian nationalists see their interpretation of religion as the source of moral authority and reject competing institutions such as science. This means that religious behavior (e.g., praying and repentance) is preferred over behavior prescribed by health or medical institutions such as social distancing or masking. Religious associational life is a source of misinformation since individuals trust information from their religious communities more than information from scientists or the CDC (Stephens, Poon, and Tan 2023). As Funk (2020) explains, distrust of scientific institutions is fueled by the feeling of a loss of control. This would seem consistent with Achterberg, de Koster and van der Waal's (2017) point that institutions are viewed with suspicions from perception of lack of control.

Data

Data for the study is compiled from the General Social Science Survey (GSS). This annual survey of adults eighteen and older has been conducted since 1972. The number of variables in the database is enormous, in the hundreds, measuring a wide range of social, economic, health, and political issues. But not all variables are consistently surveyed across the fifty years. For example, variables associated with demographic profile, income, and political activities are available since 1973. On the other hand, the survey question asking "how scientific is medicine?" is found only in two years, 2006 and 2012, which is not ideal and therefore not used here. For this reason, we use "confidence in medicine" to examine trust in medicine because it is available most years. Some questions on religion are also not available prior to 2006. In this chapter, we compare the influences of confidence of medicine between two periods: 2006–2010 and 2016–2021. This results in roughly 4,367 observations in the first period and 3,300 observations in the second period. Several of the variables were also reverse-coded to facilitate interpretation. Variables are presented in table 6.1.

Table 6.1. Description of Variables

Variable	Description	Measurement
CONMED	Confidence in medicine	1–3 (1 = hardly any, 3 = a great deal)
AGE	Age	1–8 (1 = 1–10, 8 = over 80)
SEX	Sex	1–2 (1 = male, 2 = female)
RACE	Race	1–3 (1 = White, 2 = Black, 3 = other)
MARITAL	Marital status	1–3 (1 = married, 2 = other [divorced, widowed, separated], 3 = Singapore)
EDUC	Years of education	Continuous
PARTY	Party affiliation	1–3 (1 = democrat, 2 = independent, 3 = republican)
RELIGIOUS	Strength of religious affiliation	1–4 (1 = no religion, 4 = strong)
CONFED	Confidence in executive branch of federal government	1–3 (1 = hardly any, 3 = a great deal)

Demographic, Socioeconomic, and Institutional Influences

Table 6.2 presents an idea of how trust in medicine compares to trust in other institutions. Trust in science and medicine have the highest means in both periods, at over 2.0 on a Likert Scale of 1–3, with 1 indicating hardly any trust and 3 indicating a great deal of trust; the mean also increased for trust in science in the second period. While trust in medicine declined slightly from 2.28 to 2.26, this is marginal and indicates some level of stability overall. In contrast, trust in organized religion and the executive branch of the federal government fell from 1.98 to 1.89 and 1.75 to 1.68, respectively. Notably, trust in the federal government is the lowest in table 6.2, even lower than financial and business institutions. Distrust in federal government is concerning given recent criticisms of the Department of Health and Human Services and federal agencies like the CDC. The CDC was so alarmed by disinformation suggesting that COVID-19 vaccines give citizens the disease that it began sharing tips on countering disinformation. For example, it recommended undermining trust in disinformation authors and highlighting misleading tactics.[3] Nonetheless, it is fair to say that trust

Table 6.2. Summary Statistics of Trust

Variable	Mean 2006–2010	Mean 2016–2021
Medicine	2.28	2.26
Science	2.35	2.40
Banks and financial institutions	1.97	1.91
Major companies	1.95	1.99
Organized religion	1.98	1.89
Federal government	1.74	1.68

in medicine remains reasonably high, and there is opportunity for mobilization of such trust for public health goals.

Turning to statistical analysis, we ran regressions and report the results in table 6.3. Educational level, trust in the executive branch of federal government, being Black, female, and being politically affiliated with independents are statistically significant in both periods. Those who are more educated tend to trust medical institutions. When Alesina and La Ferrara

Table 6.3. Regression Results: Influences of Trust in Medicine

Variable	2006–2010	2016–2021
AGE	0.001 (0.006)	0.008 (0.008)
EDUC	0.014 (0.003)***	0.010 (0.004) **
RELIGIOUS	0.021 (0.010)**	0.001 (0.011)
CONFED	0.213 (0.014)***	0.187 (0.017) ***
MARITAL_OTHER	–0.032 (0.024)	–0.052 (0.029) *
MARITAL_SINGLE	0.071 (0.026)***	0.044 (0.031)
RACE_BLACK	–0.118 (0.030)***	–0.151 (0.033) ***
RACE_OTHER	0.042 (0.033)	–0.0611 (0.040)
SEX	–0.052 (0.020)***	–0.058 (0.023) **
PARTY_INDEP	–0.057 (0.023)**	–0.065 (0.027) **
PARTY3_REP	–0.036 (0.027)	–0.008 (0.033)
R2	0.10	0.10

Note: Standard errors are in parentheses; *** , ** , * denote 1%, 5%, and 10% significance level.

(2002) disaggregated education into those with less and those more than sixteen years of education, they found that trust was negative in the former but positive in the latter. One explanation is to see education as raising scientific literacy and closing cognitive and information gaps because the educated are more open to scientific explanations in medicine. Sailer et al. (2022) found that science knowledge helps individuals sort through medical information and misinformation such that they are more responsive to public health guidelines. They recommend more education in science to help the public navigate pandemic crises. Raising health literacy is a potent tool for combating misinformation.

Similarly, the estimate for CONFED is positive, indicating that those who trust the federal government's executive branch are also more likely to trust medicine. Trust in government has been declining over the past six decades. Tracking the trend from 1958 to 2022, the Pew Research Center (2022) reports that over 75 percent of Americans trusted the government to do what is right most of the times in 1964. That share has fallen to 20 percent today. The issue is complex, including increased opportunity to spread mis- and disinformation in time and space using social media (Stephens, Poon, and Tan 2023). Both mis- and disinformation on the COVID-19 pandemic exploded in the last three years from conspiracy theories that justify COVID-19 denialism to the belief that COVID-19 vaccines and the pandemic were part of the work of the "deep state." A good example of a conspiracy theory that sows distrust is the narrative that the virus is the result of the enhancement of 5G mobile network by the government. Another popular conspiracy theory is that the virus does not exist but is part of global elites' desire to control the world. Former President Trump often invoked the deep state to delegitimize the work of executive branches, including federal agencies like the CDC, heaping scorn on his own scientists (Baker 2020). While this does not help in trust-building, the decline began well before his attack on federal agencies, perhaps reflecting Putnam's (2000) broader observation of fraying social and institutional capital. CONFED has the largest effect (size) on trust in medicine compared to other significant variables and cannot be ignored. As table 6.2 shows, trust in the federal government has the lowest mean of the institutions listed. Declining trust raises challenges for medical practitioners and their institutions.

Females are less likely than males to trust, and Black Americans are also more distrustful of medicine. BLACK in table 6.2 is the second largest coefficient estimate after CONFED. A major explanation is that both females and Black Americans have historically experienced discrimination (Alesina and La Ferrara 2002). A recent survey found that 52 percent of women compared to 36 percent of men considered discrimination toward patients to be serious (Today 2019). About 17 percent of women reported they had been treated differently, compared to only 6 percent of men. The same survey reports that women were more likely than men to feel that a health care provider did not take their problems seriously. Gender bias may be unintended, but, as a number of social science studies suggest, this bias may be implicit and institutionalized.

Implicit bias may also explain why the relationship between Black Americans and trust in medicine is inversely related. As we explained early, a history of callous experiments, neglect, and lack of access to health care shape Black Americans' distrust. Frenkel's (2021) report on misinformation among Black and Hispanic Americans found that introduction of Pfizer and Moderna was paralleled by a significant increase in social media mentions of Tuskegee. Moreover, vaccine outreach boomeranged because it was perceived to be a recruitment effort that treated Black Americans as guinea pigs. In his book on medical racism, Hoberman (2012) attributes health disparity between White and Black Americans to the medical establishment's political conservatism. He argues that this has led to a certain detachment and disengagement with the Black population among physicians, with little desire to establish racially sensitive relationships that can better secure medical diagnosis and compliance in treatments. Implicit bias and stereotypes—for example, the perception that Black Americans are more resistant to certain procedures—augment Black Americans' distrust of medicine (Chapman, Kaatz, and Carnes 2013).

The results for religious and political affiliations are a little more unexpected. Those who are strongly religious are also more likely to trust medicine, but this is only true in the first period. Religious affiliation plays no role in the second period. Much has been reported of the role of Christian nationalists in spurning COVID-19 health measures, from vaccines to the wearing of masks. Reasons for objection to vaccines range from susceptibility to misinformation, theological subscription (divine providence over medical intervention), to the perception that fetal cells were used in vaccine development. But being hesitant about vaccines for religious reasons does not translate into distrust of the medical institution. Curlin and his colleagues' (2005) survey of physicians revealed that physicians are relatively religious: 90 percent of doctors attended religious services occasionally, and 76 percent said they believed in God. They are part of many communities and are respected as members of these communities. Being religious does not mean that individuals are anti-science, and therefore anti-medicine. Nonetheless, the positive influence of religious affiliation vanishes by 2016–2021, and the coefficient turns insignificant. The second period has been characterized by greater resistance to public health policies associated with the COVID-19 pandemic. While this may not have diminished the trust of the highly religious, it does not seem to have helped, either.

Finally, contrary to expectation, Independents are less likely to trust medicine than Democrats. While the estimate for Republicans is also negative, it is not statistically significant. This is interesting given that the media has often blamed Republicans for perceived anti-vaccine messages and COVID-19 misinformation. The finding is also more difficult to explain but it is consistent with the above finding that vaccine hesitancy does not necessarily translate into distrust of medicine. According to the Pew Research Center (2019), Independents form the largest political group: 38 percent of Americans regard themselves to be Independents, 31 percent regard themselves as Democrats, and 26 percent as Republicans. One plausible explanation for the negative finding may be that Independents are more partisan than the term implies, with strong affiliations toward either Democrats or Republicans. They are, however, more disengaged than members of either party. It is possible that their distrust reflects this lack of engagement. Building trust, as the literature suggests, requires social capital that reduces uncertainty. Lack of engagement strengthens lack of familiarity with the expertise of medicine, which can lead to distrust.

Discussion and Conclusion

Conspiracy theories and rumors that drive misinformation and disinformation thrive in an environment of anxiety and uncertainty (Pertwee et al. 2022). The COVID-19 pandemic has seen a high level of misinformation in part because of uncertainty and anxiety about the virus and vaccines. Trusting another person or institution for information helps to reduce uncertainty, especially when anxiety is associated with the unknown due to cognitive gaps. This chapter has examined the major demographic, socioeconomic, and institutional factors that influence trust in medicine. Two variables, being a Black American and feeling confidence in the federal government's executive branch, have the largest effect. Confidence in the federal government positively affects trust in medicine, while being Black has the opposite effect. In this sense, restoring trust and confidence in the federal government and ameliorating Black Americans' distrust will go some way in encouraging individuals to trust health information and cooperate in a health crisis. In a survey of trust and distrust, Americans believe that trust in the federal government may be improved if it is more transparent, improves community cooperation, and engages in more political compromise (Rainie, Keeter and Perrin 2019).

Among Black communities with low trust, community outreach by credible messengers, specifically Black individuals trusted by the communities, should be encouraged (Peteet et al., 2022). Building social capital in these communities can help to address fears and uncertainties of vaccines and develop informational resources that are trusted by Black Americans. Access to information also explains why education positively influences trust in medicine. The highly educated are better able to filter misinformation. It also implies that simpler messages that are easy to access, communicate, and process may be relevant for segments of the population that have a lower level of education.

Some good news emerged from the analysis. Contrary to other studies, strength in religious affiliation positively affects trust in medicine in the first period. However, increased religious affiliation strength had no effect in the second period. It remains to be seen if the negative sign will turn statistically significant at some point, which could be cause for concern. On the other hand, Republicans are not more likely than Democrats to distrust medicine, but Independents are significantly more likely than Democrats to distrust medicine. Attention on differences in partisan responses ignores the finding that Independents may be the neglected group in public health policies, and one that health officials need to take increased note of in targeting their messages.

The findings from this analysis provide insight in moving forward to create new modes for communicating challenging science and health care messages when information may be distrusted. Public health, health care, and government need to engage trusted community members to disseminate important scientific and health care information. This will help build back trust and ensure that we recognize the implications of misinformation and disinformation as a result of distrust in institutions and among members of society.

Notes

1. www.aamchealthjustice.org/resources/trustworthiness-toolkit
2. Croker et al. (2013) recognize that there may be some difference between "trust" and "confidence" but point out that most surveys do not distinguish between them.
3. "How to Address COVID-19 Vaccine Misinformation," CDC.

References

Achterberg, P., W. de Koster, W., and J. van der waal. 2017. "A Science Confidence Gap: Education, Trust in Scientific Methods, and Trust in Scientific Institutions in the United States, 2014." *Public Understanding of Science* 26: 704–720.

Adesina, A., and E. La Ferrara. 2002. "Who Trusts Others?" *Journal of Public Economics* 85: 207–234.

Baker, P. 2020. "Trump Scorns His Own Scientists over Virus Data." *The New York Times*, September 16.

Bednarczyk, R. A. 2019. "Addressing HPV Vaccine Myths: Practical Information for Healthcare Providers." *Human Vaccines & Immunotherapeutics* 15, no. 7–8: 1628–1638. doi:10.1080/21645515.2019.1565267

Benson, R., J. Benson, and J. Hero. 2014. "Public Trust in Physicians: U.S. Medicine in International Perspective." *New England Journal of Medicine* 371: 1570–1572.

Bowman, K., and S. Goldstein. 2020. "Giving Vaccines a Shot?" Washington, DC, American Enterprise Institute.

Cao, J., C. Ramirez, and R. Alvarez. 2021. "The Politics of Vaccine Hesitancy in the United States." *Social Science Quarterly* 103: 42–54.

CDC. 2022. Centers for Disease Control. November 3. Accessed November 26, 2022. https://www.cdc.gov/tuskegee

Chapman, E., A. Kaatz, and M. Carnes. 2013. "Physicians and Implicit Bias: How Doctors May Unwittingly Perpetuate Health Care Disparities." *Journal of General Internal Medicine* 28L: 1504–1510.

College of Physicians in Philadelphia. 2022. "History of Anti-vaccination Movements." Accessed November 26, 2022. https://historyofvaccines.org/vaccines-101/misconceptions-about-vaccines/history-anti-vaccination-movements

Cook, T., and P. Gronke. 2005. "The Skeptical American: Revisiting the Meanings of Trust in Government and Confidence in Institutions." *The Journal of Politics* 67: 784–803.

Corcoran, K., C. Scheitle, and B. DiGregorio. 2021. "Christian Nationalism and COVID-19 Vaccine Hesitancy and Uptake." *Vaccines* 39: 6614–6621.

Croker, J., D. Swancutt, M. Roberts, et al. 2013. "Trust Increases Tolerance for Uncertainty in When Individuals Are Confronted with a Knowledge Gap." *BMJ Open* 3: e002762. doi:10.1136/ bmjopen-2013-002762

Curlin, F., J. Lantos, C. Roach, S. Sellergren, and M. Chin. 2005. Religious Characteristics of U.S. Physicians. *Journal of General Internal Medicine* 20: 629–634.

Franic, J. 2022. "What Lies behind Substantial Differences in COVID-19 Vaccination Rates between EU Member States?" *Frontiers in Public Health* 10: 1–15.

Freimuth, V., A. Jamison, G. Hancok, and S. Quinn. 2017. "Determinants of Trust in the Flu Vaccine for African Americans and Whites." *Social Science & Medicine* 193: 70–79.

Frenkel, S. 2021. "Black and Hispanic Communities Grapple with Vaccine Misinformation." *The New York Times*, March 10.
Funk, C. 2020. "Key Findings about Americans' Confidence in Science and Their Views on Scientists' Role in Society." Pew Research Center.
Gilkey, M., and McRee, A. 2016. "Provider Communication about HPV Vaccination: A Systematic Review. *Human Vaccine Immunotherapy* 12, no. 6: 1454–1468. doi:10.1080/21645515.2015.1129090
Hart Research Associates. 2022. NBC News Survey, Study #220027. Retrieved from https://s3.documentcloud.org/documents/21184709/220027-nbc-news-january-poll.pdf
Herreros, F. 2004. *The Problem of Forming Social Capital: Why Trust?* London: Palgrave Macmillan.
Ipsos. 2021. Global Trustworthiness Index 2021 (October 8).
Jones, J. 2022. "Confidence in U.S. Institutions Down; Average at New Low." Gallup, July 5.
Kennedy, B., A. Tyson, and C. Funk. 2022. "Americans' Trust in Scientists, Other Groups Decline. Pew Research Center, February 15.
Khairat, S., B. Zou, and J. Adler-Milstein 2022. "Factors and Reasons Associated with Low COVID-19 Vaccine Uptake among Highly Hesitant Communities in the US." *American Journal of Infection Control* 50: 262–267.
Konstantinou, N., S. Nicolaou, C. Petrou, and M. Pieri. 2021. "Trust in Authorities and Demographic Factors Affect Vaccine Acceptance during the COVID-19 Pandemic in Cyprus." *European Journal of Psychology Open* 80: 88–87.
Lee, J., and Y. Huang. 2022. "COVID-19 Vaccine Hesitancy: The Role of Socio-economic Factors and Spatial Effects." *Vaccines* 10: 352.
Lin, C., P. Tu, and L. Beitsch. 2020. "Confidence and Receptivity for COVID-19 Vaccines: A Rapid Systematic Review." *Vaccines* 16. www.epistemonikos.org/en/documents/c99ac6502d3ca69cee49e6309ece00445716246a
Nguyen, L., A. Joshi, D. Drew, J. Merino, W. Ma, . . . A. T. Chan. 2021. "Racial and Ethnic Differences in COVID-19 Vaccine Hesitancy and Uptake." February 28, 2021. medRxiv 02.25.21252402, 1–49. doi:10.1101/2021.02.25.21252402
Pertwee, E., C. Simas, and H. Larson. 2022. "An Epidemic of Uncertainty: Rumors, Conspiracy Theories and Vaccine Hesitancy." *Nature Medicine* 28: 456–459.
Peteet, B., V. Watts, E. Tucker, et al. 2022. "Faith, Fear, and Facts: A COVID-19 Vaccination Hesitancy Intervention for Black Church Congregations." *Vaccines* 10: 1093.
Pew Research Center. 2019. "Political Independents: Who They Are, What They Think." March 14. www.pewresearch.org/politics/2019/03/14/political-independents-who-they-are-what-they-think
Pew Research Center. 2022. "Public Trust in Government: 1958–2022." June 6. www.pewresearch.org/politics/2022/06/06/public-trust-in-government-1958-2022

Poos, L. A. 2020. "Lessons from Past Pandemics: Disinformation, Scapegoating, and Social Distancing." Brookings Institution, March 16. www.brookings.edu/blog/techtank/2020/03/16/lessons-from-past-pandemics-disinformation-scapegoating-and-social-distancing

Putnam, R. 2000. *Bowling Along: The Collapse and Revival of American Community.* New York: Simon & Schuster.

Puzio, A. 2021. "Why Is There Such a Gender Gap in COVID-19 Vaccination Rates?" June 22. FiveThirtyEight. https://fivethirtyeight.com/features/why-is-there-such-a-gender-gap-in-covid-19-vaccination-rates

Rainie, L., S. Keeter, and A. Perrin. 2019. "Trust and Distrust in America." Washington, DC: Pew Research Center.

Rajakumar, K., S. Thomas, D. Musa, and D. Almario. 2009. "Racial Differences in Parents' Distrust of Medicine and Research." *Archives of Pediatrics & Adolescent Medicine* 163: 108–114. doi:10.1001/archpediatrics.2008.521

Rowe, R., and M. Calnan. 2006. "Trust Relations in Health Care: Developing a Theoretical Framework for the 'New' NHS." *Journal of Health Organization and Management* 20: 376–396.

Salier, M., M. Stadler, E. Botes, F. Fischer, and S. Greiff. 2022. "Science Knowledge and Trust in Medicine Affect Individual's Behavior in Pandemic Crises." *European Journal of Psychology Education* 37: 279–292.

Sekimitsu, S., J. Simon, M. Lindsley, M. Jones, U. Jaiioh T. Mabogunje . . . W. Altman. 2022. "Exploring COVID-19 Vaccine Hesitancy amongst Black Americans: Contributing Factors and Motivators." *American Journal of Health Promotion* 36, no. 8. doi:08901171221099270

Sell, T., D. Hosangadi, and M. Trotochaud. 2020. "Misinformation and the US Ebola Communication Crisis: Analyzing the Veracity and Content of Social Media Messages Related to a Fear-Inducing Infectious Disease Outbreak." *BMC Public Health* 20, no. 550: 1–10. doi:https://doi.org/10.1186/s12889-020-08697-3

Shen, C., and V. Dubey. 2019. "Addressing Vaccine Hesitancy: Clinical Guidance for Primary Care Physicians Working with Parents." *Canadian Family Physician* 65, no. 3: 175–181.

Stephens, M., J. Poon, J. and G. Tan. 2023. *Misinformation in the Digital Age: An American Infodemic.* Cheltenham, UK: Edward Elgar.

Suryadevara, M., C. Bonville, P. Rosenbaum, and J. Domachowske. 2014. "Influenza Vaccine Hesitancy in a Low-income Community in Central New York State." *Human Vaccines and Immunotherapeutics* 10: 2098–2013.

Szilagyi, P., C. Albertin, D. Gurfinkel, A. Saville, S. Vangala, J. Rice . . . A. Kempe. 2020. "Prevalence and Characteristics of HPV Vaccine Hesitancy." *Vaccine* 38: 6027–6037. doi:10.1016/j.vaccine.2020.06.074

Sztompka, P. 1999. *Trust: A Sociological Theory.* Cambridge: Cambridge University Press.

Today. 2019. "Feel discriminated against at the doctor's office? TODAY survey finds you're not alone." May 13. www.today.com/health/today-survey-finds-gender-discrimination-doctor-s-office-serious-issue-t153641

Viswanath, K., M. Bekalu, D. Dhawan, R. Pinnamaneni, J. Lang, and J. McLoud. 2021. "Individual and Social Determinants of COVID-19 Vaccine Uptake." BMC Public Health 21, no. 818: 1–10. doi:10.1186/s12889-021-10862-1

Willis, D., J. Andersen, K. Bryant-Moore, J. Selig, C. Long, H. Felix . . . P. McElfish. 2021. "COVID-19 Vaccine Hesitancy: Race/Ethnicity, Trust, and Fear." *Clinical and Translational Science* 14, no. 6: 2200–2207. doi:10.1111/cts.13077

Wroe, A. 2016. Economic Insecurity and Political Trust in the United States. *American Politics Research* 44, 131–163.

Chapter Seven

Practicing Responsible Science through Community Engagement

JENNIFER ANNE SURTEES

As researchers at a public university, we have a responsibility to engage with our community. Over the past nine-plus years, we have focused on improving genome and microbiome literacy in our K–16 and adult populations. We believe that it is our responsibility to provide our citizenry with the tools and knowledge to understand, regulate, ensure ethical and equitable use of, and derive maximum benefit from the astonishing advances in these biomedical sciences. We have developed a variety of hands-on, inquiry-based activities for all ages and have developed strong community partnerships. Since the beginning of the COVID-19 pandemic, we have shifted to engaging with our community around our evolving understanding of the virus and vaccine education. Our goal is to nurture robust community partnerships to better understand the unique crosscutting needs of diverse communities and to develop an infrastructure of trust through which to communicate scientific advances, from genomic medicine to pandemic risk.

Our Challenge and Our Approach

As scientists, we are trained to ask questions about the world around us and to figure out how to answer them. We are trained in scientific techniques and approaches. We are trained to think critically and creatively. We are trained to communicate with each other through publications and seminars. But we are not typically trained to reach outward to the broader community, to share the joy and excitement of inquiry and discovery and the wonders and mysteries of our world. Here I argue that by not communicating with the public, we are depriving them of a nuanced understanding of the world, while creating the impression of exclusivity and cutting ourselves off from a shared community. In so doing, we risk ignoring areas of research that are of importance to the broader public, or specific subpopulations. As importantly, we create a vacuum, an opening and an opportunity for the spread of misinformation and disinformation. In contrast, by engaging with a broader audience, we can create and encourage trust, confidence, conversation and involvement. We can welcome everyone, at some level, into our world of discovery.

It is my belief that scientists have an obligation to become involved in our communities, to promote scientific literacy to empower the public and to help stem the tide of mis/disinformation. Further, I argue that we need to create an infrastructure within our research institutions that facilitates, supports and professionalizes this work. Three integrated elements are key to promoting science literacy and combatting science mis/disinformation through community engagement that run through this chapter: (1) learning about our communities, (2) building authentic relationships with community partners, and (3) sharing information about the scientific processes and promoting critical thinking. All require consistent, longitudinal, and direct interactions with members of the community. This, in turn, requires organizational support.

The University at Buffalo (UB)'s Genome, Environment and Microbiome (GEM) Community of Excellence is a community of faculty, students, and staff that has been charged with a grand challenge: to advance our understanding of the genome and microbiome and to use the advances to benefit humanity in a just, broad-based, and beneficial manner. This challenge required the convergence of academic disciplines and the integration of research, education, and engagement. The focus of this chapter is engagement, into which we have incorporated academic and creative research and educational methodologies. As co-director of GEM, along with Norma Nowak, PhD (UB Biochemistry), I have approached engagement through the lens of genomic and microbiome literacy: two separate but related areas of scientific pursuit. Genomic literacy refers to an understanding of what genomes are and how changes or variations within the genome can impact the overall fitness of an organism or an individual, including impacting human health (Hurle et al. 2013). The genome refers to all of the genetic information within an individual that provides a blueprint for how that individual will develop and function. All humans have the same set of genes and genetic information, with two sets of twenty-three chromosomes made up of DNA, but small variations in the DNA sequence lead to small changes in how we look and how our bodies function (Surtees et al. 2020). These variations in DNA sequence are a double-edged sword. On the one hand, these changes lead to genetic diversity, which is essential for a healthy population, and are the basis of evolution. On the other hand, some of these changes are deleterious, leading to altered function and the potential for disease, including cancers. And the combination of all these differences generates distinct genetic combinations that lead to unique individuals, with personal susceptibilities and resistance to disease (Shendure et al. 2019; Surtees et al. 2020). We can also use these differences to trace human evolution and migration through ancient history (Browning et al. 2018; Dannemann and Racimo 2018; Orlando et al. 2021; Surtees et al. 2020).

Similarly, I use the term "microbiome literacy" to refer to an understanding of microbiota as a complement of microbes that live in, on, and around us, with different communities of microbes occupying different niches in or on our bodies and in our environments (DeSalle et al. 2015) While some are pathogenic, most microbes are benign; many are beneficial and are fundamental to human health. We are still early in our understanding of which microbes comprise different microbiota (Gilbert et al. 2018). One way of defining this has been to identify microbes by genomic sequence because many microbes are not easily cultured in the lab. Thus, we refer to a microbiome, which means the complement of microbes (often primarily the bacteria) present within a microbiota community based on the presence of diagnostic DNA sequence, that is, DNA sequences specific to a particular microbe (Berg et al. 2020). In this way we can define a microbial ecosystem within the body and test the relationship between its composition and human health. The presence of certain classes of bacteria in the gut, for example, appear to enhance both physical and mental health.

Advances in our understanding of genomics, human as well as other organisms, and the microbiome have real implications for human health, agriculture, and our fundamental understanding of what it means to be human (Aggarwal et al. 2022; Auffray et al. 2019; Brand et al. 2022; D'Alessio 2022; Haber et al. 2016; Jameson et al. 2020; Liu et al. 2021; Orlando et al. 2021; Stark et al. 2019; Zhang et al. 2019). As the scientific community develops a more complete understanding of what these changes mean for health and wellness, it becomes important that the general public has some familiarity with these advances so they can both make use of the information and help to ensure the ethical and equitable use of this information. Science literacy can help us make informed personal choices and demand appropriate action and policy from elected officials and public policy makers. Most recently, genomics has been used to track the migration and evolution of the SARS-CoV-2 virus from the very beginning of the COVID-19 pandemic. By sequencing the viral genome from infected patients (and now from wastewater), we have watched the virus evolve in near real time in a massive global experiment in evolutionary biology. We have also used genomic information for vaccine and treatment development and to inform public health policy (Chiara et al. 2021; Houtman et al. 2021; Hudson and Wadsworth 2021; Lamb et al. 2021; Segelhurst et al. 2022). Developing means through which to enhance public genome and microbiome literacy has been our challenge. Our approach has been to promote and facilitate the convergence of disciplines and to integrate the principles of research, education, and engagement in order to develop impactful interventions. This has required the development and nurturing of key partnerships within the University at Buffalo (UB) and between UB and (1) K–12 schools, (2) community groups, and (3) the Buffalo Museum of Science. Here, I will highlight the rationale, development, and implementation of some key activities for each type of partnership.

In developing these partnerships and activities, it is important to define a set of goals. And when it comes to scientific literacy, it is worth asking what exactly we mean by that (Howell and Brossard 2021). What are reasonable expectations for the general public's understanding of the science? How much information or expertise can really be communicated and truly integrated into people's lives? It does not seem realistic or fair to expect community members to develop deep content knowledge about any scientific endeavor. Perhaps what is most important to communicate is the process of science—how we ask questions and how we generate and accumulate new knowledge. We have purposefully incorporated this approach into many of our literacy efforts.

The COVID-19 pandemic was an opportunity to watch science happen in real time, warts and all. Our understanding of the virus evolved over time, and scientists made mistakes, which is part of learning. But this part of the process often wasn't well-communicated to the public. There was a fundamental lack of nuance and, sometimes, humility, in some statements and guidance coming from various authorities. As a result, statements made early in the pandemic, such as the importance of washing hands to prevent spread, turned out to be inaccurate as we learned that the virus is airborne. Other statements that were accurate early in the pandemic were no longer accurate later. For example, while they remain an extremely powerful tool to fight the virus, the efficacy of vaccines has evolved along with the virus. In both cases the message to the public often ended up being static and not particularly nuanced. For some, the pandemic highlighted the power of science, with groups of scientists collaborating across the globe to understand the spread of the SARS-CoV-2 virus, the ways in which it mutates, and how that altered transmissibility and pathogenicity and, of course, the race to develop an effective vaccine. However, others found much to criticize in the scientific community, and trust in science has, in some quarters, diminished significantly (Algan et al. 2021; Parikh 2021). This has only highlighted the urgency of engaging with our communities through mindful communication, to build trust, and to empower with knowledge.

In addition to highlighting the process of learning in science, we have integrated the concept of community-level science literacy, or community literacy (National Academies of Science 2016). In this construct, individuals within a group will inhabit different places on the continuum toward genome or microbiome literacy (Surtees et al. 2020), but collectively the group is considered literate. Individuals need not attain a particular threshold of knowledge and/or skills, but the community has sufficient shared resources and abilities organized across the group such that individual's skills are distributed and deployed to benefit the entire community (National Academies of Science 2016; Ownby et al. 2014; Roth and Lee 2002). This may involve sophisticated interactions with scientists, health care professionals, institutions, and others with expert knowledge (National Academies of Science 2016).

Collaboration and Interdisciplinary Strategies for Promoting Literacy

Promoting genome and microbiome literacy across a broad swath of the population is a significant challenge. Fundamentally, difficult problems require innovative approaches and a broad range of perspectives and domain knowledge. Thus, effective engagement benefits from collaboration across the disciplines. Notably, our efforts with community engagement have included our university community. Promoting genome and microbiome literacy within the university promotes a culture of scientific literacy beyond the sciences. Bringing faculty from different disciplines together increases the diversity of thought. It has the potential to expand one's field of scholarship in unanticipated directions. And it paves the way for the development of innovative approaches to community engagement.

We have co-organized several symposia to encourage interactions across the disciplines at UB. The symposia focused on topics that can and should be explored from a variety of disciplinary perspectives. Two symposia were spearheaded by Irus Braverman, JD (UB Law). The first was "Gene Editing: Life Beyond the Human" (2016—at UB), which focused on genome editing by CRISPR technology, its potential impact on the environment, and the inadequate legal frameworks that are ill-equipped to address the attendant ethical and legal issues. In the second symposium, "Medical Posthumanities: Governing Health beyond the Human" (2021—via Zoom), the discussion focused on One Health, an approach that aims to balance and optimize the health of people, animals, and ecosystems (WHO 2021). In particular, participants explicitly aimed to push this idea of interconnectivity even further—hence "more than One Health," forcing an evaluation of the biases and assumptions underlying One Health. There was a further push to elevate views outside the sciences and beyond the human. Both symposia involved scholars from around the world in the sciences, social sciences, arts and humanities, as well as law, and were open to the public. These symposia comprised a scholarly yet accessible discussion of the relevant science and its ethical, legal, social, and philosophical implications and asked how we should approach these capabilities as a society; what are our responsibilities to society in the face of these new and powerful technologies? We need people across the disciplines to be thinking about these big questions and having these conversations in public. Each symposium resulted in a book collection of essays, allowing further dissemination of these ideas (Braverman 2018, 2023).

Irus also teaches Genetics in the Law to law students. Following the genome editing workshop, I welcomed students from this class into my laboratory, where I introduced them to genomics and they performed a simple set of experiments focused on DNA mutagenesis. This exposure to the experimental details of research as well as our discussion of genomics was intended to provide a more robust framework for genetics and genomics as they embark on law careers.

Genome and Microbiome Literacy through the Arts

Visual art: one of the first GEM initiatives was founding Coalesce: Center for Biological Art in collaboration with Paul Vanouse, MFA (Art) and the UB Department of Art. We established permanent research and teaching space and hired Solon Morse, PhD, who has a background in ecology, genomics, and teaching, to manage Colaesce. The lab-studio hybrid is dedicated to enabling hands-on creative engagement with the tools and technologies of the life sciences. Solon coordinates and facilitates research and projects generated by Vanouse and visiting artists, working closely with each artist as they realize their bioart vision.

Artists from around the world have visited and embraced the unique experience at Coalesce, where they do their own hands-on work in the lab, with guidance from Solon. Visiting artists are paired with GEM science faculty mentors and present an exhibit, talk, and/or workshop for the general public while at UB—on campus and/or in the community, connecting the arts with science to explore social and ethical questions. Coalesce collaborates with Hallwalls Center for Contemporary Art and Torn Space Theater in Buffalo, New York, to support artists and provide a venue to share their artistic work. These partnerships enhance the sustainability and impact of Coalesce activities. Coalesce has hosted dozens of artists from around the world who have presented work that originated at Coalesce at over fifty national/international exhibitions and conferences, winning awards and stimulating conversations about genomics, the microbiome, and the ethical and socials issues they involve. Vanouse created two major award-winning works at Coalesce—The America Project, and Labor (GEM 2016; Vanouse 2023). Through all of these projects and works of art, the process is paramount. The artistic process of questioning, researching, and experimenting mirrors the scientific process, with all its uncertainty.

Coalesce has driven innovation in interdisciplinary education and engagement through relationships with the Science Studies and Environmental Humanities groups at UB, and participates in the Health, Disability, Medicine, and the Arts-Humanities SUNY Network of Excellence. Coalesce and GEM co-organized another interdisciplinary symposium entitled "Microbial Aesthetics: Science, Philosophy, Ethics and Art Meet the Microbes," which focused on ways to make the invisible visible and explored the boundaries among microbes, humans, and the environment. Coalesce is also a teaching space for courses that combine arts, humanities, and life sciences. Colaesce collaborates with other classes to provide hands-on experiences, hosts high school students for UB Science Exploration Day, and led a high school student workshop, Molecular Biology in Reverse. Coalesce hosts bi-weekly Open Houses where UB classes, individuals, and the public can participate in ongoing projects, such as gene amplification and microscopy. Dr. Morse created an "adult version" of an NIH DIY strawberry DNA extraction activity (NHGRI 2015) for "DNA Cocktails with Coalesce." About forty members of the public learned about DNA and extracted DNA from strawberries using pineapple juice and rum. We have used the strawberry DNA extraction activity (minus the rum!) at many community outreach tables. The extraction process, including short wait times, provide an entry point for conversation and to introduce community members to the concept that the DNA represents the strawberry genome and the type of information that can provide and then relate it back to people—how genomic information relates to our sense of identity and/or our health.

Dance: Collaborations can develop in lots of ways—the important element is interacting with and talking to people. I developed a collaboration with another colleague, Anne Burnidge, associate professor of Dance at UB, who happens to live down the street from me. We shared a common goal of reaching and engaging people via different modalities, again in the context of genome and microbiome literacy. We were excited to try to do this by embodying the invisible (microscopic) through dance and movement (Surtees et al. 2020). These initial discussions branched out into two different but related projects. The first was an undergraduate class; the second was a dance performance and installation at the Buffalo Museum of Science.

We developed a class called "Dancing DNA" as a UB seminar course. UB seminars are designed for first-year students in their first semester at UB. They are typically small classes (less than 25 students) taught by tenure-track or tenured faculty that serve, in part, as an introduction to college. These classes are non-disciplinary—anyone in any program or major can take them—and so there is significant flexibility in the form and the content. "Dancing DNA" was an effort to reach a different kind of audience for genome literacy, with a unique approach to understanding how our bodies work at the molecular level. In the class, we introduce the students to the idea of molecular movement, shape, dynamics and activity of the proteins that maintain and express our genome. In parallel, we teach the ways in which we can and do move our bodies, the force, power and expression inherent in our own movements. At both the macro and molecular levels, we focus on speed, shape and dynamics of movement. To put these concepts into practice, the students work in small groups to collaboratively choreograph short movement pieces that use their own bodies to embody the processes of molecular biology, such as DNA replication and gene expression, which are simultaneously occurring in their bodies. As a capstone project, each student selects a genetic disease or process, researches the biology, and choreographs a movement piece, using a group of dancers. By visualizing and embodying molecular processes through movement, students experience them in 3-D and can better identify with these fundamental functions, through a visceral experience (Batson and Wilson 2014; Foster 2010; Surtees et al. 2020). The exposure to creative ways of learning deepens the students' artistic skills AND their familiarity with scientific concepts. While students are often initially wary of this unique approach to learning, they adapt and thrive over the course of the semester. The course models a collaborative, team-based approach to learning, which enriches the experience. It also highlights parallels between the artistic and scientific processes, including iterative research and experimentation (Surtees et al. 2020), and underscoring the continuously evolving nature of each.

This interdisciplinary approach to exploring the microscopic through dance led to unique creative scholarship. Focusing on microbiota, communities of microbes that live in, on, or around us, and following many discussions with me, Anne Burnidge Dance developed and choreographed "What We Leave Behind," an exploration of the human ecosystem and its attendant microbes. Through an iterative process, reminiscent of the scientific process, [Case Study 2 in (Surtees et al. 2020)] this work evolved to also include "Balancing Act," a series of choreographed vignettes exploring the impact microbes have on our world. Through dance sequences, folk-songs, video montage, and spoken text, the performance explored issues that affect the homeostasis of the human ecosystem and our communities of microbes. The work specifically looked at the human microbiome with vignettes portraying: competing media messages, trying to adopt a diet with pre- and pro-biotics, "good" and "bad" microbes, playing in the dirt, how microbes impact romantic attraction, and more. Both components were presented at the Buffalo Museum of Science in June 2018 (GEM 2018). Over 500 members of the Buffalo community learned about the human microbiome and how "good" and "bad" microbial communities impact our health and well-being, with the theme of "balance" underlying the discussion. These elements were also highlighted in a "Balancing Act" educational workshop created for third- and fourth-graders in conjunction with the installation at the museum (Buono and Burnidge 2022). This workshop explored the importance of a balanced community of microbes that each perform important tasks, through movement, improvisation, and choreography. Approximately 120 students participated in these workshops.

Partnering with Schools

Collaborations with K–12 schools are an excellent way to engage early on with explorations on the genome and the microbiome. The thoughtful development of hands-on, inquiry-based activities for even very young students instills familiarity with scientific concepts, encourages questioning and exploration (i.e., the scientific process!), and initiates partnership and pipeline building between UB and the schools. Working with children in this context has the added advantage of indirectly engaging with parents and caregivers, through formal communications (permission slips) and informal conversations between students and caregivers.

We warn children about "germs" (microbes) from a very early age, emphasizing handwashing. But what we miss is that the vast majority of microbes that live in, on, and around us (microbiota) are benign or beneficial. We wanted to broaden the way that children think about the world around them, to include the "invisible" but powerful microbes. And we wanted to do this in a way that engaged students with a variety of interests and by leveraging literary practices and social studies themes that are already part of the curriculum in elementary school. We focused on second grade. We also wanted to incorporate the arts, to engage the students in a unique way. With this perspective in mind, we developed and implemented an interdisciplinary unit targeted at second grade, in which students learned about microbes and microbial communities.

We developed a three-session introduction to microbes for second-graders that effectively integrates biological science with the arts, as well as discussions around the theme of community, urban, suburban, and rural—with different roles for individuals in each, which corresponds to core curriculum learning outcomes (Surtees et al. 2021). This aligns with the idea of microbial communities in different habitats, such as the gut or the skin, that include microbes with different functions. The sessions bring the campus into the community, with faculty, postdoctoral, graduate, and undergraduate student volunteers visiting and leading the sessions for the children in their schools. Students sample their body to generate a class microbiome, develop a hypothesis about their sampling, observe their plates, write lab reports, and share their results with their peers. They then use their knowledge about microbes and their imaginations to create their own microbes, using art supplies and storytelling. At the end of the workshop, we assemble the class microbiota—the plates and the artwork to highlight these communities. By the end of the unit, the students demonstrated knowledge of microbes and their ubiquity in our environment.

The workshop was piloted at Elmwood Village Charter School in Buffalo. It has since been delivered to students in first through third grades in eighteen schools, adapted for special-needs students, and enhanced for the Research Lab High School with whom GEM collaborates. The unit has been continually improved, based on teacher feedback. I presented this workshop at the WNY STEAM conference for teachers (2017) and it has been adapted for four elementary family STEM nights. We have also developed units/lessons on antibiotic resistance and genetics for third-, fourth-, and fifth-graders, working with elementary school teachers and colleagues in UB's Graduate School of Education to ensure that we are meeting the Next Generation Science Standards (NGSS 2013) and Common Core State Standards (CCSS 2016). For all K–12 activities, we have developed assessments of the students, including having notetakers document class discussions to assess mastery of the material, and surveys for volunteers and lead teachers so that we can improve our programs. In addition to supporting learning in schools, these initiatives provide unique opportunities for UB undergraduate and graduate students to engage with our WNY community.

GEM helped guide Buffalo Public Schools (BPS) in creating a new, science-focused high school, The Research Laboratory High School in Bioinformatics and Life Sciences (RLHS), which opened in September 2016. GEM and GEM-affiliated faculty worked with the school administrators and teachers to develop class electives, including "Advanced Microbiology and Molecular Biology Lab Skills," "Introduction to Bioinformatics," "Scientific Nomenclature," and "Bioethics." The school participates in Western New York Genetics in Research Project, a program by GEM faculty member, Steve Koury, PhD, and Norma Nowak. Students complete new research on bacterial genomes and present their research at a virtual capstone event, attended by families. Students from RLHS have worked in UB research laboratories, in positions paid through the Urban League of Buffalo, providing additional experience and preparation for students to become informed citizens.

The ongoing collaboration among scientists, science educators, dancers, and artists provide a model for engaging the public in a way that encourages exploration and collaboration. Fundamentally, everyone is learning from each other, putting everyone on an equal playing field and facilitating inquiry. It empowers the public to learn in the manner that works best for them and to question those involved in the work. While domain knowledge remains important, the collaborative, inquisitive format democratizes learning, emboldens learners, and energizes communication and community building. Here, the end goal is not simply to impart knowledge but rather to build relationships that allow us to contextualize and explore information and data together.

Going Big—Scaling our Efforts:

Part of our efforts have focused on scaling up the reach and impact of our community engagement. This has two effects. The first is simple math. It increases the number of people that we reach and teach. But the second effect is that we begin to create a community culture of genome and microbiome literacy—a community literacy. Theoretically, at least, the culture can become self-sustaining in the context of a supportive infrastructure.

As an example, as noted above, we have deployed our second-grade microbiome workshop in over eighteen schools over the past eight years. In these schools, this is now something that is part of second grade. To maintain this reach, we train interested undergraduate and graduate students, postdoctoral associates, faculty, and staff to lead these workshops. We provide the necessary supplies and coordination with schools. Similarly, Genome Day brings about 400 eighth-graders into the Jacobs School each year to mark DNA Day. Our trained volunteers lead small groups of students in extracting DNA from their own cheek cells, using a Bio-Rad kit. Students also have the opportunity to interact with scientists and shift their idea of who can be a scientist. Here again, this has become something that eighth-graders and their teachers look forward to each year.

Stand-alone outreach efforts can also have a broad reach. Family STEM (Science, Technology, Engineering and Mathematics) and STEAM (Science, Technology, Engineering, Arts and Mathematics) nights, with hands-on activities, have a broad impact. Bridget Brace-MacDonald, GEM director of outreach activities, established a GEM Student Outreach Team to engage with the general adult public at various public community events. While it can be very difficult to engage an adult audience on a science topic that they (a) think they know nothing about, and (b) tend to not find interesting, GEM has capitalized on relationships within UB and with local nonprofits to reach audiences with fun, interactive hands-on science activities that help adults understand more about the genome and the microbiome, and how their health choices related to each. Consistent presence at health fairs, arts festivals, and other community events along with engaging activities, builds community, enhances relationships, builds trust, and reduces barriers by bringing the campus into the community.

Inviting the community onto campus similarly breaks down barriers and builds trust. In collaboration with UB's Clinical and Translational Science Institute (CTSI) Community Engagement team, led by Laurene Tumiel Berhalter, PhD (Family Medicine) and the Patient Voices Network, we co-host an annual Halloween event in the main atrium of the Jacobs School. This is a fun event that provides many organizations an opportunity to connect with members of the Buffalo community. But it is also important to have difficult conversations, to encourage dialogue, and to learn from our community members. Here again, research and engagement intersect and overlap.

One approach that we have taken was to invite the community into the Jacobs School for a screening of a movie that addresses important issues in biomedical research. Our goal was to start a conversation about issues of disparity, discrimination, and racism in biomedical research, trying to tackle historical injustices head on. Building relationships requires trust, so we engage in some of these difficult conversations with our community members and provide them with a forum in which we listen. We chose to screen *The Immortal Life of Henrietta Lacks*, based on the book of the same name (Skloot 2010). Henrietta Lacks was a young African American woman diagnosed with cervical cancer in 1951 at Johns Hopkins Hospital. Despite treatment, she sadly died not long after her diagnosis. But a part of her lives on. A sample of her cervical cells was collected during a biopsy. These cells were sent to Dr. George Gey, who had been trying to grow human cells in the lab. Most died very quickly in culture, but Henrietta Lacks's cervical cells, dubbed HeLa cells, grew and divided quickly and continuously. They were (are) immortal, which makes them extremely powerful for a broad range of biomedical research. HeLa cells have been shared with labs around the world and continue to be used extensively to this day. However, the Lacks family, including Henrietta Lacks, was not made aware of the fact that these cells had been taken or that they proved to be so important for biomedical science. This has raised significant issues and concerns about privacy and consent and has contributed to mistrust of the biomedical community among African Americans. Notably, the genomes of HeLa cells have been sequenced, which raises significant ethical issues about genetic privacy for the Lacks family, who share some overlapping genetic material with HeLa cells (Callaway 2013; *Nature* 2020).

In order to have the conversation about Henrietta Lacks, we made a concerted effort to invite members of the community to the screening and discussion. We were particularly interested in engaging members of the community adjacent to the Jacobs School, in the Fruit Belt in Buffalo, which is primarily African American. Graduate students distributed door knocker invitations throughout the neighborhood. In the end, nearly 400 people attended the screening; about half were from the Fruit Belt neighborhood.

Following the screening of the movie, we held a panel discussion about the issues raised in the film and the current best practices and protections in place for human research. The panel consisted of a representative of the Institutional Review Board (IRB), which reviews and must approve all human research that occurs at UB, researchers who work with community members and community members who participate in research. The discussion was moderated by Timothy Murphy, MD (Medicine), and Pastor Kinzer Pointer of the Agape Fellowship Baptist Church in Buffalo. A robust and frank discussion took place about biomedical research in general and the treatment of African Americans in particular. This was a difficult, but necessary, conversation, and just a starting point for building a broader community. We solicited feedback through both paper surveys at the event and with a link included in a follow-up email to participants. Almost 80 percent of respondents felt they learned something about genetic research and had an improved understanding of ethical issues related to research. About 70 percent had confidence that research is conducted more ethically now than in Lacks's time. Almost 60 percent of respondents felt they improved their understanding of genetics, learned about ways in which the community can get involved in research, and would be more willing to participate in research as a result of this event. Nearly everyone (99% of respondents) claimed they would attend an event like this in the future. Respondents particularly appreciated the focus on the community and the opportunity to interact with and hear from a diverse and accessible panel. Respondents also provided some interesting ideas for future events, such as presenting more films with scientific implications followed by discussion, presentation of an overview of genetics and other basic science information for the general public, a forum for the community to share current research projects and how they impact (or could impact) the community, and seminars and information about supporting and participating in research. The feedback and responses indicated a very strong appetite in the community for engaging with UB in a meaningful way.

Community-Based Research to Learn about the Community

To promote genome literacy and to communicate effectively with the public, it is important to understand where the public stands with respect to its understanding of and attitudes about genetics and genomics research and testing. The rapid rise in the use of genomics in health care has not been accompanied by a corresponding increase in the public's knowledge of genetics and genomics. Many people struggle to define "genetics" and do not know basic information such as where genes are located. Without a basic understanding of the genome, the public is not prepared to make decisions involving genomics, one reason the National Human Genome Research Institute (NHGRI) recognizes the importance of improving the public's genomic literacy (Hurle et al. 2013). When we started this work, research was limited in investigating the public's views of fact-based, genomics-related ethical or privacy issues, and little public input on ways to improve genomic literacy had been solicited.

We assembled an interdisciplinary team of faculty, including Laurene Tumiel Berhalter, PhD, Marc Halfon, PhD (Biochemistry), and Arun Vishwanath, PhD (Communications), students and staff. We developed and deployed a survey to assess genomic literacy nationally and regionally. Little of this type of research had been done in the United States, and there was an urgent need for this information nationally. This research initiative provided important data about the knowledge of and attitudes about genetic/genomic testing and research and allows us to compare our region to the nation. It was also a critical piece for development of our community outreach and an important mechanism for assessing progress. We deployed the same survey nationally (1,504 participants) and regionally (1,000 respondents) (Jaeger et al. 2022). Specific outreach interventions were developed based on survey information, addressing fears and misconceptions and providing tools for the public to use in their own personalized decision making. Versions of this survey have been used at community events, in K–12 schools, and in UB classes.

The survey was developed to determine how well-prepared the public is to use genomic information for decision making in their lives (Jaeger et al. 2022). We assessed the public's level of genomic literacy by assessing actual and perceived knowledge, as well as their attitudes and behaviors regarding genetic and genomic testing and research. We also queried participants about their concerns about genetic and genomic testing and research and their sources for acquiring this type of information. We learned that participants had a solid basic knowledge of genetics, but noted some important barriers to literacy. For example, more than 70 percent of respondents reported a good or excellent understanding of DNA. However, less than 50 percent reported good or excellent understanding of the term "human genome"; 17 percent reported not having heard the term at all. Therefore, although people hear the terms "genome" or "genomics" routinely and are therefore familiar with them, they don't appear to have a clear understanding of their meaning. In general, participants displayed positive attitudes about the potential and promise of genomic research and testing. However, in open responses, participants also revealed significant concerns about privacy and their ability and/or willingness to trust medical and government institutions. Lack of trust was an important and recurring theme, and this was pre-COVID-19 pandemic (Czerski 2017; Tsipursky 2018). We determined that greater knowledge about and more positive attitudes toward genomics correlated with greater engagement in genetic testing and other "pro-genomic" behaviors. We concluded that both knowledge and concerns about genomics play a role in the public's ability and willingness to adopt pro-genomic behaviors. We also found that the public's level of genomic literacy could be enhanced by integrating the basic knowledge that they already have with broader and more sophisticated concepts and, importantly, how they relate to health and wellness. These insights can be used for further community engagement efforts surrounding genomic literacy, through trusted relationships.

To follow up the genomic literacy survey, I led "Community Conversations," a series of community focus groups for conversations with the public (about 400 people participated) about their knowledge and attitudes toward genomics and genetics. Community Conversations helped us connect with the community and will help us to develop ways to enhance public genomic literacy. One of the key findings from our discussions with community members was that they had a deep mistrust of government and were not confident that physicians were qualified or capable of providing guidance with respect to genomics. This aligns with research that has demonstrated that health care providers are ill-prepared to do this, both through a lack of knowledge and a lack of confidence in what they do know. On the other hand, focus group participants were more likely to trust UB scientists to provide this information. Another key finding was that a significant proportion of participants had serious concerns about how genomic information would impact their sense of identity, socially and culturally, which tied in with concerns about structural racism in biomedicine. There were also concerns about ill-defined authority figures with respect to genetic testing. Finally, much discussion occurred on the subject of genetic determinism with respect to genetic testing, and a consequent sense of powerlessness. "Community Conversations" has taught us some critical societal and cultural factors and concerns that must be considered in order to engage with the community effectively and to develop interventions to foster enhanced public genomic literacy

COVID-19 Education and Engagement

We leveraged our partnerships with schools, the CTSI, and the Buffalo Museum of Science to assemble resources related to COVID-19 and remote work and learning for community members through a newsletter that was shared widely across platforms. We also established a K–12 COVID-19 Chat series. UB GEM faculty, students, and staff, with a wide range of expertise related to different aspects of COVID-19, spent an hour chatting virtually with kids about their expertise and answering questions. The topics included bioinformatics, infectious diseases, respiratory therapy, zoonotic diseases, microbiology, virology, and vaccine development. K–12 students, their teachers, and their families, joined in the discussion and asked questions of the experts. These highly engaging discussions helped demystify aspects of SARS-CoV-2 and allowed us to share the ways in which we are learning about the virus through the pandemic and learning how to keep ourselves, and them, safe.

As the COVID-19 vaccine roll-out began, vaccine hesitancy was a significant problem—across the country between 40 and 60 percent of people surveyed were not inclined to get vaccinated, including health care workers. We pivoted to developing educational programming about COVID-19 vaccines using the COVID-19 chat series as a model. We again partnered with the CTSI and the Buffalo Museum of Science to develop, implement, and deliver these educational interventions that will be targeted to middle and high school students, families, adult community members, and health care workers, who had exhibited significant vaccine hesitancy to this point. Working with researchers, students, and trainees, we developed literature, talking points, resources (slides, video, cartoons), and training to facilitate a wide range of volunteers and a wide range of audiences—from middle school students to adults, families, and community members. All of our materials are available at www.buffalo.edu/gem. In partnership with the Buffalo Museum of Science, we convened a "Conversations in Science"

Zoom session focused on vaccines and how they work, with a focus on describing the new mRNA versions used for many COVID-19 vaccines. In all of our vaccine education, we maintained a clear focus on the process for developing and testing the different types of vaccine, how they work, what we know and, importantly, what we do not know about how they will work long-term. Without the community, infrastructure, and partnerships built through GEM over the past five years, we would not have been able to so quickly pivot to develop COVID-19–related educational offerings, which have had an important impact on our community.

A key, overarching question for community engagement to promote scientific literacy is—what works? What engages folks in different contexts, formal versus informal settings and classroom versus recreational (voluntary) spaces? To address this, it is necessary to assess and evaluate the different efforts through surveys and interviews, as we have done in developing educational materials, following public events and through formal survey and focus group research. This data can then be used to improve, enhance, and/or expand efforts to reach different communities. A community advisory board is critical. Working with community members who represent the target populations provides important perspectives on where community priorities, knowledge, and interests lie, which in turn informs outreach efforts and interventions.

Fundamentally, we must be willing to listen and learn from our communities. Strong communication underlies all efforts for effective community engagement, including promoting scientific literacy and combatting mis/disinformation. But it does take time and purposeful effort to establish lines of communication and build relationships that lead to trust. It often also requires learning to speak and share with a new disciplinary language or vocabulary. Using accessible language is essential and shows respect for the audience. But it does take work and practice—it's a new way to interact with people. We have learned that direct, face-to-face interactions (in person or virtual) are critical for building collaborations and partnerships—among scholars and with community partners. And it is important to think broadly about who we interact with—and spread our networks through existing networks. We shouldn't assume that we know people's interests (or lack of interest) or knowledge.

We have also found that students can be tremendous drivers of community engagement. Both undergraduate and graduate students have been highly motivated to step outside their course of study or thesis research to develop educational materials, to lead new research, and to engage with the people that make up our community. It is truly inspiring and can lead to increased faculty engagement as well.

Through all of this, support and resources are absolutely critical. This means both administrative and organizational support and financial resources. It is critical for building trust relationships that we maintain connections with K–12 schools and community partners over time in a consistent and systematic manner. We need materials and supplies for activities. It is also often appropriate to compensate student ambassadors and community members who share their time and expertise with us. We have been extremely fortunate to have support from UB to develop and support a broad range of community engagement efforts. With these resources, we have built a network of partnerships and relationships within our community that we can and will leverage to promote scientific literacy and combat mis/disinformation on several fronts.

Acknowledgments

This work was generously supported by the Office of the Provost and the Office of the Vice-President for Research and Economic Development at the University at Buffalo (State University of New York at Buffalo). I am grateful for the partnership and mentorship of my GEM co-director, Norma Nowak. I am also grateful to Marc Halfon and Robert Genco, PhD (deceased) for their collaboration in shepherding GEM into existence. None of the work discussed in this chapter would have been possible without the support of Sara Thomas, GEM administrator, Bridget Brace-MacDonald, GEM Director of Outreach Activities, and Sandra Small, PhD, GEM Education Manager. This team, along with myself and Norma, has functioned as an integrated, collaborative unit, which is critical in fostering the thoughtful integration of our tripartite mission of research, engagement and education. The team successfully built partnerships and networks across the UB campuses and in our WNY community, to an extent that would not be possible for faculty alone. This provides a platform for faculty and students who seek to engage meaningfully and purposefully with our schools and community. I am also grateful to faculty members mentioned throughout this chapter who were willing to step outside their comfort zone and engage in purposeful interdisciplinary research and scholarly activities to promote genome and microbiome literacy in our UB and WNY community. Finally, I am in awe of the dozens of undergraduate, graduate and professional students and postdoctoral associates who devoted time, effort and intellectual resources into developing and implementing hands-on activities and other educational resources and who engaged with K–12 and adult community members over the past nine years.

References

Aggarwal, N., S. Kitano, G. R. Y. Puah, S. Kittelmann, I. Y. Hwang, and M. W. Chang. 2022. "Microbiome and Human Health: Current Understanding, Engineering, and Enabling Technologies." *Chemical Reviews*. https://doi.org/10.1021/acs.chemrev.2c00431

Algan, Y., D. Cohen, E. Davoine, M. Foucault, and S. Stantcheva. 2021. "Trust in Scientists in Times of Pandemic: Panel Evidence from 12 Countries." *Proceedings of the National Academy of Sciences* 118, no. 40: e2108576118. https://doi.org/doi:10.1073/pnas.2108576118

Auffray, C., J. L. Griffin, M. J. Khoury, J. R. Lupski, and M. Schwab. 2019. "Ten Years of Genome Medicine." *Genome Medicine* 11, no. 1: 7. https://doi.org/10.1186/s13073-019-0618-x

Batson, G., and M. Wilson. 2014. *Body in Motion: Dance and Neuroscience in Conversation*. Chicago: University of Chicago Press.

Berg, G., D. Rybakova, D. Fischer, T. Cernava, M.-C. C. Vergès, T. Charles, X. Chen, and M. Schloter. 2020. "Microbiome Definition Re-visited: Old Concepts and New Challenges." *Microbiome* 8, no. 1: 103. https://doi.org/10.1186/s40168-020-00875-0

Brand, C. M., L. L. Colbran, and J. A. Capra. 2022. "Predicting Archaic Hominin Phenotypes from Genomic Data." *Annual Review of Genomics and Human Genetics* 23, no. 1: 591–612. https://doi.org/10.1146/annurev-genom-111521-121903

Braverman, I. (Ed.). 2018. *Gene Editing, Law and the Environment: Life Beyond the Human*. New York: Routledge.

———. 2023. *More-than-One Health: Humans, Animals, and the Environment Post-COVID*. New York: Routledge.

Browning, S. R., B. L. Browning, Y. Zhou, S. Tucci, and J. M. Akey. 2018. "Analysis of Human Sequence Data Reveals Two Pulses of Archaic Denisovan Admixture." *Cell* 173, no. 1: 53–61.e59. https://doi.org/10.1016/j.cell.2018.02.031

Buono, A., and A. Burnidge. 2022. "Dancing Our Microbiome at the Science Museum: A Dance/STEAM Collaboration." *Journal of Dance Education* 22, no. 2: 98–107. https://doi.org/10.1080/15290824.2020.1790568

Callaway, E. 2013. "Most Popular Human Cell in Science Gets Sequenced." *Nature*. https://doi.org/10.1038/nature.2013.12609

CCSS. 2016. Common Core State Standards Initiative. www.corestandards.org

Chiara, M., A. M. D'Erchia, C. Gissi, C. Manzari, A. Parisi, N. Resta, F. Zambelli, E. Picardi, G. Pavesi, D. S. Horner, and G. Pesole. 2021. "Next Generation Sequencing of SARS-CoV-2 Genomes: Challenges, Applications and Opportunities." *Brief Bioinform* 22, no. 2: 616–630. https://doi.org/10.1093/bib/bbaa297

Czerski, H. 2017. "A Crisis of Trust Is Looming between Scientists and Society—It's Time to Talk." *The Guardian.* www.theguardian.com/science/blog/2017/jan/27/a-crisis-of-trust-is-looming-between-scientists-and-society-its-time-to-talk

D'Alessio, V. 2022. "Ancient DNA Brings Us Closer to Unlocking Secrets of How Modern Humans Evolved." *Horizon: The EU Research & Innovation Magazine.*

Dannemann, M., and F. Racimo. 2018. "Something old, something borrowed: admixture and adaptation in human evolution." *Curr Opin Genet Dev*, 53, 1–8.

DeSalle, R., S. Perkins, and P. Wynne. 2015. *Welcome to the Microbiome: Getting to Know the Trillions of Bacteria and Other Microbes In, On, and Around You.* New Haven, CT: Yale University Press.

Foster, S. 2010. *Choreographing Empathy: Kinesthesia in Performance.* New York: Taylor & Francis.

GEM. 2016. *Coalesce Center for Biological Art.* www.buffalo.edu/genomeenvironmentmicrobiome/coalesce.html

GEM. 2018. "2 Minutes with the Microbiome: Embodied Research through Dance." www.youtube.com/watch?v=wEWR_p49xlM&t=127s

Gilbert, J. A., M. J. Blaser, J. G. Caporaso, J. K. Jansson, S. V. Lynch, and R. Knight. 2018. "Current Understanding of the Human Microbiome." *Nat Med* 24, no. 4: 392–400.

Haber, M., M. Mezzavilla, Y. Xue, and C. Tyler-Smith. 2016. "Ancient DNA and the Rewriting of Human History: Be Sparing with Occam's Razor." *Genome Biology* 17, no. 1: 1. https://doi.org/10.1186/s13059-015-0866-z

Houtman, J., R. Glassman, L. Shultz, J. Rivera, E. Bass, and R. Bright. 2021. "Genomic Surveillance Is Essential to Track Covid-19 Variants in Both Unvaccinated and Vaccinated Populations." www.rockefellerfoundation.org/blog/genomic-surveillance-is-essential-to-track-covid-19-variants-in-both-unvaccinated-and-vaccinated-populations

Howell, E. L., and D. Brossard. 2021. "(Mis)informed about What? What It Means to Be a Science-Literate Citizen in a Digital World." *Proceedings of the National Academy of Sciences* 118, no. 15: e1912436117. https://doi.org/doi:10.1073/pnas.1912436117

Hudson, A., and C. Wadsworth. 2021. "Genomic Sequencing: Here's How Researchers Identify Omicron and Other COVID-19 Variants." https://theconversation.com/genomic-sequencing-heres-how-researchers-identify-omicron-and-other-covid-19-variants-172935

Hurle, B., T. Citrin, J. F. Jenkins, K. A. Kaphingst, N. Lamb, J. E. Roseman, and V. L. Bonham. 2013. "What Does It Mean to Be Genomically Literate?"

National Human Genome Research Institute Meeting Report. Genet Med 15, no. 8: 658–663.

Jaeger, J., A. Hellwig, E. Schiavoni, B. Brace-MacDonald, N. A. Lamb, L. Tumiel Berhalter, M. S. Halfon, A. Vishwanath, and J. A. Surtees. 2022. "Challenges in Improving Genomic Literacy: Results from National and Regional Surveys of Genomic Knowledge, Attitudes, Concerns, and Behaviors." bioRxiv, 2022.2008.2026.505444. https://doi.org/10.1101/2022.08.26.505444

Jameson, K. G., C. A. Olson, S. A. Kazmi, and E. Y. Hsiao. 2020. "Toward Understanding Microbiome-Neuronal Signaling." *Molecular Cell* 78, no. 4: 577–583. https://doi.org/https://doi.org/10.1016/j.molcel.2020.03.006

Lamb, N. A., J. E. Bard, A. Pohlman, A. Boccolucci, D. A. Yergeau, B. J. Marzullo . . . J. A. Surtees. 2021. "Genomic Surveillance of SARS-CoV-2 in Erie County, New York." medRxiv, 2021.2007.2001.21259869. https://doi.org/10.1101/2021.07.01.21259869

Liu, Y., X. Mao, J. Krause, and Q. Fu. 2021. "Insights into Human History from the First Decade of Ancient Human Genomics." *Science* 373, no. 6562: 1479–1484. https://doi.org/doi:10.1126/science.abi8202

National Academies of Science. 2016. *Science Literacy: Concepts, Context and Consequences*. Washington, DC: The National Academies Press. https://doi.org/https://doi.org/10.17226/23595

Nature. 2020. "Henrietta Lacks: Science Must Right a Historical Wrong" [Editorial]. *Nature* 585: 7. https://doi.org/10.1038/d41586-020-02494-z

NGSS. 2013. "Next Generation Science Standards: For States, by States." The National Academies Press. https://doi.org/https://doi.org/10.17226/18290

NHGRI. 2015. "How to Extract DNA from a Strawberry." NHGRI. www.genome.gov/Pages/Education/Modules/StrawberryExtractionInstructions.pdf

Orlando, L., R. Allaby, P. Skoglund, C. Der Sarkissian, P. W. Stockhammer, M. C. Ávila-Arcos . . . C. Warinner. 2021. Ancient DNA analysis. *Nature Reviews Methods Primers* 1, no. 1: 14. https://doi.org/10.1038/s43586-020-00011-0

Ownby, R. L., A. Acevedo, R. J. Jacobs, J. Caballero, and D. Waldrop-Valverde. 2014. "Quality of Life, Health Status, and Health Service Utilization Related to a New Measure of Health Literacy: FLIGHT/VIDAS." *Patient Educ Couns* 96, no. 3: 404–410. https://doi.org/10.1016/j.pec.2014.05.005

Parikh, S. 2021. "Why We Must Rebuild Trust in Science." *Trend Magazine*. www.pewtrusts.org/en/trend/archive/winter-2021/why-we-must-rebuild-trust-in-science

Roth, W.-M., and S. Lee. 2002. "Scientific Literacy as Collective Praxis." *Public Understanding of Science* 11, no. 1: 33–56. https://doi.org/10.1088/0963-6625/11/1/302

Segelhurst, E., J. E. Bard, A. N. Pillsbury, N. A. Lamb, C. Zhu, A. Pohlman, A. Boccolucci . . . Y. Ye. 2022. "Improved Robustness of SARS-CoV-2 Whole-Genome Sequencing from Wastewater with a Nonselective Virus

Concentration Method." medRxiv, 2022.2009.2007.22279692. https://doi.org/10.1101/2022.09.07.22279692

Shendure, J., G. M. Findlay, and M. W. Snyder. 2019. "Genomic Medicine—Progress, Pitfalls, and Promise." *Cell* 177, no. 1: 45–57. https://doi.org/10.1016/j.cell.2019.02.003

Skloot, R. 2010. *The Immortal Life of Henrietta Lacks*. New York: Crown Publishing Group.

Stark, Z., L. Dolman, T. A. Manolio, B. Ozenberger, S. L. Hill, M. J. Caulfied, Y. Levy . . . K. N. North. 2019. "Integrating Genomics into Healthcare: A Global Responsibility." *American Journal of Human Genetics* 104, no. 1: 13–20. https://doi.org/https://doi.org/10.1016/j.ajhg.2018.11.014

Surtees, J. A., T. Russo, and A. H. Burnidge. 2020. "Interpreting the Meaning in Our Genomes: Perspectives from Biochemistry, Genetics, Infectious Disease, and Dance," in ed. K. H. Smith and P. K. Ram, *Transforming Global Health: Interdisciplinary Challenges, Perspectives, and Strategies*, 213–228. New York: Springer International Publishing. https://doi.org/10.1007/978-3-030-32112-3_14

Surtees, J. A., S. K. Small, J. N. Tripp, and L. E. Shanahan. 2021. "Microscopic Communities: Interdisciplinary Exploration of Microbes in the Classroom." *J Microbiol Biol Educ* 22, no. 1. https://doi.org/10.1128/jmbe.v22i1.2207

Tsipursky, G. 2018. "(Dis)trust in Science. Can We Cure the Scourge of Misinformation?" *Scientific American*. https://blogs.scientificamerican.com/observations/dis-trust-in-science

Vanouse, P. 2023. Paul Vanouse: .com(posite), .org(anism). www.paulvanouse.com

WHO. 2021. "Tripartite and UNEP support OHHLEP's definition of 'One Health' Joint Tripartite (FAO, OIE, WHO) and UNEP Statement." www.who.int/news/item/01-12-2021-tripartite-and-unep-support-ohhlep-s-definition-of-one-health

Zhang, H., L. Klareskog, A. Matussek, S. M. Pfister, and M. Benson. 2019. "Translating Genomic Medicine to the Clinic: Challenges and Opportunities." *Genome Medicine* 11, no. 1: 9. https://doi.org/10.1186/s13073-019-0622-1

Afterword

Trusting Fiction's Truth

CHRISTINA MILLETTI

> The only reason the phrase "fictional truth" is not an oxymoron as "fictitious truth" would be is that fiction is a genre whereas lies are not. Being a genre, it rests on conventions, of which the first and perhaps only one is that fiction specifically, but not always explicitly, excludes the intention to deceive.
>
> —Michel Riffatterre, *Fictional Truth*

The Power of Story

In 2011, the Defense Advanced Research Projects Agency (better known as DARPA) announced a new, seemingly "lo-fi" program for the normally cutting-edge tech wing of the US Department of Defense best known for its ingenious "sci-fi" inventions.[1] The "STORyNET" workshop—otherwise known as "Stories, Neuroscience and Experimental Technologies: Analysis and Decomposition of Narratives in Security Contexts"—had a single distinctive focus: to study "narrative" and "story-telling" and their impacts on "vexing security challenges such as radicalization, violent social mobilization, insurgency and terrorism." In effect, the Department of Defense was interested in how stories sway their listeners, particularly when those stories have been intentionally weaponized. Covered widely in mainstream journals like *Wired* and *The New Yorker*, it's not unduly surprising that the DARPA workshop gave writers and scholars (not to mention readers and citizens) cause to feel as much wonder as alarm at the resources the US Department of Defense was willing to spend on the subject of "stories"—a conventionally humanities-based field of interest—but also on questions about "narrative" that have been the subject of ongoing discussion and debate among literary scholars as far back as Plato. Seemingly without irony, DARPA described their inquiry as "a matter of great import and some urgency" (Sterling 2011).

While a number of articles at the time satirically warned of forthcoming "military-industrial fiction" (Vanasco 2011) and "weaponized Dr. Seuss" (Eddy 2011) arising from DARPA's corridors, instead it was Donald Trump's presidency a few years later (2016) that introduced "fake news" into the country's rhetorical armory, successfully demonstrating DARPA's concerns on US soil. Since then, "fake news" has become just one insidious arm of an embedded misinformation crisis that has impacted the public and a wide range of industries: intensifying vaccination hesitancy, injuring corporate bottom lines, increasingly fracturing the news industry and its politically polarized readership, and worst of all, generating violent encounters around the globe. Now, a little over a decade since the "STORyNET" workshop, our hope for Truth-Seeking in our Age of (Mis)Information Overload is not only to showcase the treacherously wide reach of misinformation but also to demonstrate the powerful potential that a Venn diagram of research between creative writers, literary scholars, mathematicians, artists, and social and computer scientists can offer when they explore the same issue within their specific fields but in a pose of deliberate and enlightened exchange. Here, their differing approaches shines a wide spotlight on both the impact and consequences of misinformation but also offers some guidance on potential paths through what is rapidly becoming (arguably, already is) a global emergency.

As a partnership between University at Buffalo's Humanities Institute and Center for Information Integrity, the work in this volume also represents an unusual form of scholarly engagement that showcases a rigorously dynamic "convergent" conversation between the humanities and the sciences (mirrored in this Afterword's intentionally "convergent" content). What becomes evident after reading the chapters in this volume addressing the misinformation crisis on (for instance) deficiencies and over-reliance on neural networks (Pitman), the dangers of government by algorithm (Ziarek), how to teach the public about the subtleties of the scientific process (Surtees and Ophir-Velho-Tzivian), or how to use emotional connections in media to teach about the ecological crisis (Fiege and Kenyon) is that artists, social scientists, film-makers, mathematicians are—surprisingly—all asking similar questions about the impact and effects of narrative on varied "audiences" (readers, viewers, subjects, and patients) in our very different fields. While determining a course of action to correct the mosaic of problems that has arisen in the wake of the misinformation crisis remains a hydra-headed beast of contention in its own right, it is more than apparent that a once controversial idea originating in the humanities now has an embedded and broad appeal across disciplines with researchers of all stripes. Stories have power. Words are also often actions. Narratives—for better and worse—create change.

What is even more curious, while the typical question that is usually asked in response to the misinformation crisis—how can we correct lies with "truth"—nearly every article in this volume takes a deliberate sidestep to reshape the terms of the problem at hand. While our conflict, at present, appears to be one about truth, the volume's contributors frequently assert a key companion problem that arises: truth's equally important sibling—trust.

Put another way: how do we trust the truth when we encounter it?

Why Fiction

As a fiction writer, I'm most interested in how narrative calibrates credibility: how a story, in other words, seems real or "true" to its readers. What effects in crafting language create the appearance of things on the page we believe to be true and real? How is it that, as William Gass reflects, the description of a peach makes the "mouth water . . . while the real peach spoils" (Gass 1979, 32)? And how do writers further exploit such effects to make even the impossible seem as ordinary and common as, say, a cup of coffee with breakfast?

Given the subject of this volume, I am particularly intrigued by fiction's ability to convey truth as much as its counterpart, nonfiction, whose truthfulness (arising from fact) is generally not the subject of debate. As the misinformation crisis has in many ways colonized the world of fiction at this contemporary moment, and lies are now broadcast to the public every day at an unprecedented, consumptive pace (a now well-known 2018 MIT study of Twitter usage has proven that not only are false stories "70% more likely to be retweeted than true stories," but that real news takes six times as long to reach its audience[2]), I'd like to take a moment to pressure how truth arises in fiction by considering two conventional genres that, historically, have been marked by their relation to the truth in order to better understand where we might not only find it, but perhaps also how to trust it when we do. In this way, nonfiction—as a genre based in fact—might be viewed here as a kind of "control" variable in this experiment examining fiction's truth.

At the level of craft, writing fiction and nonfiction isn't all that different: there are characters and plots, scenes and dialogue. Good writing—fiction and nonfiction—requires research: an attention to history as much as place, furniture, and weather formations, the trees outside a window as much as the subtle twitch in a crooked smile. The distinction between the genres, then, might be said to be one of "expected" versus "intended" authenticity. From a fiction writer's perspective, nonfiction is a fiction that purports to be true, whereas fiction mirrors realistic relationships and details in order to make an imagined story appear real, credible—*true*—to readers. Both genres, in short, use similar techniques to "coordinate" with the truth, if from neighboring originating positions. In this light, I'd propose that fiction and nonfiction are not the oppositional forms their names suggest: nonfiction exists in relation to fiction, and both relate lyrically to the truths they portray. As Thomas Leitch has said, "Whatever the opposite of fictional discourse might be, it is neither nonfictional discourse nor truth" (1986, 193). My aim, here, is to clarify that fiction and nonfiction are not binary genres: both are inflected by their earned veracity. You might even say, it's the oxygen that allows their narratives to take up residence, to live for a time, in the minds of the reader.

If, as novelist Amitava Kumar reflects, fake news has become "the specter haunting the writing of fiction" (2019) it is crucial—for both writers and readers—to not only feel confident in how fiction is situated with respect to genres like "fake news" narratives (similarly based in unreal information) or nonfiction (based in fact) in order to begin considering how to intervene in the misinformation crisis, particularly if "story" seems to be both the source of the problem as well as a lever, as I'd like to suggest, that we might trigger to disrupt it. My effort, then, isn't merely rhetorical in addressing these genre's crucial subtleties: I'm proposing that fiction and nonfiction are much closer to one another in their "appeal" to truth (though they use information "creatively") than to fake news narratives, which demand acceptance as truth. In fact, unlike fake news narratives, fiction (or nonfiction) dares readers to discover new truths for themselves. As Kumar reflects elsewhere in his essay "How Fiction Can Defeat Fake News":

> Unlike literary fiction, fake news offers nothing that is new. Instead, it conforms to existing popular prejudices. It is formulaic, often sentimental, and has a quality of sickening repetitiveness. . . . Genuine surprise, of the sort one finds in a story by, say, Anton Chekhov or Alice Munro, shakes us out of our complacent understanding of the world. It makes us skeptical of what we thought we knew about ourselves and, more than that, about others. . . . Good, meaningful fiction does not confirm preexisting beliefs; its entire raison d'être is to disturb and challenge such beliefs.

This "challenge" is what William Gass might call the fundamental "medium of fiction" in his essay by the same name. As he notes, works of fiction and the concepts they contain are designed to "take [us] up . . . [to] invade us as we read . . . The purpose of the literary work is the capture of consciousness, and the consequent creation, in you, of an imagined sensibility, so that when you read you are that patient pool or cataract of concepts which the author has constructed" (Gass 1979, 32–33). While fiction and fake news may seem similar to some readers, based as they are in imaginary constructs, they in fact are entirely distinct: one challenging, inhabiting, sensitizing, and the other confirming, warping, exploiting. As Gass reflects elsewhere, "Works of art confront us the way few people dare to: completely, openly, at once. They construct, comprise, our experience; they do not deny or destroy it; and they shame us, we fall so short" (Gass 1979a, 283). Perhaps the only questions are: Are we capable of confronting ourselves as much as others? If so, are we up to that challenge?

This "truth" of fiction—its innate and underrated ability to create surprising encounters with ourselves and others—is the basis for Samuel Johnson's allegory about the birth of fiction. His "Truth, Falsehood, and Fiction" offers convincing insight into the unexpected truth in stories. Written in 1751, Johnson's depiction of "the present corruption of mankind" in which there are "many incitements to forsake truth" sounds uncannily familiar, as if ripped from contemporary headlines. For instance: "Truth is, indeed, not often welcome for its own sake; it is generally unpleasing, because contrary to our wishes and opposite to our practice; and as our attention naturally follows our interest, we hear unwillingly what we are afraid to know, and soon forget what we have no inclination to impress upon our memories" (Johnson, 1751). As Johnson's allegory evolves, the battle between Falsehood and Truth grows heated, mankind becomes fully captivated by Falsehood and

Truth gives up—sound familiar?—ready to abandon mankind until, in an inspired turn, the Muses weave "a loose and changeable robe, like that in which falsehood captivated her admirers; with this they invested truth, and named her fiction." As Jonathon Arac artfully describes Johnson's dramatic turn: "Truth prevailed by imitating the falsehood of Falsehood, which imitated the truth of Truth" (Arac 2000, 1088). You might say, fiction clothes truth so that readers can experience it, test it out, learn for themselves—rather than hearing it programmatically and parroting it.

In more contemporary times, writers such as Virginia Wolf, Kathy Acker, and Percival Everett have each presented arguments about the nature of fiction that echo these sentiments. Kathy Acker particularly pressures how fiction—for better and worse—can confront and critique the status quo, while others merely support it.

> If I'm going to tell you what the real is by mirroring it, by telling you a story that expresses reality, I'm attempting to tell you how things are. By letting you see through my own eyes, I give you my viewpoints, moral and political. In other words, realism is simply a control method. . . . behind every literary or cultural issue lies the realm of the political, of political power. And whenever we talk about narrative, narrative structure, we're talking about political power. (Acker 2004, 17–18)

To Acker's mind, readers must be aware of how authors' perspectives shape truths on the page. David Castillo, co-editor of this volume, and William Egginton call this state of heightened readership "fictional awareness," reminding us that the arts have the "power to infect our beliefs with the self-knowledge that keeps us from being enthralled by them" (2017, 141).

A recent example of such a challenge can be found in prolific writer Percival Everett's novel *The Trees*. Characterized in book reviews as a "revenge fantasy" (Lorentzen 2021), a dark satire about the history of lynching in America—the entire jet-fueled impetus of the plot makes readers question the history of embedded racism in the United States by inverting racist tropes as the ghost of Emmett Till haunts a pair of Black detectives while they investigate a spree of murders of White people in Mississippi. As Everett reflects in an interview, that challenge isn't always met with enthusiasm because truth-telling can be confrontational: "the novel lives as much in turning around stereotypes as it does in revealing the truth of lynching. I'm happy to say I've pissed off a lot of people for my stereotyping of the white characters. Someone in an interview [objected] and my response was: 'Good, how does it feel?'" (Cummins 2022). Perhaps it's not so surprising, then, that narrative is the core of our current misinformation crisis. Falsehood is sly and persuasive. Truth hurts and is often unwelcome. Fiction threads our way across this spectrum and offers opportunities, with sufficient self-engagement, to cauterize the danger misinformation poses all of us. If, as Hernan Diaz, the author of 2022's Pulitzer prize–winning novel *Trust*, reflects: fiction "rather than presenting us with truthful content, shows us how we experience truth, then reading challenging fiction may provide readers with an enduring toolkit to help them work their way through the slippery rhetorical gamesmanship of fake news narratives that we all now encounter every day" (2021, 57).

Fiction's Trust

David Halpern—"nudge theory guru" and CEO of the UK's Behavioral Insight Team (also known as the "Nudge Unit"), a social policy consultant organization—reflects that "trust" is the "dark matter of the economy and society: it matters greatly yet we don't focus on it much" (Dubner 2016). As he goes on, trust is social capital, and perhaps most surprisingly, a direct predictor of a country's economic growth. We therefore ignore trust between our communities at our personal, national, and global peril. How then do we learn to trust, particularly among and across communities that have long histories of distrust between them? The only simple response to this complex question is that there is no easy answer to re/building trust. Innumerable business workshops and seminars are devoted to increasing trust in order to increase efficiency and profits. There are trust falls at corporate retreats as well as middle school mindfulness sessions. Meanwhile, the "Edelman Trust Barometer" delivers annual reports that help all kinds of organizations "navigate trust in a polarized world" (unsurprisingly, the forecast for 2023 is grim; Edelman 2023). Health sciences fields are replete with studies on how to increase vaccination rates among underserved communities who have been historically violated by medical research. Whatever guide you read, from whichever field it originates, the idea of "building" trust is anchored by several similar principles: honesty, vulnerability, and authenticity (Lord 2019). The message is clear: trust is earned; it takes time.

  This volume (and the form of this Afterword) is meant to showcase that effort in trust: that "unsiloed" from our fields—by drawing from, and trusting in, work that crosses disciplines—scholars may forge new paths in addressing the problems that have arisen from the misinformation crisis, rather than strictly remaining within the safety of our disciplines. Such work is deeply uncomfortable and defamiliarizing, and suspicion is often warranted. Would anyone be surprised, for instance, if STORyNET (and the subsequent DARPA iteration "Narrative Networks" [N2]) studied narrative not only for defensive purposes but offensive objectives as well? Meanwhile, various business sectors far too often seem palpably interested in solving mistrust in racial and gender inequity in order to exploit larger, more profitable, markets.

Into these scenarios of marked distrust, I'd like to propose that fiction can play an unexpected role. If the world of fiction showcases truths in simulation, then we may find "drafts" of possibility in the works of writers who have saturated their worlds with division. As Amy Dockser Marcus (a journalist covering the health sciences) notes, Raymond Carver's story "Cathedral" may be a case in point (Marcus 2023). Carver's minimalist fiction is best known for creating uneasiness in the most ordinary of circumstances, particularly between intimate characters who should, but fail, to understand each other. That opacity is a deep well that Carver draws from to create gutting fictions about alcoholics and divorcees, bad parents and terrible husbands. As Larry McCaffery writes, "Watching Carver's characters interact is . . . similar to the experience of spending an evening with two close friends who you know have had a big fight just before you arrived: even the most ordinary gestures and exchanges have transformed meanings, hidden tensions, emotional depths" (2012, 228).

"Cathedral," however, offers a surprising potential for exchange by narrating the ordinary if uncanny space of the dinner table—in this case, after a long-lost friend of the narrator's wife comes to visit. Robert is blind, and the unnamed husband manages to assert a roster of prejudices even before his guest arrives: the husband is not only patronizing to his wife and demeaning about her differently abled friend, but he also manages to lather the atmosphere between them all with racist language before Robert even steps through the door. As the husband notes: "My wife finally took her eyes off the blind man and looked at me. I got the feeling she didn't like what she saw" (1989, 215). The reader isn't surprised. The husband is distinctly unlikeable.

Later, however, after the three have eaten and chatted and smoked some dope, the husband selects a program on TV about churches in the middles ages. As the television begins to silently showcase the architecture of different cathedrals, the staging ground that Carver has carefully built throughout the uncomfortable meal for the narrow-minded husband finally comes to a head as he begins to painfully narrate what he's seeing on TV. Words, however, fail him, and frustrated, he gives up until Robert asks to try an experiment. Instead of describing the cathedral, he asks his host to draw it. Putting his hand over the husband's hand, and with Robert's stoned encouragement, the husband then begins to draw and, soon, gets lost in the work, as much as the intimate connection he's created with his wife's friend. The husband draws everything, from gargoyles to flying buttresses, and finally, the blind man counsels the husband to close his eyes as he's drawing—to better see what they're drawing together. In the final lines of the story, Robert tells the husband to open his eyes and to look at the drawing, asking: "What do you think?" Remarkably, the husband chooses to keep his eyes closed, and the last words of the story—a simple and stunned reply that sounds flat when pulled from the emotionally wrought context—are heavy and laden with unadorned meaning: "It's really something" (228).

However the reader chooses to interpret this moment, it's clear that an unanticipated, startling new connection has arisen between the two men who, at the outset of the story, were fathoms apart. At the beginning, Robert is unable to see, and the husband is unwilling to see. Yet, softened by a joint and strawberry pie, the husband relaxes just enough to allow himself to not only try to see as Robert sees while he draws, but also to understand Robert's differing perceptiveness, and maybe something about his own potential growth as well. Carver showcases in "Cathedral" how trust and connection can suddenly and robustly cleave from distrust, offering not a blueprint so much as a north star to aim for, to guide us, on our journey. Simply put: this is the truth that fiction offers about trust—when fact is not enough.

Stories then, and fiction in particular, have a crucial role in working through what we should perhaps rechristen our "trust crisis." Fiction can guide our way, teach us how to view others, even present a toolkit to judge the language that describes our truths. As Robert reflects early in "Cathedral," signaling the direction the story will take: "Learning never ends. It won't hurt me to learn something tonight" (222).

Notes

1. DARPA, for instance, invented ARPANET, the first computer network, which became the internet and, more recently, inventions such as the "EXACTO program," a defense system based on in-flight "self-steering" bullets.

2. The same study also proved that humans—not bots—are the key perpetrators of the spread of disinformation. See: https://news.mit.edu/2018/study-twitter-false-news-travels-faster-true-stories-0308

References

Acker, Kathy. 2004. "The Killers," in *Biting the Error: Writers Explore Narrative*, ed. Mary Burger, Robert Gluck, Camille Roy, and Gail Scott, 14–18. Toronto: Coach House Books.

Arac, Jonathon. 2000. "Truth." *PMLA* 115, no. 5 (October) 1085–1088.

Carver, Raymond. 1989. *Cathedral*. New York: Vintage.

Castillo, David, and William Egginton. 2017. "The Screen behind the Screen: A Penultimate Response to a Polemical Companion," HIOL Debates, ed. Bradley J. Nelson and Julio Baena, vol. 8, 132–146. https://cla.umn.edu/hispanic-issues/debates/polemical-companion-medialogies-reading-reality-age-inflationary-media

Cummins, Anthony. 2022. "Percival Everett: 'I'd love to Write a Novel Everyone Hated.'" *The Guardian* (March 12). www.theguardian.com/books/2022/mar/12/percival-everett-id-love-to-write-a-novel-everyone-hated

Diaz, Hernan. 2022. *Trust*. New York: Riverhead Books.

Diaz, Hernan. 2021. "The Heart of Fiction: Storytelling, Experience, and Truth." *The Yale Review* 109, no. 2: 53–67.

Dizikes, Peter. 2018. "Study: On Twitter False News Travels Faster than True Stories," MIT News. https://news.mit.edu/2018/study-twitter-false-news-travels-faster-true-stories-0308

Dubner, Stephen. 2016. "Trust Me," Freakonomics [podcast], episode 266 (November 10). https://freakonomics.com/podcast/trust-me

Eddy, Max. 2011. "DARPA Seeks to Understand Storytelling; Weaponized Dr. Seuss Imminent." *The Mary Sue* (February 10). www.themarysue.com/storynet-darpa

Edelman. 2023. "Edelman Trust Barometer Special Report: Business and Racial Justice." www.edelman.com/trust/2023/trust-barometer/special-report-business-racial-justice

Everett, Percival. 2022. *The Trees*. New York: Graywolf Press.

———. 1991. "Signing to the Blind." *Callaloo* 14, no. 1: 9–11.

Gass, William H. 1979. "The Medium of Fiction," in *Fiction and the Figures of Life*, 27–33. Boston: David R. Godine.

———. 1979a. "The Artist and Society," in *Fiction and the Figures of Life*, 276–288. Boston: David R. Godine.

Johnson, Samuel. 1751. "Truth, Falsehood, and Fiction: An Allegory." *The Rambler* 96. www.johnsonessays.com/the-rambler/falsehood-fiction-allegory

Kumar, Amitava. 2019. "How Fiction Can Defeat Fake News." *Columbia Journal Review* (Fall). www.cjr.org/special_report/fiction-defeat-fake-news.php
———. 2021. "How Can You Write Fiction That Fights Fake News?" *Lithub Quarterly* (October 5). https://lithub.com/amitava-kumar-how-can-you-write-fiction-that-fights-fake-news
Leitch, Thomas. 1986. *What Stories Are: Narrative Theory and Interpretation*. University Park: Pennsylvania State University Press.
Lorentzen, Christian. 2021. "Hillbilly Effigy: Percival Everett's Slapstick Revenge Fantasy." *Book Forum* (September). www.bookforum.com/print/2803/percival-everett-s-slapstick-revenge-fantasy-24618
Lord, Kristin. 2019. "Six Ways to Repair Declining Social Trust." *Stanford Social Innovation Review* (January 31). https://ssir.org/articles/entry/six_ways_to_repair_declining_social_trust
Marcus, Amy Dockser. 2023. "The Cathedral of Science: On the Struggle to Find Clear and Satisfying Solutions." *Literary Hub* (June 12). https://lithub.com/the-cathedral-of-science-on-the-struggle-to-find-clear-and-satisfying-solutions
Marcus, Ben. 2003. "On the Lyric Essay." *The Believer Magazine* (July). New York: McSweeneys.
McCaffery, Larry. 2012. "An Interview with Raymond Carver." *Mississippi Review* 39, no. 13: 228–247.
Riffaterre, Michel. 1990. *Fictional Truth*. Baltimore, MD: Johns Hopkins University Press.
Sterling, Bruce. 2011. "Design Fiction: Special Notice DARPA-SN-11-20: Stories, Neuroscience and Experimental Technologies (STORyNET): Analysis and Decomposition of Narratives in Security Contexts," *Wired* (Febryary 11). www.wired.com/2011/02/design-fiction-special-notice-darpa-sn-11-20-stories-neuroscience-and-experimental-technologies-storynet-analysis-and-decomposition-of-narratives-in-security-contexts
Vanasco, Jeanine. 2011. "Why Is the U.S. Government Interested in Storytelling?" *The New Yorker* (March 14). www.newyorker.com/books/page-turner/why-is-the-u-s-government-interested-in-storytelling
Wachtel, Eleanor. 2023. "An Interview with Percival Everett." *Brick: A Literary Journal* 111 (Summer). https://brickmag.com/an-interview-with-percival-everett/

Contributors

Editors

David R. Castillo is Professor of Spanish and co-director of the Center for Information Integrity at the University at Buffalo where he served as Chair of the Department of Romance Languages and Literatures from 2009 to 2015 and Director of the Humanities Institute from 2016 to 2022. He is the author of *Un-Deceptions: Cervantine Strategies for the Disinformation Age*, *Baroque Horrors: Roots of the Fantastic in the Age of Curiosities* and *Awry Views: Anamorphosis, Cervantes, and the Early Picaresque*, and co-author of *Medialogies: Reading Reality in the Age of Inflationary Media*, *Zombie Talk: Culture, History, Politics* and *What Would Cervantes Do? Navigating Post-truth with Spanish Baroque Literature*. Castillo has also coedited *Reason and Its Others: Italy, Spain, and the New World*, *Spectacle and Topophilia: Reading Early and Postmodern Hispanic Cultures*, *Writing in the End Times: Apocalyptic Imagination in the Hispanic World*, *Continental Theory Buffalo: Transatlantic Crossroads of a Critical Insurrection*, and the forthcoming *Anti-Disinformation Pedagogy*. Castillo is a recipient of the UB Exceptional Scholar Award for Sustained Achievement. His work in early modern literature and cultural history focuses on the damaging effects of inflationary media, including the proliferation of deceptive illusions and manipulative disinformation, and what we can learn from the "reality literacy" strategies of Miguel de Cervantes and other authors of the Spanish Golden Age to help us navigate our post-truth age.

Siwei Lyu is a SUNY Empire Innovation Professor in Computer Science and Engineering, at the University at Buffalo. He is director of UB's Media Forensic Lab, and co-director of the Center for Information Integrity. Lyu's research interests include digital media forensics, computer vision, and machine learning. Lyu has published over 190 refereed journal and conference papers. Lyu's research projects are funded by NSF, DARPA, AFRL, NIJ, UTRC, IBM, and the Department of Homeland Security. As a leading expert on media forensics, he testified at the US House of Representatives Hearing on Online Imposters and Disinformation (September 2019) and the NYS State Senate Hearing on Protecting Consumer Data and Privacy on Online Platforms (November 2019). He served as an Academic Advisor of the Global DeepFake Detection Challenge. Lyu was the recipient of the NSF CAREER Award (2010), the Best Paper Award of IEEE Signal Processing Society (2010), the President's Award for Excellence in Research of the University at Albany (2017), the SUNY Chancellor's Award for Excellence in Research and Creative Activities (2018), the Google Faculty Research Award (2019), and IEEE Region 1 Technological Innovation (Academic) Award (2021). Dr. Lyu is a Fellow of IEEE, IAPR, and AAIA, a Distinguished Member of ACM, a Senior Member of the Sigma Xi Society, and a Member of the Omicron Delta Kappa society.

Christina Milletti's novel *Choke Box: A Fem-Noir* won the Juniper Prize for Fiction from the University of Massachusetts Press. Her fiction, articles, and reviews have appeared in many journals and anthologies, including *Best New American Voices*, *The Iowa Review*, *The Master's Review*, *Denver Quarterly*, *The Cincinnati Review*, *Studies in the Novel*, *Zeta*, the *Brooklyn Rail*, *American Letters & Commentary*, *Experimental Fiction*, and the *Buffalo News* (among others). She is an Associate Professor of English at the University at Buffalo where she is currently the Executive Director of UB's Humanities Institute. She also co-curates the Exhibit X Fiction Series, a reading series based at Hallwalls for students and the wider WNY community. Recently, she won the Patron's Prize from Thornwillow Press who published her winning fiction, "The Girling Season," in a special letterpress chapbook edition. With the help of a residency at Saltonstall Foundation of the Arts, she will soon complete her latest book, a collection of stories called *Now You See Her*

Cynthia Stewart is founding Program Manager for the Center for Information Integrity at the University at Buffalo. She is an interdisciplinary scholar with interests across many disciplines, both non-STEM and STEM—especially in the places where they touch on the big, philosophical questions. Stewart has over twenty-five years' experience helping interdisciplinary teams work together successfully. Her previous positions at UB include Director of Administration for the Institute for AI and Data Science, and Managing

Director of the Creative Arts Initiative. Prior to her arrival at UB, Stewart served as Director of Strategic Projects at Antioch University Santa Barbara, where she was responsible for managing all cross-departmental projects, Assistant Dean of the Clinical Psychology program at Fielding Graduate University, and coordinator of *The International Bible Commentary: A Catholic and Ecumenical Commentary for the Twenty-First Century* (1998), where she copy edited and published the *edition princeps* version.

Contributors

John Fiege is a film director, cinematographer, photographer, and podcaster whose work explores our relationships with one another and the rest of life on Earth. His award-winning films have played at Hot Docs, SXSW, Big Sky, MoMA, Cannes, and many other venues, receiving distribution on Netflix, iTunes, Amazon, Sundance Now, and other platforms. He has received numerous fellowships, grants, and residencies, including from University at Buffalo's College of Arts and Sciences, The Redford Center, Doc Society, University at Buffalo's Humanities Institute, Austin Film Society, CrossCurrents Foundation, Film Society of Lincoln Center, Carleton College, Princess Grace Foundation, The University of Texas, University Film and Video Association, Kodak, and Smithsonian Institution. He hosts the Chrysalis podcast, which is a space for transformative conversations about our physical and spiritual relationship to the rest of life on Earth. He holds a BA from Carleton College, an MS in geography from The Pennsylvania State University, and an MFA in film production from The University of Texas at Austin, where he also worked as a lecturer. He is currently Assistant Professor in the Department of Media Study and an affiliate of the Department of Environment and Sustainability at the University at Buffalo, State University of New York.

Matt Kenyon is a Buffalo-based artist whose work has been exhibited nationally and internationally in such venues as the Museum of Modern Art, New York, MOCAD Detroit, Science Gallery Dublin, Centre de Cultura Contemporània de Barcelona, and the International Print Center. He is a TED Fellow, a MacDowell Fellow, and his work has been awarded the FILE Prix Lux. His work has been featured in *The New York Times*, *Wired*, and *Gizmodo*, and has also appeared in edited volumes such as *A Touch of Code* (Gestalten Press) and *Adversarial Design* (MIT Press). He lives and works in Buffalo, New York, where he is an Associate Professor in the Department of Art at the University at Buffalo, Art and Technology Program Director, Director of Graduate Studies, and part of PLATFORM, UB's socially engaged design studio.

Yotam Ophir is an Assistant Professor of Communication at the University at Buffalo. His work combines computational methods for text mining, network analysis, experiments and surveys to study media content and effects in the areas of political, science, and health communication. Ophir is the head of the Media Effects, Misinformation, and Extremism (MEME) lab, a member of the Center for Information Integrity at the University at Buffalo, and a distinguished fellow at the Annenberg Public Policy Center at the University of Pennsylvania. His work on misinformation includes studying disinformation and conspiracy theories online and in mainstream media, the politicization of science, and extremist discourse among white nationalists on the far-right.

E. Bruce Pitman is a Professor in the Department of Materials Design and Innovation at the University at Buffalo. The author or co-author of more than 100 research articles and reports, he has been a principal investigator or co-investigator on $16M of research and equipment awards. An expert in mathematical modeling, for the last two decades he has been studying uncertainty quantification—techniques for understanding uncertainty in models of physical or biological systems, and how computing can account for these uncertainties. In addition to his research and teaching activities, Pitman served as Vice-Provost for Educational Technology from 2000–2003, and as Associate Dean for Research and Sponsored Programs in the College of Arts and Sciences from 2003–2011. He served as Dean of CAS from 2011–2016. He joined MDI in 2016. During 2019–2021, Pitman served as Interim Director of the Institute for Computational and Data Science.

Jessie Poon is Professor at the Department of Geography at the University at Buffalo. She has published more than 100 articles on firms, trade and investment, is editor of *Environment and Planning A*, and serves on several editorial boards. Poon currently chairs the Regional Studies Association. Her recent work explores the socioeconomic factors that influence misinformation. Her co-authored book *Misinformation in the Digital Age: An American Infodemic* was published in 2023. This book explores how misinformation in the digital age calls attention to the multiple geographic dimensions of online fictions, conspiracy theories, trade, climate misinformation, and political disinformation. She is working on a project that examines misinformation in the context of Singapore, which strictly regulates online discourses.

Jennifer Anne Surtees is Professor in the Department of Biochemistry in UB's Jacobs School of Medicine and Biomedical Sciences and is an expert in mechanism of genome stability. She has served as co-director of the Genome, Environment and Microbiome (GEM) Community of Excellence at UB since 2015, which advances understanding of the genome and microbiome and their interaction with the environment through research, education, community programs, and art. Dr. Surtees is currently the Associate Deam for Undergraduate Research and STEM Outreach in the Jacobs School. During the COVID-19 pandemic, Surtees has worked with UB colleagues and several COVID-19 testing partners to conduct genomic sequencing of virus samples in Western New York. These efforts have aided the region's COVID-19 response, identifying the arrival of new variants and helping the community understand how SARS-CoV2 infections are changing locally as the virus evolves. She also collaborated with faculty, students, and staff to provide SARS-CoV-2 and vaccine information for all ages. Surtees has assembled a strong interdisciplinary team, with expertise in genetics, environmental engineering, and mathematical modeling, communications, and public health, to develop an early warning system for infectious diseases that integrates multiple types of ecosystem data from a wide range of stakeholders, including the community.

Laurene Tumiel Berhalter is Associate Professor and Director of Community Translational Research in the Jacobs School of Medicine and Biomedical Sciences, Department of Family Medicine. An epidemiologist by training, she has over twenty-five years of experience conducting community-based participatory research and health disparities research to improve chronic disease self-management and cancer prevention among underserved communities. She has worked with a variety of partners from both urban and rural communities. For over thirteen years, she has worked with the Patient Voices Network (PVN), a grassroots group of patients receiving care from safety-net practices, to design and implement programs to improve the delivery of health care using a Patient Ambassador model, a peer support model to empower patients in their own care and address social determinants of health. As Co-Director of the Community Stakeholder Engagement Research Module Core at the UB Clinical and Translational Science Institute (CTSI), she is committed to building infrastructure to facilitate community engagement and community partnered research. A major part of this work is to develop and communicate culturally relevant and appropriate information to diverse community groups.

Lilian Tzivian is a full professor and head of the Academic Master program in Epidemiology and Medical Statistics at the Faculty of Medicine, and a lead researcher at the Institute of Clinical and Preventive Medicine of the University of Latvia (Riga, Latvia). Her work at the University of Latvia is related to the quality of life of patients. She is certified as an Epidemiologist and a Head of Epidemiological Projects by the German Society for Epidemiology and the German Society for Medical Informatics, Biometry, and Epidemiology. Tzivian is also a lead investigator at the Institute of Occupational, Social, and Environmental Medicine, Center of Health and Society, University of Dusseldorf (Dusseldorf, Germany). She specialized there in environmental epidemiology and mental health. Tzivian is the author of more than forty scientific publications in highly influential scientific journals as well as several book chapters.

Raphaela M. Velho is currently a doctoral student at the University at Buffalo Department of Communication. Her interests include political communication, misinformation, and media effects.

Ewa Plonowska Ziarek is Julian Park Professor of Comparative Literature at UB and a Visiting Faculty in the Institute for Doctoral Studies in the Visual Arts Maine. She co-authored with Rosalyn Diprose *Arendt, Natality and Biopolitics: Towards Democratic Plurality and Reproductive Justice* (2019), a book awarded Book Prize of Symposium: Canadian Journal for Continental Philosophy. Her other books include *Feminist Aesthetics and the Politics of Modernism* (2012); *An Ethics of Dissensus: Feminism, Postmodernity, and the Politics of Radical Democracy* (2001); *The Rhetoric of Failure: Deconstruction of Skepticism, Reinvention of Modernism* (1995); and numerous co-edited volumes, including *Intermedialities: Philosophy, Art, Politics* (2010); *Time for the Humanities* (2008), and *Revolt, Affect, Collectivity: The Unstable Boundaries of Kristeva's Polis* (2005). Her interdisciplinary research interests include feminist political theory, modernism, and algorithmic culture.

Index

access, to health care, 120, 125
accountability, of AI, 26–27
Acker, Kathy, 162
Administrative Conference, US, 37
Aesop, 75, 91
affiliation, religious, 125, 127
African American community, 145–146
Agape Fellowship Baptist Church, 146
agency, political, 32–35
Ahearn, Ashley, 83–84
AI. *See* artificial intelligence
"algorithmic governmentality," 9–10
algorithmic modeling, 10, 31
algorithmic racism, 33
algorithmic technologies, 29–31, 33, 34, 36, 42, 43
algorithms, 3, 18, 20, 29; government by, 35, 37–38; harms of, 32; probabilistic, 23
"Alternative Rule" (artwork), 109–112, *110, 112*
Amazon, 17, 20
"The America Project" (art), 139
American Association of Medical College, 11, 115
Anne Burnidge Dance, 141
anti-vaccine movement, 116
Arac, Jonathon, 162

Ardent, Hannah, 31, 33, 39–42, 43, 46
Aristotle, 82
ARPANET, 165n1
artificial intelligence (AI), 1, 2; accountability of, 26–27; complexity of, 38; explainability and interpretability of, 24, 25, 26; explaining model of, 22; failures of, 17–18; fake content with, 3–4; humans working with, 20, 24, 26; illusions generated by, 12–13; legal regulation of, 37; successes of, 18; systems, 9, 18–19, 20, 24–25; Trustworthy, 24–25; unsupervised, 26–27
arts, 139–143
artwork: "Alternative Rule," 109–112, *110, 112*; "The Burning of the House of Commons," 101; "Cloud," *98*, 98–99; "Giant Pool of Money," 99–102, *100*; "Spore," 96–98, *97*; "Supermajor," *105*, 105–107; "Tap," 107, *108*, 109; "Tide," *102*, 102–103, 104–105
Association of Physicians, 59
Atlas of AI (Crawford), 33
automated judgements, 39, 44–46
awareness, fictional, 162

176 | Index

"Balancing Act" (performance), 141
Baton Rouge, Louisiana, 102–103, 105, 110
Bauerlein, Mark, 78–79
behaviors, science-consistent, 53–54, 56
Benjamin, Ruha, 33
Bernholz, Lucy, 36
Berns, Thomas, 38
Bhattacharya, Jayanta, 60
Biafra, Jello, 95
Bio-Rad kit, 144
biomedical research, 145–146
Bitcoin miner, 100f, 101
Black Americans, 119, 124–125, 126–127
"black box" models, 24
"black box societies," 9, 33–34, 38
"Black Lives Matter," 89
Bodmer Report, 55
Bolsonaro, Jair, 58
bookkeeping, double-entry, 100–101
BPS. *See* Buffalo Public Schools
Brace-MacDonald, Bridget, 144
Braverman, Irus, 138
brittleness, of DNNs, 19–20, 24
Brown, Wendy, 35, 36
Buffalo Museum of Science, 140, 141
Buffalo Public Schools (BPS), 143
building trust, 151, 163
Burnidge, Anne, 140, 141
"The Burning of the House of Commons" (artwork), 101
Bush, George W., 61

Camargo, Layel, 88
Campbell, Joseph, 75
"candle in the dark," science as, 62
capital, social, 120, 124, 126
capitalism, digital, 34
Carr, Nicholas, 81
Carson, Rachel, 61

Carver, Raymond, 164–165
Castillo, David, 162
"Cathedral" (Carver), 164–165
Cattaneo, A. G., 108
CCSS. *See* Common Core State Standards
Center for Disease Control and Prevention (CDC), 117, 118, 119
Center for Health Justice, American Association of Medical College, 11, 115
Center for Humane Technology, 12
Center for Information Integrity, 8, 158
Center for Information Integrity, UB, 8
Central Bank, 117
Cervantes, Miguel de, 5–6
ChatGPT, 4
Cheney, Dick, 104
children, school-age, 110–111, 142
China, 4
Christians, 61–62, 121
Chrysalis (podcast), 11, 76, 79, 84–86, 89–91
classifier: Gaussian Process, 23, *23*; GoogLeNet, *19*; of simple neural network, *21*, 22–23
Clean Air Act, 90
Clean Water Act, 90
climate: action, 10, 54, 85; change, 61–62, 75–77, 89–90, 102–103, 105; communication deficit model, 85; crisis, 80, 84, 85, 88; denialism, 77; racism and, 89
climate movement, 88
Clinical and Translational Science Institute (CTSI) Community Engagement team, UB, 145, 149
Clinton, Hillary, 78
"Cloud" (artwork), *98*, 98–99
Coalesce (lab-studio), 139–140

collaboration, 137–138, 142–144
collateral data, 34
Columbine High School shooting, 111
Common Core State Standards (CCSS), 143
communication, 13; climate, 85; science, 10–11, 54–56, 62, 65, 66, 127
communities, 32, 75; African American, 145–146; engagement with, 134, 137–138, 142–145, 146, 148–151; literacy of, 144; outreach to, 140–141; partnerships with, 133–134, 136; religious, 87–88; trust in, 8
community-based research, 147
"Community Conversations" (focus groups), 148–149
COMPAS, 42
complex society, 98
complexity: of algorithmic technologies, 38; of climate change, 89; of culture, 89–90
Comte, Auguste, 64
confidence, 127n2; data, *122*; in federal government, 126; in medicine, 117–118, 121
Congress, US, 4
Constructive Institute, 82
constructive journalism, 82–83
contamination, of groundwater, 109
contradictions, to democracy, 35–36
control: gun, 111; loss of, 121
convergence research, 7–8
conversations, generative ecological, 84
"Conversations in Science" Zoom session, 149–150
cooperation, 57, 76, 84, 118, 120
Cornwall Declaration on Environmental Stewardship, 62
counter technology, 7
COVID-19, 54, 61, 62, 64–65, 118–119. *See also* vaccines; education on, 149–150; pandemic, 96, 101, 116–117, 124, 126, 133, 136–137; politicization of, 57–60
Crawford, Kate, 30, 33
creativity, generative, 81, 92
crisis: climate and cultural, 80, 84, 85, 88; ecological, 75–77, 80; housing, 98–99; media on environmental, 76–77, 91; public health, 115; Syrian refugee, 78; trust, 165
CRISPR technology, 138
"Crosseyed and Painless" (song), 95
CTSI. *See* Clinical and Translational Science Institute Community Engagement team
cultural crisis, 85
cultural diversity, 88
culture, 81, 88–89
Cuyahoga River, 107–108
cyberattacks, 3–4

dance, 140–141
"Dancing DNA" (course), 140–141
DARPA. *See* Defense Advanced Research Projects Agency
Darwin, Charles, 63
data, 121; collateral, 34; training, 22–23; on trust, *123*; variables in confidence, *122*
data-driven system, 97
debunking, fact-checking and, 6–7, 8
deep neural networks (DNNs), 3, 18, 22, 23, 25–26; brittleness of, 19–20, 24
deep state, 58, 124
Deep Thought (fictional computer), 17, 25
DeepFakes, 3–4, 7
Defense Advanced Research Projects Agency (DARPA), 22, 157–158, 164, 165n1
Deficit Model, 10, 53–55, 85

democracy, 12–13, 29; characteristics of, 39; contradictions to, 35–36; threats to, 9, 33, 34, 36, 37
Democrats, US, 58
denialism, 75–76, 77
Department of Art, University of Buffalo, 139
Department of Defense, US, 157–158
Department of Health and Human Services, US, 122
Diaz, Hernan, 163
digital capitalism, 34
digital reading, 81–82
Diprose, Rosalyn, 40
Discourse (Epictetus), 77
discrimination, of patients, 124–125
disinformation. *See* specific topics
disparities, health, 116, 125
distrust: in government, 59; in medical scientists, 116; in public health authorities, 60; in science, 57–58, 61–62
diversity: in culture, 88; genetic, 135; in perspectives, 91
DNA, 135, 140–141, 144; genetics and, 146–148
"DNA Cocktails and Coalesce" (workshop), 140
DNA Day, 144
DNNs. *See* deep neural networks
dominant culture, 88
double-entry bookkeeping, 100–101
"Dumb Hicks Are America's Greatest Threat," 78
dynamics of movement, 140–141, 142

Earth Day, 89–91
Easterly, Doug, 96
ecological chorus, 91
ecological crisis, 75–77, 80
economic modeling, 104
economic security, 120
economics, trickle-down, 101, 104
ecosystem: information, 30, 31, 32, 34; self-contained, 96
"Edelman Trust Barometer," 163
education, 119, 123–124, 127; on COVID-19, 149–150; impact of school shooting on, 109–112; school-age children and, 110–111, 142; virus and vaccine, 133
Egginton, William, 162
elementary schools, collaboration with, 142–144
Elmwood Village Charter School (Buffalo, NY), 143
emotional correctness, 77–78, 79–80
Endangered Species Act, 90
engagement: community, 134, 137–138, 142–145, 146, 148–151; public, 12
"enlarged mentality," 39, 40–41
environment: ecological crisis, 75–77, 80; media on crisis of, 76–77, 91; wildfires, 88
Environmental and Climate Justice Program, 89
environmental crisis, media on, 76–77, 91
environmental movement, 89
Environmental Protection Agency (EPA), 61, 89–90, 107–108
Epictetus, 77, 79
ethical issues, 145–146
eureka moments, 63
European Union, 4, 59
Evangelical church, 87
Evangelical Climate Initiative, 10, 66
evangelical messengers, 86–87
Everett, Percival, 162–163
everyday human activities, 29
evolution, human, 56, 63–64, 135
"EXACTO program," 165
experiment, Tuskegee syphilis, 119, 125

explainability, of AI, 24, 25
explaining model, of AI, 22

fact-checking, 6–7
failures, of AI, 17–18
fake content, with AI, 3–4
fake news, 95, 158, 160–161, 163
falsehood, 163
falsifiability, 64
Family STEM/STEAM nights, 144
Fauci, Anthony, 65
FDA. *See* American Food and Drug Administration
federal government, US, 122, 126. *See also branches of government; specific departments*
fiction, 159–160, 164–165; trust of, 163; truth of, 161–162
fictional awareness, 162
Fictional Truth (Riffaterre), 157
Fiege, John, 10–11
finance, global, 99, 101
financial and business institutions, 122
flash flood, Baton Rouge, LA (2016), 102
Food and Drug Administration, US (FDA), 54–55
forensics, of DeepFakes, 7
fossil fuels, 107
Foucault, Michel, 30
"The Four Oxen and the Lion" (Aesop), 75
Fox News, 77
fracking, 108–109
Frestón (fictional character), 5
Freud, Sigmund, 64
Fruit Belt of Buffalo, NY, 146
Fujimura, Makoto, 81

Gander, Forrest, 91
Gap Model, 55
Gass, William, 159, 161

Gaussian Process classifier, 23, *23*
Gawker (blog), 78
GEM. *See* Genome, Environment and Microbiome Community of Excellence, UB
"Gene Editing" (symposium), 138
General Social Survey (GSS), 11, 115, 118, 121
generative creativity, 81, 92
generative ecological conversations, 84
generative event, 90
generative media, 79–80, 82, 91–92
generative podcast, 84
generative stories, 80, 81
genetic diversity, 135
genetics, 146–148; genomics research, 147–148; HeLa cells, 145; human genome, 148; microbiome literacy and, 144
The Genius of Earth Day (Rome), 89
Genome, Environment and Microbiome (GEM) Community of Excellence (UB), 134, 139, 143, 144, 150
Genome Day, 144
genomic literacy, 133, 134–136, 137–138, 139–143, 144, 147–149
genomics research, 147–148
Gey, George, 145
"Giant Pool of Money" (artwork), 99–102, *100*
global finance, 99, 101
global petroleum industry, 107
goals, public health, 123
The Godfather, Part II, 104
Golumbia, David, 42, 43
Google, 19
GoogLeNet classifier, *19*
government: by algorithm, 35, 37–38; distrust in, 59; trust in, 124; US, 30, 122, 126
"Government by Algorithm," 37–38

Graduate School of Education, UB, 143
Great Barrington Declaration, 60
Greater Sage-Grouse (bird), 83–84
Griffin, Jack (fictional character), 96, 112
groundwater, contamination of, 109
Grouse (podcast), 83–84
GSS. *See* General Social Survey
gun control, 111
gun laws, racism and, 111
Gupta, Sunetra, 60

Halfon, Marc, 147
Hallwalls Center for Contemporary Art, 139
Halpern, David, 163
Hamming, Richard, 17, 25
Hannity, Sean, 77
Harari, Yuval, 12, 13
harms, algorithmic, 32
Harris, Tristan, 12, 13
Head of the Vaccination Bureau, Latvia, 59
health, 116, 125, 135. *See also* public health
health care, 117, 119, 120; patient discrimination in, 124–125
health care providers, 117
Heavy Expanded Mobility Tactical Truck (HEMTT), 102
HeLa cells, 145
HEMTT. *See* Heavy Expanded Mobility Tactical Truck
hesitancy, around vaccines, 115–119, 120, 125–126, 149
Hitchhiker's Guide to the Galaxy, 17
Home Depot, 96–97
House of Commons, 100–101
Houser, Heather, 85
housing: bubble, 97; crisis, 98–99; market, 103

"How Fiction Can Defeat Fake News" (Kumar), 160–161
Hsu, Tiffany, 4
Humanities Institute, UB, 8, 158
humans: activities, 29; evolution, 56, 63–64, 135; genome, 148; health, 135; research, 146; spreading disinformation, 166n2; working with AI, 20, 24, 26
Hume, David, 64

ideas, qualitative, 44–45, 46
illusions, 106–107; AI generated, 12–13; self-sustaining, 5
The Immortal Life of Henrietta Lacks, 145
income, socioeconomic status and, 120
Independents (political), 126, 127
industry: global petroleum, 107; whaling, 106
influences of trust, *123*
Info Ops, 2
information: ecosystems, 30, 31, 32, 34; integrity of, 10, 29–31, 35, 36, 44, 45; sources of, 1
InfoWars, 111
Infowhelm (Houser), 85
infrastructure of trust, 133
institutional influence, 122
Institutional Review Board (IRB), 146
integrity, of information, 10, 29–31, 35, 36, 44, 45
internet, 1, 2, 95, 165n1
interpretability of AI, 24, 26
"The Invisible Man," 11, 96, 112
invisible power, 96, 112
Ipsos (company), 11
IRB. *See* Institutional Review Board

Jacobs, Abigail Z., 44–46
Jacobs School, 144, 145–146
Johns Hopkins Hospital, 145

Johnson, Samuel, 161–162
Johnson & Johnson vaccine, 65
Jones, Alex, 111
journalism, 2, 82–83
judgements, 41–43; automated, 39, 44–46; political, 39–40

K-12 COVID-19 Chat series, 149
Kahan, Dan, 54, 56
Kant, Immanuel, 39–40, 41, 42
Kenyon, Matt, 11
Klein, Ezra, 81–82
Knights of Malta, 99–100
knowledge, power of, 53, 56, 65
Kohn, Sally, 77–78, 79–80
Koury, Steve, 143
Kulldorff, Martin, 60
Kumar, Amitava, 160–161
Kushner, Robert, 81

"Labor" (art), 139
Lacks, Henrietta, 145–146
Laffer, Arthur, 104
Laffer Curve, 104
The Lancet, 64
Landemore, Hélène, 36
landscape, media, 8
language, use of, 87
Latvia, 59–60
legal regulation, of AI, 37
Leitch, Thomas, 160
"Let's Try Emotional Correctness," 77
literacy: of communities, 144; genomic and microbiome, 133, 134–136, 137–138, 139–143, 144, 147–149; science, 55, 66, 134–138, 150–151
living organism, 97–98
logicality, 41–42, 43, 46
López Obrador, Andrés Manuel, 58–59
loss of control, 121
Lycos (search engine), 2

machine learning (ML), 18, 24, 43–44
Mambrino (fictional character), 6
Marcus, Amy Dockser, 164
Marx, Karl, 64
mass media marketing, 102
Mayo tribe, 88
McCaffery, Larry, 164
media: on environmental crisis, 76–77, 91; generative, 79–80, 82, 91–92; landscape, 8; Latvian, 59–60; marketing and mass, 102; new, 1–2; power of, 95; Russian, 60; science in, 63; social, 1, 2–4, 95, 116–117, 159; trust in, 1, 3, 4–5; users of, 7
medical institutions, trust in, 121, 122
"Medical Posthumanities" (symposium), 138
medical scientists, 11–12, 115–118, 148
medicine: confidence in, 117–118, 121; racism in, 125, 145, 148; trust in, 125–127
metrics, quantitative, 98
Mexico, 58–59
Meyaard-Schaap, Kyle, 86–88
"Microbial Aesthetics" (symposium), 139
microbiome literacy, 133, 134–136, 137–138, 139–143, 144
Microsoft, 17
Milletti, Christina, 8
Mills, Charles W., 35
Minister of Health, Latvia, 59
misclassification, of panda, *19*, 20, 22–23
misinformation. *See specific topics*
ML. *See* machine learning
modeling: algorithmic, 10, 31; economic, 104
Moderna vaccine, 60, 125
monetary national income analog computer (MONIAC), 103–104, 105

money, 100–102, 120
MONIAC. *See* monetary national income analog computer
monoculture, 88
Morse, Solon, 139, 140
movement: anti-vaccine, 116; Black Lives Matter, 89; climate and environmental, 88, 89; dynamics of, 140–141, 142; positivist, 64; slow art, 81
Mozilla Foundation, 33, 47n1
mRNA, 150
Murphy, Timothy, 146
Myers, Steven Lee, 4
myth, 75–76

N2. *See* "Narrative Networks"
NAACP. *See* National Association for the Advancement of Colored People
narrative, storytelling and, 157–159, 163, 164
"Narrative Networks" (N2), 164
National Association for the Advancement of Colored People (NAACP), 89
National Human Genome Research Institute (NHGRI), 147
National Science and Technology Council, 30
National Science Board, 55
NBC, 118
Network of Excellence, SUNY, 139
neural network, 99. *See also* deep neural networks; research, 25; simple, 20, *21*, 22–23
neurons, 19–20
New Bedford Whaling Museum, 105–106
new media, 1–2
New York Times, 4, 12
New Zealand, 86, 104
Next Generation Science Standards (NGSS), 143

NHGRI. *See* National Human Genome Research Institute
Nixon, Richard, 61
Nobel Prize, 85
Nolan, Hamilton, 78
NON AES SED FIDES' (Not Money But Trust), 100
non-fiction, 160
North Dakota, 83
Nowak, Norma, 134, 143
NPR, 83–84
Numerical Methods for Scientists and Engineers (Hamming), 17
nutrition facts labels, 54–55

observation, systemic act of, 63, 64
oil mining, 106
On Being (podcast), 79–80
One Health, 138
O'Neil, Cathy, 35, 43
Ophir, Yotam, 10
organism, living, 97–98
organized religion, 122
outreach, community, 140–141

panda misclassification, *19*, 20, 22–23
pandemic, 10. *See also* COVID-19
pareidolia, 99
partnerships, community, 133–134, 136
patient discrimination, 124–125
Patient Voices Network, 145
Patterson, Jacqui, 89
Perignon, Dom, 101
perspectives, diversity in, 91
Pew Research Center, 118, 124, 126
Pfizer vaccine, 60, 125
Phillips, Bill, 103, 105
Phillips hydraulic computer, 103, 105
pipeline, of machine learning, 43–44
Pitman, E. Bruce, 9
plasma speakers, 108–109
Plato, 158

podcast: On Being, 79–80; Chrysalis, 11, 76, 79, 84–86, 89–91; generative, 84; Grouse, 83–84; Wolf, 81–82
Pointer, Pinzer, 146
polarization, of science, 61–62
political agency, 32–35
political judgements, 39–40
politicization: of COVID-19, 57–60; of science, 54, 61–62, 65
Politico, 78–79
Poon, Jessie, 11
Popper, Karl, 64
positivist movement, 64
power: invisible, 96, 112; of media, 95; of stories, 157–159, 165; systems of, 47n1; technologies of, 29, 33, 34, 36–37, 38, 42–43; wealth and, 112
"pre-bunking," 8
prediction products, 34
Principles of Trustworthiness, American Association of Medical College, 11, 115
privacy, 148; data, 9, 33; genome, 145, 147
probabilistic algorithms, 23–24
process of learning, in science, 136–137
Proust, Marcel, 81–82
Ptolemaic star system, 63
public engagement, 12
public health: authorities, 60; crisis, 115; goals, 123
Public Health Service, US, 119
Putnam, R., 120, 124

Q-Anon, 58
Q-Knights, 5, 6
qualitative ideas, as automated judgement, 44–45, 46
quality, of health care, 119
quantitative metrics, 98

Quixote, Don (fictional character), 5–6

racism, 162; algorithmic, 33; climate change and, 89; gun laws and, 111; medical, 125, 145, 148; in search engines, 33
Raskin, Aza, 12, 13
Reader, Come Home (Wolf, M.), 81
Reich, Rob, 36
relationship: social, 29, 32; symbiotic, 97
religion, organized, 122
religious affiliation, 125, 127
Religious and Conservative New Right, 61
religious communities, 87–88
"Remain in Light" (album), 95
Republicans, US, 58, 61, 62, 78, 120–121, 126–127; administration, 90; campaign, 104
research: biomedical, 145–146; community-based, 147; convergence, 7–8; genomics, 147–148; human, 146; neural network, 25
The Research Laboratory Program in Bioinformatics and Life Sciences (RLP), 143
resistance, to science, 53–54, 56, 57
Riffaterre, Michel, 157
RLP. *See* The Research Laboratory Program in Bioinformatics and Life Sciences
"Roadmap for Researchers on Priorities Related to Information Integrity Research and Development," 30–33, 35
Robert (fictional character), 164–165
Roman Empire, 77
Rome, Adam, 89–90
Rouvroy, Antoinette, 38
Royal Society Committee, 55
Rudin, C., 22, 24
Rumsfeld, Donald, 104

Sancho (fictional character), 5–6
Sandy Hook school shooting, 111
Sapiens (Harari), 12
SARS-CoV-2 virus, 136–137, 149
school shooting, 109–112
science: as "candle in the dark," 62; communication, 10–11, 54–56, 62, 65, 66, 127; literacy, 55, 66, 133, 134–138, 139–143, 144, 147–149, 150–151; in media, 63; politicization and polarization of, 54, 61–62, 65; process of learning in, 136–137; resistance to, 53–54, 56, 57; self-correcting in, 66; trust and distrust in, 54, 57–58, 61–62, 63–64, 65–66, 124
science-consistent behaviors, 53–54, 56
Science Exploration Day, UB, 140
Science Studies and Environmental Humanities groups, UB, 139
scientific knowledge, 65
scientific revolution, 62–63
scientists, 11–12, 115–118, 133–134, 148
search engines, racism in, 33
security, economic, 120
"Seeing the Generative Story of Our Time," 80
self-contained ecosystem, 96
self-correcting, in science, 66
self-sustaining illusions, 5
Semenova, L., 24
"Seven Sisters," 107
The Shallows (Carr), 81
Shelterwood Collective, 88–89
shooting, school, 109–112
Silent Spring (Carson), 61
simple neural network, 20, *21*, 22–23
skeleton, whale, 105–106
slow art movement, 81
social capital, 120, 124, 126

social media platforms, 1, 2–4, 95; false medical information on, 116–117; Twitter, 159
social relationships, 29, 32
society, complex, 98
solutions journalism, 82–83
Solutions Journalism Network, 82
Sonoran Desert, 88
sources, of information, 1
speakers, plasma, 108–109
"Spore" (artwork), 96–98, *97*
Standing Rock, North Dakota, 83
statistics, of trust, *123*
STEM/STEAM nights, Family, 144
Stiegler, 38
stories: generative, 80, 81; power of, 157–159, 165
"STORyNET" workshop, 157–158, 164
Student Outreach Team, GEM, 144
Studies of Work Atmospheres and Mass Production (SWAMP), 95–96
successes, of AI, 18
SUNY Network of Excellence, 139
"Supermajor" (artwork), *105*, 105–107
Surtees, Jennifer Anne, 12
SWAMP. *See* Studies of Work Atmospheres and Mass Production
"the Swedish approach," 60
symbiotic relationship, 97
Syrian refugee crisis, 78
systems: of AI, 18–19, 20; data-driven, 97; of power, 47n1; Ptolemaic star, 63

Talking Heads, 95
tally-sticks, 100–101
"Tap" (artwork), 107, *108*, 109
technologies: algorithmic, 29–31; counter, 7; CRISPR, 138; digital, 1; of power, 29, 33, 34, 36–37, 38, 42–43

TED talk, 77, 79
Tesla, 17
Thompson, Stuart A., 4
threats, to democracy, 9, 33, 34, 36, 37
"Tide" (artwork), *102*, 102–103, 104–105
Till, Emmett, 162
Time, 107–108
Tippett, Krista, 79–80, 81
tobacco products, 56
Torn Spaces Theater, 139
"Toward a Democratic Theory of Judgement" (Zerilli), 39
training data, 22–23
transformation, 76
The Trees (Everett), 162–163
trickle-down economics, 101, 104
Trump, Donald, 58, 61, 78–79, 83, 124, 158
Trump supporters, 58
trust, 13, 127n2; in AI systems, 9, 24–25; building, 151, 163; in communities, 8; crisis, 165; data on, *123*; of fiction, 163; in government, 124; influences and statistics of, *123*; infrastructure of, 133; in media, 1, 3, 4–5; in medical institutions, 121, 122; in medical scientists, 11–12, 115–118, 148; in medicine, 125–127; in money, 100; in science, 54, 57, 63–64, 65–66, 124; truth and, 159–160; in vaccines, 119
Trust (Diaz), 163
Trustworthy AI, 24–25
truth, 95, 163, 164; of fiction, 161–162; trust and, 159–160
"Truth, Falsehood, and Fiction" (Johnson), 161–162
Tumiel-Berhalter, Laurene, 11, 145, 147

Turner, J. M. W., 101
Tuskegee syphilis experiment, 119, 125
Twitter, 159
Two Continents Restaurant, 104
Tzivian, Lilian, 10

UB. *See* University of Buffalo
underwater mortgage, 103
Undoing the Demos (Brown), 35
United States (US), 147; Administrative Conference of, 37; Congress, 4; Democrats, 58, 126, 127; Department of Defense, 157–158; government, 30, 122, 126; Public Health Service, 119; Republicans, 58, 61, 62, 78, 90, 104, 120–121, 126–127
United Technology Physical Sciences Laboratory, 108
University of Buffalo (UB), 136, 138, 142–143, 144, 151; Center for Information Integrity, 8; Clinical and Translational Science Institute (CTSI) Community Engagement team, 145, 149; Department of Art, 139; Genome, Environment and Microbiome Community of Excellence, 134, 139, 143, 144, 150; Graduate School of Education, 143; Humanities Institute, 8, 158; Science Exploration Day, 140; Science Studies and Environmental Humanities groups, 139
unsupervised AI, 26–27
UPIs. *See* user profile information
Urban League of Buffalo, 143
US. *See* United States
use of language, 87
user profile information (UPIs), 34
users, of media, 7

vaccines, 57–58, 60, 64; COVID-19, 122; education on, 133; hesitancy around, 115–119, 120, 125–126, 149; Johnson & Johnson, 65; Moderna and Pfizer, 60, 125; mRNA, 150; trust in, 119
validity, question of, 44–46
values, 56–57, 86–88; of money, 100–102
Vanouse, Paul, 139
variables, in confidence data, *122*
vegetarianism, 86
Velho, Raphaela, 10
violence, 110–111
virus. *See also* COVID-19: education on, 133; SARS-CoV-2, 136–137, 149
Vishwanath, Arun, 147

Wakefield, Andrew, 64
Wallace, Alfred Russel, 64
Wallach, Hanna, 44–46
wars, culture, 81
Washington, DC, 5, 104

wealth, power and, 112
Weapons of Math Destruction (O'Neil), 35
Western New York Genetics in Research Project, 143
whale skeleton, 105–106
whaling industry, 106
"What We Leave Behind" (dance), 141
White House, 78
Wi-Fi, 96
wildfires, 88
WNY STEAM conference, 143
Wolf, Maryanne, 81
Wolf (podcast), 81–82
Wroe, A., 120

Yahoo, 2
Yaqui tribe, 88
"yellow journalism," 2

Zerilli, Linda, 39, 40
Ziarek, Ewa, 9, 40
Zuboff, Shoshana, 8